Strategic Marketing Decisions 2008–2009

Strategic Marketing Decisions 2008-2009

Isobel Doole and Robin Lowe

AMSTERDAM • BOSTON • HEIDELBERG • LONDON • NEW YORK • OXFORD
PARIS • SAN DIEGO • SAN FRANCISCO • SINGAPORE • SYDNEY • TOKYO

Butterworth-Heinemann is an imprint of Elsevier

Butterworth-Heinemann is an imprint of Elsevier
Linacre House, Jordan Hill, Oxford OX2 8DP, UK
30 Corporate Drive, Suite 400, Burlington, MA 01803, USA

First edition 2008

Notice
No responsibility is assumed by the publisher for any injury and/or damage to persons
or property as a matter of products liability, negligence or otherwise, or from any use
or operation of any methods, products, instructions or ideas contained in the material
herein.

British Library Cataloguing in Publication Data
A catalogue record for this book is available from the British Library.

Library of Congress Cataloguing in Publication Data
A catalogue record for this book is available from the Library of Congress.

ISBN: 978 0 7506 8972 4

For information on all Butterworth-Heinemann publications
visit our website at http://www.elsevierdirect.com

 Designed and typeset by P.K. McBride

Printed and bound in Italy
08   09   10   11   12   10   9   8   7   6   5   4   3   2   1

Contents

Unit 1
Introduction to strategic marketing decisions

Learning objectives

Strategic marketing decisions need to be made throughout the marketing planning process, as well as at critical times in response to the competitive challenges facing the company. At these times strategic marketing decision-making may not necessarily be within the formal planning or budgeting cycle, but part of the iterative process of strategy development. In this module, the development of a sustainable competitive advantage is viewed as a continual process requiring a constant stream of strategic marketing decisions to be made that are individually sound and that collectively contribute to the marketing planning process and add value for shareholders and other stakeholders.

In this unit you will:

1.1 Examine the role of life cycles in strategic decisions to manage competitive advantage across global, international and domestic markets.

1.2 Examine the influence of market position on strategy and performance.

1.3 Critically appraise the changing dimensions of strategic decisions made to sustain competitive advantage in today's global markets.

1.4 Assess how product/market/brand/customer life cycles can be managed strategically across markets.

1.5 Examine the role of competitive relationships and how organizations compete to achieve customer preference.

Having completed this unit you will be able to:

◆ Appraise a range of corporate and business visions, missions and objectives and the processes by which they are formulated, in the light of the changing bases of competitive advantage across geographically diverse markets.

◆ Demonstrate the ability to develop innovative and creative marketing solutions to enhance an organization's global competitive position in the context of changing product, market, brand and customer life cycles.

This unit relates to the statements of practice:

Bd.1 Promote a strong market orientation and influence/contribute to strategy formulation and investment decisions.

Gd.1 Select and monitor channel criteria to meet the organization's needs in a changing environment.

Key definitions

A stakeholder – is anyone who has an interest in or an impact on an organization's activities.

Strategic marketing decisions – are the decisions made as part of the iterative process of strategy development. A company makes these decisions in response to the changing dimensions of the marketing environment to ensure a sustainable competitive advantage. These are part of the problem-solving process and are required throughout the process of analysis, strategic choice and implementation.

A sustainable competitive advantage – is the achievement of a company to develop a superior, differentiated position in the market place that creates superior value for customers, shareholders and stakeholders and that they are able to maintain over a period of time.

Hard-edged marketing – is the process by which marketing managers ensure they make decisions that create superior value for all stakeholders, especially customers and shareholders and prove the value of marketing's contribution to business by the use of meaningful marketing metrics.

Market/competitive life cycles – describe the cyclical nature of the demand and competitive activity in markets. Life cycles are based on the notion that during the lifetime of a market, it passes through a number of distinct phases, each of which has particular characteristics with regard to the nature of competitor activity, the demand for a product and the type of strategies that are appropriate to meet the distinct characteristics of the phase.

Study guide

This coursebook is critical to the overall understanding of the Strategic Marketing Decisions syllabus. It will help you to develop the knowledge and skills necessary to contribute to strategic marketing decisions in the formulation of a competitive marketing strategy. The end point of the module is a set of strategic decisions for the organization that may be built into a marketing or business plan. The module builds on the skills you have developed in the Marketing Planning module at Professional Diploma in Marketing and the Analysis and Evaluation module at Professional Postgraduate Diploma in Marketing. The knowledge and skills you develop in studying this module will be then taken forward into implementation in the Managing Marketing Performance module. This study guide incorporates an examination of the relevant knowledge and understanding of strategic decisions within domestic, international and global contexts. The knowledge and skills you acquire can then be applied in the Strategic Marketing in Practice module.

The Strategic Marketing Decisions module examines how, in this dynamic environment, competitive advantage might be developed through strongly differentiated positioning that is exploited in a cost-effective manner. Its emphasis is on where and how the organization competes, and, in doing this, it highlights the strategic marketing significance of brands, innovation, alliances and relationships and e-marketing. While the syllabus is divided into five elements, as a whole it incorporates two important building blocks:

The development of the capabilities within an organization to make effective strategic marketing decisions.

The development of innovative marketing solutions that enhance an organization's competitive position in its chosen markets while delivering superior value to the customers and to the shareholders of the company.

This study guide focuses on the key components of the syllabus that will enhance your ability to develop a more innovative approach to the strategic development of an organization, which is committed to building a competitive advantage that will create added value for customers, shareholders and other stakeholders. Table 1.1 gives you an indication of the learning outcomes and the units in which they are covered. However, it is necessary for participants to study the guide in an integrated way and view the complete strategic decision process of identifying new marketing opportunities, areas for innovation and value creation in an organization as an iterative and continuous process. As you go through the guide we will help you apply the lessons of good practice discussed through the activities and questions that you should try to apply to your own organizations as well as others that operate in different contexts from your own.

In each unit we have tried to direct the reader to the main components of the syllabus and incorporated questions and activities to help develop your learning. The core textbook for the syllabus that accompanies this workbook is Doole and Lowe (2005) *Strategic Marketing Decisions in Global Markets*, Thomson Learning, 978-1844801428.

To fully study the concepts and material of the syllabus you do need to read this textbook, to ensure you have the necessary in-depth knowledge you will require for the examination.

Question 1 of the CIM examination for the Strategic Marketing Decisions is case study based and integrative in nature. This question accounts for 50 per cent of the marks and so it is important you practise a number of different case study questions from different contexts. In every unit of this coursebook, we have included a number of case studies with questions for you to practise your skills. Throughout each unit we have included a number of practical activities and short questions which are also good preparation.

In each unit we have specified which examination questions since 2004 are most relevant to that unit. Examination questions are integrative in nature and to answer a question you may need to draw on the knowledge you have developed in a number of units. You need to practise these questions to help you build your skills as you progress through the book, however be prepared to draw from a variety of sources to answer the question not just from what is in specific units.

Table 1.1: Learning outcomes/unit guide

Learning outcomes	Study units/syllabus reference
Appraise a range of corporate and business visions, missions and objectives and the processes by which they are formulated, in the light of the changing bases of competitive advantage across geographically diverse markets	Units 1, 2, 3, 5, 6, 7
Identify, compare and contrast strategic options and critically evaluate the implications of strategic marketing decisions in relation to the concept of 'shareholder value'	Units 2, 5, 7, 10, 11, 12
Evaluate the role of brands, innovation, integrated marketing communications, alliances, customer relationships and service in decisions for developing a differentiated positioning to create exceptional value for the customer	Units 3, 4, 8, 9, 10, 12
Demonstrate the ability to develop innovative and creative marketing solutions to enhance an organization's global competitive position in the context of changing product, market and brand and customer life cycles	Units 1, 2, 4, 6, 7, 8, 9, 10
Define and contribute to investment decisions concerning the marketing assets of an organization	Units 4, 6, 8, 9, 11
Demonstrate the ability to re-orientate the formulation and control of cost-effective competitive strategies, appropriate for the objectives and context of an organization operating in a dynamic global environment	Units 5, 6, 10, 11, 12

The table is meant only to be indicative. It is important that students understand that the learning outcomes at the Postgraduate Professional Diploma and particularly for Strategic Marketing Decisions are integrative in nature and are developed by building skills across the units of this coursebook. They are not necessarily outcomes of any individual units. The module requires the student to develop the ability to synthesize material from across the units and apply it to the context given in the examination question.

Introduction

To develop the capabilities within an organization to make effective strategic marketing decisions, a company needs to have the ability to understand the changing dimensions of the market in which it operates and the impact this has on its competitive advantage (syllabus element 1). It needs to be able to challenge traditional thinking and develop an innovative culture through learning and knowledge management to reorientate and reformulate competitive strategies to sustain its advantage in the market (syllabus element 2). Finally it must have the ability to appraise strategic marketing decisions and assess strategic options with regard to the potential return on any investments made (syllabus element 5).

To sustain a competitive advantage over time, companies need to develop innovative marketing solutions that enhance an organization's competitive position while delivering superior value to the customers and to the shareholders. To achieve this, a company must build its knowledge and understanding of the strategic issues involved in leveraging competitive capability across global markets (syllabus element 3) and it needs the skills and the capabilities necessary to manage a marketing portfolio across global markets (syllabus element 4). In creating innovative marketing solutions a firm must also ensure it has the necessary budgetary and planning control systems and appropriate performance measurement systems to ensure that in the execution of strategies, a positive contribution is made to shareholder value (syllabus element 5).

The development of strategies that build upon and leverage an organization's competitive position globally is fundamental to the achievement of a sustainable competitive advantage. The challenges of doing this across a spectrum of fast moving and geographically and culturally varied markets in an effective manner represent a significant intellectual challenge and require the development and refinement of decision-making skills. In this unit we examine how strategic marketing decisions need to be taken at critical times in response to the competitive challenges faced by companies and not necessarily only within the formal planning or budgeting cycle. As said earlier, in this syllabus, it is recognized that the development of a marketing strategy is a continuous process, requiring a constant stream of strategic decisions to be made that are individually sound and that collectively contribute to the marketing strategy planning process of an organization.

Question 1.1

What capabilities do you think a company needs to make effective strategic decisions?

Changing dimensions of competitive advantage

The emergence of a more open world economy, the globalization of consumer tastes and the unabated construction of global electronic highways all increase the interdependency and interconnections of nations' economies across the globe. The marketplace is becoming increasingly complex, as some markets become more saturated and fragmented, the competitive pressures increase and survival and growth become more difficult to sustain. The need for managers to develop the skills to respond to these pressures affects companies of all sizes.

The global marketing environment is becoming increasingly complex. Global wealth overall is increasing, and this is again reflected in changing demand structures across markets. Increasing affluence and demand means that consumers are now actively seeking choice across the globe with the result that the competitive landscape is changing as companies compete to win the battle for disposable income. Commercial dynamism has seen nations across Asia, South America and Eastern Europe emerge as high growth economies, and their companies increasingly seek new markets globally and so they themselves are emerging as powerful competitors in today's global markets.

The global marketplace is simultaneously becoming interdependent, economically, culturally and technically through the consistent thrust in technological innovation. The Internet in particular is helping to level the playing field among large and small firms in B2B and B2C e-commerce. Information moves anywhere in the world at the speed of light, and what is becoming known as the global civilization is being facilitated by the convergence of long-distance telecommunications and cuts in the cost of electronic processing and the growth of Internet business.

Question 1.2

What are the main environmental factors impacting on the way companies are now seeking a sustainable competitive advantage?

On the supply side, there is a trend towards globalization, seeking world standards for efficiency and productivity. This in itself has led to companies reconfiguring as they endeavour to realign themselves to better position themselves globally. In many industries we have seen the rationalization and consolidation of global competitors. This means that to sustain a competitive advantage, companies cannot rely on historical data and simply extrapolate it to forecast the trends of the future. Nor can they simply assume that their competitors will behave in the way they have done so in the past. Changes in the environment and in the structure of competitor activity mean the basis on which companies compete has also changed and the competitive game has become harder to win. The performance of a company is determined by not only its own actions but the actions and reactions of competitors, customers, governments and other stakeholders. As the environment becomes more complex these have become much harder to predict and more difficult in themselves to manage.

The dimensions on which marketing managers achieved their competitive advantage used to be very much focused on the transaction itself. However, if companies are to sustain a competitive advantage in today's market, the focus has to be on the total integrated marketing effort delivering superior customer value in the market. Marketing, over the past decades, has evolved through several stages from the early days of transaction marketing through to the concept of value-based marketing. According to Doyle (2000) in doing this, marketing thinking has travelled through four stages:

1 **Transactional marketing** – Where the focus was on the actual exchange and building short-term profits for the company. The main performance indicator was sales volume, and so marketing decisions were primarily concerned with enhancing the efficiency and effectiveness of that sale.

2 **Brand marketing** – In this stage the focus was on building of the augmented product where value was built through the brand image and related product benefits. In brand marketing, customer loyalty is built by building an emotional relationship between the customer's lifestyle and the lifestyle built around the brand.

3 **Relationship marketing** – In relationship marketing, customer retention is the key strategic objective. It is based on the notion that profitability is sustained by building customer loyalty and so achieving customer retention. The focus is on getting existing customers to buy more and to keep them in the habit of buying the companies' products through loyalty schemes such as store cards and rewards for loyal customers.

4 **Value-based marketing (VBM)** – It recognizes the need for a totally integrated marketing effort that manages the whole of the marketing process to deliver customer value and so builds value for the shareholders of the company. Proponents of value-

based marketing argue that to compete effectively, a company needs to do more than build a brand or build relationships – it has to build value. Thus while relationships and brands are important, markets are changing the basis for competition and new types of competition are emerging, which means that to achieve a sustainable competitive advantage companies need to offer a total value proposition to their customers.

Activity 1.1

What approach to achieving competitive advantage predominates in your company? What do you see as the strengths and weaknesses of the approach taken by your company in the way it has built its competitive advantage?

The concept of value-based marketing is examined in some depth in Unit 2 of this coursebook. In this unit what is important for you to understand in studying for this module is that, because of the changing dimensions of competitive advantage, to be successful, organizations need to put a great deal of effort not into learning just about their customers and competitors but also into developing a detailed understanding of environmental factors. These will impact on their markets and the perceptions and expectations of their partners in their supply chain and other relationships they may need to form, to help them build a strategy that will deliver competitive advantage. In achieving this strategic marketing decision-makers have now to deal with certain priorities that, according to Wilson and Gilligan (2004), are:

◆   The pace of change and the need for marketing managers to rapidly respond with innovative solutions with regard to products, services and marketing processes.

◆   Fragmented markets and the increasing need for customization to smaller targeted niches.

◆   The delivery of superior customer value as a basic ingredient of competitiveness.

◆   Information, market knowledge and the ability to learn as the premier source of competitive advantage.

◆   The strategic significance of new types of partnerships and new networks of relationships in the supply chain.

Biofuels – Utopia or just another environmental disaster?

The USA and Europe are promoting biofuels, made from cereals, sugar, oilseeds and vegetable oils, as a major part of the solution to climate change. The EU wants to see plants generating 10 per cent of road fuel by 2020. Ethanol production in the USA, made mainly from domestic corn is expected to double by 2016 and in 10 years, Brazil, currently the fastest growing ethanol producer will increase production by almost 150 per cent. Governments in developing countries are working with biofuels firms to release land for agrofuel crops. The Indian government proposes to plant 14 million hectares, Brazil has 120 million and 15 African countries, 379 million.

However, a charity called Grain claims that this is causing huge environmental damage. The land grab is expropriation on an unprecedented scale, leading to hundreds of thousands of indigenous people being pushed off their land. Food prices for poor countries will inevitably rise significantly and there are claims that some biofuels save very little on carbon emissions, compared to fossil fuels. Indeed, agro farming itself is a major cause of global warming due to the use of chemical fertilizers that release nitrous oxide into the air.

Adapted from: R Harrabin, Charity attacks rush for biofuels BBC News Online 29 June 2007, and Biofuels 'to push farm prices up', BBC News Online, 4 July 2007

Organizations therefore need to devote significant resources to building their knowledge capability on all these aspects, to ensure a sustainable competitive advantage can then be based upon a genuine understanding. They also need to make sure these capabilities are then fed into the strategic marketing decision process of the company. You can read in some detail in Chapter 2 of the core textbook for this syllabus (Doole and Lowe (2005) *Strategic Marketing Decisions in Global Markets*) how the development of a learning organization underpins the development of these capabilities within it. In the following section we will discuss the implications of the changing dimensions of competitive advantage on strategic marketing decision-making.

The changing dimensions of strategic marketing decisions

The challenges outlined mean it is now vital that marketing within companies takes on a much more strategic role and has a more prominent influence in the corporate strategic direction the company takes. The boundary lines between marketing and other functions areas such as operations, finance and human resources are much more blurred as marketing takes this more strategic role within an organization. Anthony Brown of IBM (*Marketing Business*, December 2003) suggests there are two types of corporations, those with marketing departments and those with marketing souls.

If companies are to have a marketing soul then strategic marketing decisions need to involve everyone in the company not just the marketing department and should be concerned with bringing together all the business processes that contribute to the design and development of the marketing offering to deliver superior value in the market. All of this has implications for a company's approach to strategic marketing decision making.

The need for innovative thinking

Senior marketing managers need not only the ability to develop problem-solving strategies but also the mindset that enables them to reinvent periodically the basis on which an organization can compete in response to changes in their markets. The challenges of the new competitive environment cannot be met if marketing decision-makers follow the same linear rational planning procedures that have been propagated in the last decades. The challenges in today's marketing environment require managers to be innovative and creative in their thinking if they are to build a sustainable competitive advantage.

Question 1.3

Explain what is meant by innovative and creative thinking. Why is such thinking important in strategic marketing decision-making?

The need to take a more strategic role

If marketing decision-makers are to take on a more strategic role, then they have a responsibility to show how the marketing decisions taken can deliver better revenue growth, more profit and increased customer satisfaction. In today's highly competitive marketplace, marketing managers are required to be much more accountable for their actions, show the cost effectiveness of marketing tactics and show how marketing strategies add to the shareholder value of an organization. The concept of shareholder value will be examined in Unit 2.

The CIM firmly believe if marketing is to take on a more strategic role it has to become 'hard edged'. This means marketing has to help companies make better decisions and become more influential in driving a business forward. 'Hard-edged marketing' is the process by which marketing managers ensure they make decisions that create superior value for all stakeholders, especially customers and shareholders, and prove the value of marketing's contribution to business by the use of meaningful marketing metrics. CIM research found that out of the top 20 companies in Fortune 500, only one, General Electric, had a chief marketing officer representing marketing at board level. One of the reasons for this they feel is the perception that the benefits of marketing activities are not measured in terms of profitability. They argue that marketing managers have a responsibility to make a demonstrable contribution to the success of the business. Thus it is important for students of the Postgraduate CIM Diploma to show they understand that marketing does not operate in either a commercial or a creative vacuum. Strategic marketing decisions have to be related to organizational goals and the impact of marketing activities has to be judged against the organization's key performance indicators.

The need to take a more strategic role at the board level of organizations has therefore focused the dimensions of strategic marketing decisions. Hard-edged marketing requires the application of robust marketing metrics to marketing decisions (see Units 11 and 12 of this coursebook) and it requires marketing decisions that deliver an effective strategy and a performance that creates demonstrable superior value for all stakeholders. This theme is the focus of all the units examining the design, development and implementation of strategic marketing decisions throughout this coursebook. However, central to the theme of hard-edged marketing is that if strategic marketing decisions are to drive business success, then the executives making those decisions must undergo a fundamental change in attitude and direction. It is important then that you, the reader, as a student of the CIM Postgraduate Diploma, are able to understand and overcome the obstacles faced in marketing, achieving influence at a board level and show how, in the strategic marketing decisions you make, you have embraced marketing metrics as an integral part of the decision-making process.

Activity 1.2

Consider the manner in which your organization makes strategic marketing decisions. How hard edged do you think your organization is in making such decisions?

The role of life cycles

One of the first requirements in making optimal strategic marketing decisions that focus creativity in the right places and drive the business forward is understanding the nature of the market/competitive life cycle in which the products/services of a company are competing. Thus to make appropriate decisions, managers need to have an understanding of the role of life cycles in managing competitive advantage across global, international and domestic markets.

The reader of this coursebook will be well acquainted with the concept of the product/market life cycle for the Professional Diploma of the CIM syllabus. However, in making strategic decisions with regard to a company's marketing strategy it is important not just to understand the product life cycle but how all life cycles, be it the market life cycle, the competitive life cycle or the brand and customer life cycles, affect the company's strategic position in the marketplace.

Market/industry life cycle

There are four distinct stages to the market/industry life cycle:

1   There is little or no market concentration. Newly deregulated firms, start-ups and industries spun off from others are all present at this stage.

2   In this stage, leading companies start to emerge, and concentration of competitive activity increases.

3   In this stage, companies extend their core businesses, eliminate secondary operations or swap them with other companies for assets closer to their core activity.

4   By this stage there has been a process of rationalization as weaker competitors have withdrawn from the market and the leading companies have consolidated to dominate the market.

Wilson and Gilligan (2004) suggest that it is the market/industry life cycle that should be the focus of attention of strategic marketing decision-makers and not so much the product life cycle. It is this cycle that helps decision-makers identify how the market is likely to evolve and how it will be affected by changing needs, new technology, developments in the channels of distribution and so on.

Activity 1.3

Consider the life cycle of an industry or market known to you. Can you identify the stages as outlined in the section above? What characteristics were most predominant at each stage? What shape do you think the life cycle took?

Demand/technology life cycles

The stage of industry/market life cycle is the starting point for understanding the inter-relationships of the other life cycles such as the demand life cycle and the technology life cycle. It is the demand life cycle that is concerned with the underlying need within a market. The technology life cycle, by contrast, is concerned with the particular ways in which this need is satisfied. Doole and Lowe (2005, Chapter 3) illustrate this by looking at the need for a data processing capability. The demand life cycle for this has been there for many long years and is still growing. While the actual growth rate itself has slackened in recent years the overall demand for faster data processing capability still continues on its upward trend. However, the way that need has been satisfied over the years and the technology used to process data has changed substantially and itself gone through several life cycles from paper-based technology to mechanical aids, to larger computers and then to smaller and smaller but faster and faster computers. Each of these phases had a technology life cycle in itself within the overall framework of the demand life cycle. The demand life cycle therefore is concerned with the evolution of the need itself, whereas the technology life cycle is concerned with the detail of how the need is met.

Royal Mail delivering a different message

Organizations progress through life cycles, ultimately coming to the point where their strategy must be reinvented. For a number of years Royal Mail, the UK state owned postal services business has been facing terminal decline due to a number of factors. However, its heritage, strong brand and reputation for reliability, albeit less than satisfactory in recent years, made it potentially the great business turnaround story. The reasons for its decline are well known. The changing communications market, particularly the Internet has meant that Royal Mail have had to question whether their traditional core capabilities will be the basis of their future competitiveness too. The market has been opened up to other business services and logistics companies that for the first time have been allowed to compete with Royal Mail in their most lucrative markets. Many argue that state ownership has made it difficult for Royal Mail's management to make the necessary decisive strategic decisions, starved it of the cash needed for investment in new opportunities and provided staff with an employment 'security blanket'.

Allan Leighton was brought in to save the company five years ago. As profits declined in response to private sector competition he developed a plan, which would save costs, but result in the loss of at least 15,000 jobs. This led to a nationwide strike, and the closure of thousands of post offices, leading to protests particularly in rural communities, which considered rural post offices as a 'lifeline'. At the same time Leighton had to improve the reliability of the service. Therefore the key task for Royal Mail to ensure the sustainability of the strategy was to add value for customers, in the process removing unnecessary costs.

Source: Robin Lowe, from publicly available resources

Question 1.4

What decision areas need to be addressed by Royal Mail?

The competitive life cycle

The pattern of the market, demand and technology life cycles will also impact on the competitive life cycle within a market. In the beginning of the competitive life cycle the company that is the pioneer in the market may have achieved a first mover advantage and so may be, if only for a short time, the sole supplier and so have no direct competitors. As the market progresses, as we discussed previously, competitors move in and the market share of the first mover may be affected. As more competition penetrates the market, price competition tends to increase, with the result that the scope for premium pricing on the part of the pioneer declines. As the market develops yet further and more firms enter the market, the perceived value of the product tends to decline, with the result that there is a gradual shift towards what Wilson and Gilligan (2004) refer to as commodity competition.

Question 1.5

Far from providing a useful insight it is thought by many that the life cycle concept is misleading and not helpful to managers making strategic marketing decisions for future time horizons. Fully discuss this statement using examples from your own experience.

Managing life cycles across the globe

Companies competing globally will have a plethora of such life cycles to manage simultaneously as life cycles across the globe may well be at differing stages. This makes managing life cycles across global markets extremely challenging in some markets. Competition today in many markets is global rather than domestic for many products and services. Consequently, there is a reduced time lag between product research, development and production, leading to the simultaneous appearance of a standardized product in major world markets. While many companies simultaneously launch new products across the globe, the shape and patterns of the life cycles that emerge as markets develop can vary enormously. Firms operating globally still need to develop an understanding of how to manage such life cycles across their markets.

Activity 1.4

Look at a product life cycle for a product or service that is known to you, which is sold across a number of international markets. In what ways does the life cycle vary across the key markets? Looking at the product from a market perspective draw the shape of the life cycle and plot the positions of the various countries at the different stages they have reached.

How organizations compete to achieve customer preference

In order for companies to compete effectively to achieve customer preferences, according to Treacy and Wieresma (1995), they need to focus on achieving operational excellence, product leadership, customer intimacy and brand leadership.

Operational excellence – Companies that pursue this may well offer middle market products at the best price with the least inconvenience. Thus they do not seek to be the technological innovators in the market but compete by targeting a customer preference for value for money. It is this no-frills approach that characterizes many of the retailers such as Wal-Mart, Matalan and Gap and airline companies such as Ryanair and EasyJet. In highly competitive and largely mature markets, for example, an ever greater number of organizations have to compete directly against competitors who offer almost identical products across 70–80 per cent of the range.

Product leadership – Involves focusing upon developing and offering products that consistently push at the boundaries of innovation; both Intel and Nike are examples of this. Offering innovative solutions with the latest product developments requires a high investment in research and development (R&D) and a strong innovation capability. This means employing the leading researchers in the field and building an organizational culture where creativity can flourish. Examples of such companies are Microsoft, Glaxo, SmithKline Beecham, Procter and Gamble and 3M.

Customer intimacy – In a time when technology has allowed marketers to move from mass marketing to mass customized marketing, companies now have the technical capability to target on an individual basis and so create customer value through the illusion of having an individual personal relationship with their customers. Lastminute.com, Amazon and a number of other Internet suppliers are able to offer individual buying solutions through the information built from purchasing profiles. However, customer intimacy is much more prevalent in B2B marketing when customers often require high value bespoke solutions to technical problems.

Brand leadership – The global brands of Nike, Sony and McDonald's have become worldwide phenomena by pursuing such a policy. However, brand leadership is only sustainable if it offers superior value to the customer. Companies basing their strategic positioning on brand leadership need to work actively to deliver an extra value proposition that is valued by the customer to sustain brand leadership over a period of time.

Insight: From cheap and cheerful to market leader

When Kim Sang Su took over as chairman of LG in 2003 the white goods business was losing money. LG had gained a reputation for manufacturing products that were sold in large volumes and were relatively inexpensive but were not distinctive in specification or reputation. Since 2003, the LG white goods business has been transformed despite the rapid raw material increases and strong Korean currency. It is now the third largest household appliance maker in the world with profitability twice that of Whirlpool, the largest company. It is the leader in home air conditioners, canister vacuum cleaners and microwave ovens and hopes to become number one in system air conditioners, front-loading washing machines and side-by-side refrigerators.

The transformation has been achieved by a broad-based innovation programme throughout the company, instituted by the chairman. Innovation has helped LG to attack the global high-end market. LG refrigerators, for example, are available in ten colours and one product incorporates a crystal display that provides a five-day weather forecast based on satellite information.

Adapted from: Tee-Gyu K. LG looks to double world's best products by 2010, *Korea Times*, September 2006

Question 1.6

In the above section it is suggested that to compete for customer preference, companies should aim to achieve operational excellence, brand leadership or customer intimacy. Identify the strengths and weaknesses of using each of these to achieve a customer preference.

Case study: Sony and German chip designer join forces

One may think it strange that a Japanese electronics giant, Sony, should need to work with a German firm, Qimonda, on such a fundamental component of their business as memory chips. In their high-tech world, innovation is critical in the race to build a global and sustainable competitive advantage. There is a constant stream of new applications for the technology in the form of leading edge products. Memory chips are used to store information on products such as mobile phones, MP3 players and digital cameras. However, their price has been falling due to over-supply in the industry, squeezing the profits of manufacturers. Moroever, there is a huge design and set-up cost to manufacturing, and increasingly, manufacturers wish to share these costs (and risks too). Despite these problems, Sony is intent on boosting its expertise in this area and believes that integration of the two companies' technological strength will lead to unprecedented levels of creativity and design in the future.

Adapted from: Sony in memory chip joint venture, *BBC News Online*, 2 October 2007

Question 1.7

Explain the reasons why companies participate in high technology joint ventures. Why are such relationships so important in the high-tech market?

The role of competitive relationships

The question facing many companies in today's global market is whether they can effectively compete for customer preference alone or whether some kind of relationship with competitors is required to sustain a competitive advantage over time. Companies such as General Motors, General Electric, Glaxo and SmithKline Beecham have maintained their market leadership, but an integral part of their strategy to do so has been either the acquisition of companies or the formation of strategic alliances they perceived they needed to help them compete more effectively in the marketplace. In today's marketing environment when competing for customer preference, companies (as we discuss further in Unit 10 of this coursebook) not only have to identify who it is they are competing against but also need to identify which competitors they may conceivably compete with, to deliver superior value to their customers.

There are a number of driving forces for this trend:

◆ Companies do not have sufficient resources alone to realize their full global potential and so may form a relationship to achieve better operational excellence or perhaps greater customer intimacy.

◆ The pace of innovation and market diffusion is ever more rapid and so to achieve global brand leadership; relationships may be formed so that new products and services can be exploited quickly by effective diffusion into the global market.

◆ High R&D costs mean it is increasingly difficult, costly and risky for companies to develop breakthrough innovations alone. Thus to achieve product leadership, relationships may be formed in R&D as in the Sony/Philips alliance, which produced the mini disc player.

◆ In mature markets such as the car and airline industries, operational excellence has been achieved by the formation of alliances, mergers and takeovers to rationalize competition, achieve economies of scale and achieve cost leadership in the industry.

◆ Some companies use relationships to acquire the capability to access new markets where they have little expertise or experience so they are better positioned to compete for customer preference in those markets.

The formation of customer and supply chain relationships is examined in some depth in Unit 10. However, the important concept for the reader to familiarize themselves with at this stage is that in strategic marketing decisions, to compete for customer preference, the manager needs to question the assumption that this is something the company will achieve alone. It may be that in many markets today it is the company that understands the strategic significance of partnerships and has a network of relationships that is most able to effectively compete for customer preference.

Activity 1.5

What approach to developing potential relationships with your competitors does your company take?

See CIM SMD Examination December 2004 Q.2 and December 2005 Q. 2

In preparing for the SMD examination it is necessary for you to tackle questions that expose you to a number of different contexts. The senior examiner will always try to ensure candidates are presented with varying situations in the examination. This question looks at a B2B service provider making strategic marketing decisions in a fast-moving and uncertain environment and so is a good one to help you prepare for such questions.

Summary

◆ The development of a sustainable competitive advantage is viewed as a continual process requiring strategic marketing decisions to be made that are individually sound and collectively add value for shareholders as well as other stakeholders.

◆ It is necessary for participants to study this coursebook in an integrated way and view the complete strategic decision process of identifying new marketing opportunities, areas for innovation and value creation in an organization as an iterative and continuous process.

◆ Strategic marketing is about the development of innovative marketing solutions that enhance an organization's competitive position in its chosen markets while delivering superior value to the customers and to the shareholders of the company.

◆ It is now vital that marketing within companies takes on a much more strategic role and has a more prominent influence in the corporate strategic direction the company takes.

◆ In making strategic decisions it is important to understand how all life cycles, be it the market life cycle, the competitive life cycle or the brand and customer life cycles, affect the company's strategic position in the marketplace.

◆ In competing for customer preference companies not only have to identify who it is they are competing against but also need to identify which competitors they may conceivably cooperate with to deliver superior value to their customers.

Further study

For a more detailed treatment of what strategic marketing decisions making is about you should read:

Doole, I. and Lowe, R. (2005), *Strategic Marketing Decisions in Global Markets*, Thomson Learning, Chapters 1 and 3.

Doyle, P. (2000) *Value-Based Marketing: Marketing Strategies for Corporate Growth and Shareholder Value*, Wiley, Chapter 1.

Wilson, R.M.S. and Gilligan, C.T. (2004) *Strategic Marketing Management: Planning Implementation and Control*, Butterworth-Heinemann, 3rd edition, Chapters 1 and 2.

Hints and tips

The concept of 'hard-edged marketing' is central to the whole of the CIM Chartered Diploma. In this module this means that you need to show that you understand that if strategic marketing decisions are to drive business success then marketing has to take a strategic role in the organization. This means in the examinations you will need to show that for the case study/scenario provided you can make marketing decisions of the calibre required by a company at board level. It is important therefore that you can show how the decisions you make help deliver superior customer value and that you understand that the application of marketing metrics is an integral part of the strategic marketing decision-making process.

Bibliography

Doole, I. and Lowe, R. (2005) *Strategic Marketing Decisions in Global Markets*, Thomson Learning

Doyle, P. (2000) *Value-Based Marketing: Marketing Strategies for Corporate Growth and Shareholder Value*, Wiley

Treacy, M. and Wieresma, F. (1995) *The Discipline of Market Leaders*, London: Harper

Wilson, R.M.S. and Gilligan, C.T. (2003) *Strategic Marketing Planning*, Butterworth-Heinemann

Wilson, R.M.S. and Gilligan, C.T. (2004) *Strategic Marketing Management: Planning Implementation and Control*, Butterworth-Heinemann, 3rd edition

Unit 2 Challenging traditional strategic thinking

The CIM syllabus for Strategic Marketing Decisions emphasizes the need for candidates to show that they can do more than simply go through the traditional marketing planning process. You need to be able to demonstrate you can rethink market boundaries and product/service boundaries that prevail within the market and create innovative strategies that change the basis on which a company can compete.

In this unit you will:

2.1 Examine the significance and application of new marketing thinking to strategic decisions.

2.5 Determine drivers for realignment in strategic thinking.

2.6 Explore the alternative approaches to strategic marketing decisions (e.g. formal/ analytical approach vs. transformation approaches).

2.10 Examine issues in strategic marketing decision-making in SMEs.

4.1 Explain and evaluate the contribution of value-based marketing.

Having completed this unit you will be able to:

◆ Appraise a range of corporate and business visions, missions and objectives and the processes by which they are formulated, in the light of the changing bases of competitive advantage across geographically diverse markets.

◆ Identify, compare and contrast strategic options and critically evaluate the implications of strategic marketing decisions in relation to the concept of 'shareholder value'.

◆ Demonstrate the ability to develop innovative and creative marketing solutions to enhance an organization's global competitive position in the context of changing product, market, brand and customer life cycles.

This unit relates to the statements of practice:

Bd.2 Specify and direct the strategic planning process.

Gd.1 Select and monitor channel criteria to meet the organization's needs in a changing environment.

Key definitions

Breakpoints – occur in markets as a consequence of a major change in the environment or the competitive nature of the market that results in a previously successful strategy being made obsolete.

Value-based marketing – a marketing strategy that is based on a totally integrated marketing effort that delivers superior value to customers and so in turn delivers superior value to shareholders.

Shareholder value principle – asserts that marketing strategies should be judged by the economic returns they generate for shareholders, the returns being measured by dividends and increases in the company share price.

Emergent strategies – a pattern of action that develops over time in an organization in the absence of a specific mission and goals, or despite a mission and goals. Mintzberg (1994).

Study guide

By reading and completing the questions and activities in this unit you should start to build the skills to develop innovative and creative strategies that deliver added value to customers. Most of the concepts introduced in this unit will be revisited in some depth in later units of the coursebook. At Professional Diploma of the CIM syllabus you developed the skills and knowledge to undertake a rigorous marketing plan. These skills are still important, but in this module you need to build on this knowledge and develop the ability to apply the skills to difficult competitive situations that may need added flair and creativity while at the same time ensuring any strategic decisions made are viable in terms of adding value to the customers and shareholders of a company. Using the driving analogy, at Professional Diploma, you learnt the mechanics of driving a car and have successfully passed your test. At this stage it is akin to taking an advanced driving test and so you need to show that you can apply those skills to adverse weather conditions and in complex situations where you have to be able to anticipate difficult situations ahead and respond quickly and appropriately to maintain the safety and well-being of your company.

Drivers for realignment in strategic thinking

Activity 2.1

Before you start to read the next section consider the environmental factors in a market or industry known to you that are requiring a company to realign their strategic thinking.

The drivers for strategic alignment centre on four emergent needs:

Rising customer expectations

The drive for increased revenue and growth from the market place

The intensification of global competition

The need for innovation and creativity.

In the global marketing place there are a number of environmental factors giving rise to the drivers outlined above:

◆ **The increasing globalization of the market place** – means all companies, even if they operate in one national market, are subject to international competitive pressures. As trade barriers reduce, markets become increasingly open to international competitors. In the European Union (EU), the accession of Central and Eastern European countries, while increasing market opportunity, also means companies in the high cost countries of Western Europe will be increasingly subject to the competitive pressure from competitors with a high level of technical capability and much lower labour costs. The accession of China to the World Trade Organization (WTO) signals China's intention to further develop as a serious international competitor.

◆ **The emergence of the global village** – is a culmination of the visible trends that social and cultural differences between countries become much less of a barrier and global needs that transcend political and national boundaries are satisfied by an increasing number of global brands such as Microsoft, Intel, Coca-Cola, McDonald's, Nike and so on.

◆ **The growth and movement in populations across the globe** – While the world population is growing dramatically, the growth patterns are not consistent around the world. The significant variations in changing populations are heralding social changes across the globe. 85 per cent of the world's population live in developing countries. There are also visible moves in the population within many countries leading to the formation of huge urban areas where consumers have a growing similarity of needs across the globe. The population of Greater Tokyo is just under 30 million and Mexico 20 million. Cities such as Lagos, Buenos Aires and Jakarta will soon outstrip cities such as Paris, London and Rome.

◆ **The growing body of international law** – affects the marketing strategies developed by companies. International conventions and agreements from world institutions such as the IMF, the World Bank and WTO increasingly impact on how companies compete globally. The harmonization of legal systems within regional economic groupings such as the EU is increasingly impacting on how companies operate in such markets.

◆ **Piracy** – in markets with limited trademark and patent protection is a serious challenge for global competitors. Increasingly, international laws are being developed to cover things such as piracy, patents and trademarks legislation. For many companies in the high-tech industries this is vital if they are to compete effectively in the growth markets around the world. Bootlegged software constitutes 87 per cent of all personal computer software in use in India, 92 per cent in Thailand and 98 per cent in China, resulting in an nnual loss of US$8 billion for software makers.

◆ **Shrinking communications** – means, increasingly, that in the global marketplace, information is power. At the touch of a button we can access information on the key factors that determine our business. Manufacturers wanting to know the price of components around the globe or the relevant position of competitors in terms of their share price or in terms of new product activity have it at their immediate disposal.

◆ **The Internet and the access gained to the World Wide Web** – are revolutionizing international marketing practices. An estimated 1.26 billion people now have access to the Internet. The United Nations estimates that global e-business is now worth well over US$10 trillion. Most of this is B2B marketing as opposed to B2C marketing.

Case study: Defence business attacking new markets

Defence equipment manufacturers are constantly seeking ways of diversifying in order to reduce their dependency on a small number of arms customers, typically governments that frequently go through periods of investment and cutbacks in arms purchasing. BAe Systems benefited from heavy US spending in Iraq for seven years, but as support for US involvement in Iraq decreased among the electorate, cutbacks in the US budget were expected. In 2007 the US accounted for 50 per cent of BAe's £15 billion revenue compared to 32 per cent from the British Ministry of Defence.

The best option for such companies is to push defence equipment into civilian markets – in some cases to deal with problems that the industry has itself caused! It is estimated that a million hand-held missile devices are circulating in the world and each rocket is capable of bringing down a passenger airliner. There have already been a number of attempts made. The worst case was in 2002 when an Israeli jet carrying 261 passengers out of Mombasa in Kenya was brought down by two missiles. Military aircraft are usually armed with counter measures but this would not be acceptable for civilian airlines that pass over cities. BAe has developed Jeteye, a laser defence system that will 'blind' incoming missiles and the US Homeland Security was reported to be trialling the system. The problem is that as each system costs $1 million and increases fuel consumption because of increased 'drag'. There will be reluctance amongst airlines to use them until there is a serious attack, when it is likely to be already too late.

There are alternatives for BAe Systems. They have supplied New York with a fleet of diesel-electric hybrid buses and the New York authorities are ready to order 850 more. Other cities are also adopting the technology and London is expected to have a fleet of 1000 for the London Olympics in 2012. Alongside its naval work BAe is also carrying out refits of Disney, Princess and Carnival cruise liners in US repair yards.

Adapted from: D Robertson, Anti-missile system in airline's sights, *The Times*, 10 December 2007.

Question 2.1

What do you see as the main drivers for the strategic realignment of BAe Systems? How do you think the competition will respond and how can BAe manage its military and non-military markets?

Question 2.2

How far do you think the growing access to the Internet has been a driver for strategic alignment?

Significance and application of new marketing thinking to strategic decisions

The changes in the marketing environment discussed above and the changes brought by the growth of e-business have all contributed to a global environment where the competitive landscape is much more complex; product, market and brand life cycles are shorter; and the search for competitive advantage by companies is more difficult to sustain over time. This has led to the changing dimensions in competitive advantage and the changing dimensions in strategic marketing decision-making we discussed in Unit 1 of this coursebook. Consequently, marketing managers have had to rethink the way they approach marketing decisions and incorporate new values into the marketing strategy process.

Insight

According to a global Web-based survey by Interbrand, the Google brand had the most impact on people's lives. Google's influence has overtaken some of the best established brands such as Coke and Apple. Some commentators believe the success of brands, such as Google has huge lessons for marketing managers as the tools and approaches used offline often do not work on the Web. Catchphrases are of little use as most Internet users are searching for information.

Many companies use websites to boast of their achievements that are of no interest to potential consumers surfing the Net wanting instant access to the simple and functional information they are searching for.

Equally a new generation is now growing up, skilled in accessing the world through their computer screens. Their motivations, the way they seek information and the stimuli they react to are of a completely different character to that of the previous generation. This in turn is impacting on how such consumers should be targeted offline and requiring marketing managers to rethink their traditional marketing tools.

Question 2.3

Critically evaluate the implications of the Internet on the offline strategic marketing decisions of the future. Do you think this will require a total realignment of offline marketing strategies?

The need for innovative thinking

To respond to the environmental challenges, strategic marketing decision-makers have had to rethink the market boundaries in which they operate and base their market definition in terms of the customers they serve rather than the product market they are in. This has meant they have had to break free of the notion that they have a localized customer base and so seek new customers globally and they have had to break free of their thinking in terms of the product/service boundaries that prevail within the market so they can create innovative strategies that change the basis on which they compete.

With the drivers for strategic realignment discussed above it is almost inevitable that at some stage marketing managers will face the problems of breakpoints. According to Wilson and Gilligan (2004) these could arise for a number of reasons:

◆ Changes in the demographics or social structure of a market that herald changes in customer needs, their values and/or expectations of the product and services they seek.

◆ Technological breakthroughs that provide the innovative organization with a major competitive advantage but which, in turn, put competitors at a disadvantage.

◆ The identification of new business opportunities by companies that redefine the market boundaries and cause a rethink among competitors as to how they should now compete.

◆ Shifts within the distribution network that lead to changes in the balance of power between manufacturers and retailers and very different sets of expectations – this could sometimes mean changes in the supply chain that offer scope for major reductions in cost.

◆ Indirect competitors developing a new resource capability and so becoming direct competitors bringing into the competitive landscape a different set of skills as well as a different perspective on the market.

◆ A mature market where companies are facing increasing price competition and so declining returns that force a radical rethink of how the company is operating and how it should develop in the future.

Activity 2.2

In the company in which you work or for a company known to you, what breakpoints can you identify that rendered the company's strategy obsolete? What strategic decisions did the company make to overcome the breakpoints?

It also means, as discussed in Unit 1, that to compete effectively in today's marketing environment, marketing decision-makers need to take on a more strategic role and ensure they are able to show how the marketing decisions taken can deliver better revenue growth, more profit and increased customer satisfaction. As said previously, in today's highly competitive marketplace marketing managers are required to be much more accountable for their actions, be able to show the cost effectiveness of marketing tactics and show how marketing strategies add to the shareholder value of an organization.

According to Piercy (2002), if strategic marketing decisions made by marketing managers are to clearly show how they contribute to shareholder value, this means companies have to develop customer-focused strategies based on offering value to customers, which in turn enhances company performance and so increases shareholder value. This means strategic marketing decisions need to be concerned with:

◆   **How to create value** – Piercy views this as the key issue in achieving and sustaining competitive success, particularly in relation to branding and customer relationship management given the increasing demands made by customers.

◆   **How to harness the power and impact of the Internet** – Particularly in relation to the need to develop integrated and multi-channel routes to a company's markets.

◆   **How to achieve a totally integrated marketing effort** – The need to ensure the strategic decisions made exploit all the company's resources and capabilities to deliver value to the customer.

◆   **How to engender creativity in the strategy of a company** – Piercy argues the focus of strategic decision-making should be on *strategizing and creativity* and not on the bureaucracy and structures of formal planning.

Question 2.4

Explain what is meant by a totally integrated marketing effort. How can a company achieve this?

The need to deliver shareholder value

According to Doyle (2000), by delivering shareholder value, marketing is more able to influence strategic decisions in the boardroom at a corporate level. Shareholder value marketing offers a way for managers to show how marketing strategies increase the value of the firm as well as provide a framework and language for integrating marketing more effectively with other functions of the business. Doyle suggests the need to deliver shareholder value redefines the marketing concept as:

> The marketing concept states that the key to creating shareholder value is building relationships with target customers based on satisfying their needs more effectively than competitors. (Doyle, 2000, p. 75)

The traditional marketing objectives of increasing market share and building customer loyalty, he argues, are not enough in themselves, unless they can be linked to the increasing of shareholder value and higher financial performance. The techniques and tools for assessing the viability of strategic marketing decisions and measuring shareholder value are examined more thoroughly in Unit 11 of this coursebook. In this unit we are simply concerned with introducing the concept of the shareholder value principle and discussing the implication for strategic marketing decision-makers.

The shareholder value principle asserts that marketing strategies should be judged by the economic added value they generate for the company, be it owned by shareholders or privately – the returns being measured by dividends and increases in the company value. This is based on two principles:

The primary obligation of managers is to maximize returns for shareholders and owners.

The stock market value of a company is based on the investors' expectations of the cash-generating abilities of the company.

Question 2.5

What do you understand by the term shareholder value/economic value added? Why is such a principle important to strategic marketing decisions?

This of course means that the role of marketing managers therefore is to deliver marketing strategies that maximize the cash flow of a company over time and so create value. The essence of the shareholder value principle is that managers create economic added value that in turn generates greater return than their cost of capital. If marketing managers are to make decisions that deliver economic added value, they need to harness the thinking of value-based marketing.

Case study: The added value of technological innovation

The need for innovation is critical to success, but how long is anything innovative and leading edge? The colour television in 1954 was heralded as a breakthrough, high-tech innovation and yet today it is seen as little more than a commodity – unless it has a plasma flat screen. Today the cost of a new flat screen television is not dissimilar to the price of a colour television in 1954 – about £750. Over the years the standard colour television has plummeted in price and now can be purchased for less than £50.

DVD players only a few years ago were the fastest-ever selling technological innovation and yet today the price of these has plummeted to such an extent that they are seen almost as a commodity where any brand will do and more often than not they can be picked free through promotional offers, something that the consumer picks up as a bonus for buying another product. Thus the commoditization process that took place over 50 years of the life cycle of the colour television has taken less than 5 years for the DVD player. Indeed most consumers have moved on at least two steps beyond with the next innovation – the DVD recorder – to an easily programmable hard drive recorder linked to their satellite television system.

Question 2.6

How does a company continue to maximize shareholder/stakeholder value in a market of tumbling prices?

Look at your own organization and identify the potential obstacles to applying the economic value added principle to your company. What are the reasons for this and what are the implications for strategic marketing decisions?

The concept of value-based marketing

Value-based marketing recognizes the need for a totally integrated marketing effort that manages the whole of the marketing process to deliver customer value and so build value for the company. Proponents of value-based marketing argue that to compete effectively a company needs to do more than build a brand, or build relationships, it has to build value. Thus while relationships and brands are important, markets are changing the basis for competition and new types of competition are emerging, which mean that to achieve a sustainable competitive advantage, companies need to offer a total value proposition to its customers. As Doyle (2000) says, it is 'by delivering superior value to customers that management can in turn deliver superior value to shareholders'.

According to Doyle (2000), delivering value-based marketing takes four major steps:

1   The development of a deep understanding of customer needs, operating procedures and decision-making processes.

2   The formulation of value propositions that meet the needs of customers and create a differential advantage.

3   Building long-term relationships with customers so that a level of loyalty and trust is built based on satisfaction and confidence in the supplier.

4   An understanding that the delivery of superior value to customers requires superior knowledge, skills, systems and marketing assets.

Incorporating this concept redefines marketing as being:

The management process that seeks to maximise returns to shareholders by developing and implementing strategies to build relationships of trust with high value customers and create a sustainable differential advantage. (Doyle, 2000, p. 70)

Question 2.7

What are the main components of value-based marketing?

According to Treacy and Wiersema (1995) if managers are to harness the thinking of value-based marketing, they need to come to terms with making three key strategic marketing decisions:

◆   **What is its value proposition?** – The implicit promise the company is going to make to customers to deliver its particular combination of values.

◆   **What is its value-driven operating model** – The combination of operating processes, management systems, structure and culture the company feels it needs to have if it is to have the ability to deliver on its value proposition.

◆ **What are its value disciplines?** – In other words what is the way the company is going to combine its operating models and value propositions to achieve a differential competitive advantage in its markets?

Activity 2.4

Does your company hold core values? If so, identify three or four value disciplines that you think are considered important in making strategic marketing decisions within your company.

If you think your company does not have any core values, then consider the implications of this to their strategic marketing decision-making.

Value disciplines are an important element of the work carried out by Collins and Porras (1997) and Collins (2000), in their six-year longitudinal study of high-performing companies in the United States. They found that businesses with long-standing reputations for business excellence had a strong core ideology. The ideology, they suggest, consists of three components: core values, core purpose and an envisioned future.

1 **Core values** – are sets of guiding principles that have intrinsic value and importance to those inside the organization.

2 The **core purpose** – is seen to be the fundamental reason for being a company, the reason the firm exists. Collins and Porras view an effective purpose as reflecting the importance people attach to the company's work.

3 **An envisioned future** – is viewed as the defining direction of the firm's strategy, a view of the future that comprises big hairy audacious goals (BHAGs).

The core ideology therefore has implications for how strategic marketing decisions should be led by the executive and it will also determine the orientation of the company to its strategic decision-making processes.

Insight: Space tourism

Is space tourism the ultimate in market niches? A number of smaller firms see this as the ultimate market niche, if they can build the capability to design a reusable launch system that is not too expensive and has guaranteed safety. Richard Branson's Virgin Galactic at www.virgingalactic.com is already gearing up for this market. Branson has successfully completed his space flight training course. In the United States, market analysts suggest that there are at least 10,000 potential space tourists willing to spend $1 million for the two-hour trip into space. However, NASA has explicitly stated it has no interest in this market. Foster and Partners have won an international competition to design the first spaceport in New Mexico and so the question remains: Could there be huge rewards for the first into the market or will the rewards be outweighed by the risks?

Alternative approaches to strategic marketing decisions

While there are many different approaches to the making of strategic decisions to formulate and develop a strategy, the two we will discuss in this unit are the rational formal approach and the emergent strategy approach.

The key component of the rational planning approach is that it is a highly formal linear sequence that requires a highly formalized approach to strategic marketing decision-making and a mechanical programming approach to implementation of those decisions. Underlying the rational approach is the assumption that the process of strategy development is like a machine, if each of the component parts are executed as specified, then the end product, that is the resultant strategy, will be effective and efficient. In terms of strategic decision-making there will be a strict hierarchy of decisions that need to be made in a particular sequence. The implementation of those decisions, while important, is perceived as being something that is considered as a consequence of the strategic decisions and not necessarily as part of the decision-making process. This means that the rational formal approach has certain characteristics such as:

◆　Strategies result from a controlled conscious process of formal planning that incorporates a sequence of distinct steps in the decision-making process.

◆　Responsibility for the whole process rests with the chief executive, but the implementation is the responsibility of operational managers and the two are seen as separate.

◆　Strategies are comprehensive and highly detailed and quite explicit in nature. This means they can then be implemented through detailed operational plans specifying objectives, action plans, budgets and control measures.

The emergent school of strategy development on the contrary believes strategies are formed and not necessarily formulated. In other words, strategies are built from a number of little actions and decisions made by different managers in an organization, sometimes with little thought to the strategic consequences. Taken together over time these small changes produce a major shift in direction. Thus the strategy emerges from the various corners of an organization and forms itself, as over time these small changes crystallize and take shape until they reach a form when they can be clearly articulated as a strategy.

In making strategic marketing decisions to meet the challenges of today's markets, firms in many ways need to make strategic decisions as to how they will proactively develop new markets and new strategies, while at the same time making decisions as to how they should react to changes and developments in the marketplace. This is much akin to the emergent strategy development process proposed by Mintzberg (1973). He distinguishes between deliberate strategy (rigid plans set from above) and emergent strategy that changes as new market insights arise. Mintzberg sees strategy development as something that emerges through the creative and iterative process of crafting a strategy of proactively seeking new opportunities while reacting to the challenges faced in the marke place stating that strategy '... is developed through long experience and commitment. Formulation and implementation merge into the fluid process of learning through which creative strategies emerge.'

Strategy development therefore is a multidimensional iterative process that can be built from any aspect of the marketing process and transcend up an organization rather than being dictated from above. There has to be thorough systematic analysis, but it also requires intuition and experience, innovation and creativity from all the persons involved in the company's operations.

Question 2.8

Evaluate the two approaches to strategic marketing decision-making outlined in the section above. Making reference to examples, show how each of the approaches can be used by marketing decision-makers.

See CIM SMD Examination December 2004 Q.4 and June 2005 Q4

As we have seen in the study text, a major criticism of marketing teaching has been the focus on simply the rational planning approach that is viewed as a highly formal linear sequence. In the SMD syllabus you need to think about alternative approaches and show an appreciation of the implications of different approaches to strategy formulation on strategic marketing decisions. These questions allow you to prepare for questions on this subject.

Issues of strategic marketing decision-making in small- and medium-sized enterprises

Small- and medium-sized enterprises (SMEs) face particular problems in decision-making in that they have limited resources of time, finance and professional expertise. This means they often do not have the capacity to set up the formal knowledge management systems of many larger organizations. In many SMEs, the managing director may have sole responsibility for all marketing decisions. This means such persons should have the capacity within themselves to generate ideas, assess options and clarify the best route forward. They do not have the luxury of bringing together teams of experts and professionals within the organization to help them analyse information and share the responsibility of the decision-making. Thus the responsibility of making strategic decisions can be a lonely and onerous one. Consequently they take a much more emergent approach to decision-making. Many commentators would argue this is a much healthier approach to strategic marketing decisions and gives SMEs an inbuilt flexibility to quickly respond to challenges in the marketing environment.

To overcome their limited resources, many SMEs create a *virtual organization* by developing a network of lateral partnerships through which they can access information, clarify their assessment of strategic options and can seek assurance the decisions being made are appropriate. Partnerships are formed by SMEs with an array of organizations such as consultants, universities, government agencies, banks, professional bodies and contacts in the market they perceive as being valuable to their business.

Thus in developing long-term relationships, firms develop an extended flexible organization, almost a virtual structure. They build a network of partnerships of varying degrees of intensity and use these relationships to enhance their capability to compete in their markets. The added value created through these relationships is based on the ability it gives

SMEs to gain access to both markets and information, to build barriers to competition as well as to ensure they can effectively service their markets.

If used effectively, such relationships can play a huge part not only in advising SMEs in decision-making but also in the provision of information on which to base decisions and helping to validate any decisions made as appropriate to the market conditions. These relationships therefore play an important role in strategic marketing decisions as part of the iterative strategy development process. Relationships both *inform* the strategy development process and *add form* to the strategy.

Insight: Not such a Red Letter Day for stakeholders

Red Letter Days was set up by Rachel Elnaugh, who was 24, to sell memorable experiences, such as driving a Formula 1 car or climbing a mountain. The gifts are sold in major retail stores such as Boots and Debenhams. The experiences are provided by a network of suppliers to Red Letter Days. However, after fighting for two and a half years to save the firm, it went into administration on 1 August 2005. It was a spectacular high profile crash because Elnaugh was one of the Dragons on television's *Dragons' Den*, dispensing tough advice to would-be entrepreneurs. Two years on she feels let down by business associates and former employees, with many selling their stories to the press and she has no immediate desire to go back into running a company. Instead she prefers to pass on the lessons she has learned.

Entrepreneurs are natural optimists and so it is vital to get in specialist advisers, such as a good lawyer, early on to maintain the balance. To keep a company afloat it is necessary to keep several options open – if you chose one and pursue that alone, it might fail. Also no one can be trusted, because many people can benefit from the failure of a multi-million pound business given the amount of money and opportunities at stake.

Adapted from: R Bridge, Failure is not the end of the road, *The Sunday Times*, 9 December 2007

Activity 2.5

Interview the managing director of a SME. Discuss with them the process of strategic marketing decision-making within the firm and the issues and problems they face in making such decisions.

Summary

◆ In the global marketing place there are a number of environmental factors driving the realignment of strategic thinking. Consequently, marketing managers have had to rethink the way they approach marketing decisions and incorporate new values into the marketing strategy process.

◆ The drivers for strategic realignment mean it is almost inevitable that at some stage marketing managers will be faced with a breakpoint that renders their current strategy obsolete.

◆ Marketing managers have to show how they contribute to shareholder value through customer-focused strategies based on offering value to customers, which enhances company performance and so increasing economic added value. By delivering enhanced value, marketing is more able to influence strategic decisions in the boardroom at a corporate level.

◆ Value-based marketing recognizes the need for a totally integrated marketing effort that manages the whole of the marketing process to deliver customer value and so build value for the shareholders and owners of the company.

◆ There are two principal views as to how strategic decisions are formulated, the rational linear approach and the iterative emergent approach. Mintzberg suggests strategy development is something that emerges through a creative and iterative process.

◆ SMEs face particular issues in making strategic marketing decisions as they generally do not have formal procedures and so need to form external relationships to contribute to the validation of the decision-making process.

Further study

For a more detailed treatment of the issues discussed in this unit you should read:

Doole, I. and Lowe, R. (2005) *Strategic Marketing Decisions in Global Markets*, Thomson Learning, Chapters 1 and 3

Doyle, P. (2000) *Value-Based Marketing: Marketing Strategies for Corporate Growth and Shareholder Value*, Wiley

Wilson, R.M.S. and Gilligan, C.T. (2004) *Strategic Marketing Management: Planning Implementation and Control*, Butterworth-Heinemann, 3rd edition

Hints and tips

The Strategic Marketing Decision examination paper requires candidates to apply their learning to a specific case study or industry scenario. In discussing the concepts examined in this unit it is important that candidates recognize that not all organizations are the same. You should therefore make sure that your answers reflect the size and competitive position of the companies specified in the scenario or case study provided in the examination. To build your skills in this it is a good idea to contextualize your learning as much as possible by applying the concepts learnt to different organizations in varying competitive situations. Reading marketing journals and the quality press can help you to build a portfolio of situations to which the concepts can be applied. In the examination if you are able to provide examples to illustrate your points, you can ensure that you make your answers as applicable to the situation specifics.

Bibliography

Collins, J. (2000) *Good to Great: Why Some Companies Make the Leap...and Others Don't*, Century

Collins, J.C. and Porras, J.I. (1997) *Built to Last: Successful Habits of Visionary Companies*, Century

Doyle, P. (2000) *Value-Based Marketing: Marketing Strategies for Corporate Growth and Shareholder Value*, Wiley

Hamel, G. and Prahalad, C.K. (1994) *Competing for the Future*, Boston, MA: Harvard Business School Press

Mintzberg, H. (1994) The *Rise and Fall of Strategic Planning*. New York, NY: The Free Press.

Mintzberg, H. (1973) *The Nature of Managerial Work*, New York: Harper & Row

Piercy, N.F. (2002) *Market Led Strategic Change: A Guide to Transforming the Process of Going to Market*, Oxford: Butterworth-Heinemann, 4th edition

Porter, M.E. (1985) *Competitive Advantage: Creating and Sustaining Superior Performance*, New York: Free Press

Treacy, M. and Wiersema, F. (1995) *The Discipline of Market Leaders*, London: Harper

Wilson, R.M.S. and Gilligan, C.T. (2004) *Strategic Marketing Management: Planning, Implementation and Control*, Oxford: Butterworth-Heinemann, 3rd edition

Unit 3

Competitive strategy as a learning process

Learning objectives

To score well in this examination you need not only to show you have an understanding of the SMD syllabus but that you can evaluate situations presented in an examination, identify decision areas and formulate solutions to dilemmas. Practising such a technique is good preparation for the examination.

In this unit you will:

2.7 Explore competitive marketing strategy as an emergent/learning process.

2.8 Examine the role of knowledge management in sustaining competitive advantage.

2.9 Evaluate the incorporation of customer-led Internet marketing into marketing strategies.

3.9 Appreciate the value of effective knowledge management in creating competitive advantage.

Having completed this unit you will be able to:

◆ Appraise a range of corporate and business visions, missions and objectives and the processes by which they are formulated, in the light of the changing bases of competitive advantage across geographically diverse markets.

◆ Evaluate the role of brands, innovation, integrated marketing communications, alliances, customer relationships and service in decisions for developing a differentiated positioning to create exceptional value for the customer.

This unit relates to the statements of practice:

1 Promote a strong market orientation and influence/contribute to strategy formulation and investment decisions.

2 Specify and direct the strategic marketing planning process.

Key definitions

Market orientation – the presence of a culture within an organization, which is focused towards the understanding of customer and competitors and so can create superior value for consumers.

Learning organization – an organization that has an effective learning capability and is able to efficiently manage its knowledge base to re-orient strategies and respond to competitive challenges and so reshape themselves to sustain their competitiveness.

Signal learning – it is concerned with monitoring the environment and the signalling of challenges and changes in a firm's markets and its performance in that market.

3R learning – the 3Rs stand for reflect, re-evaluate and respond. 3R learning occurs in anticipation of, and in response to, critical events occurring in a firm's markets. It is this type of learning that firms that successfully reinvent themselves undergo in reflecting on the demise of their traditional basis for competitive advantage.

Knowledge management – the systematic management of the knowledge gained through rigorous approach to the research and analysis undertaken. To make effective strategic decisions, it is of paramount importance that the knowledge built is trustworthy, credible and verifiable and that it is accessible to all the managers involved in the decision-making process.

Study guide

The concepts studied in this unit underpin the strategic marketing decision process in any successful company. Without a strong learning capability and an effective knowledge management system it is difficult for a company to build a sustainable competitive advantage. In the analysis and evaluation module of the Postgraduate Diploma of the CIM syllabus you will have studied in some depth the techniques and processes of carrying out an external analysis of the marketing environment and an internal audit of a company's capabilities. This unit builds on the skills and knowledge you have developed in that particular module and examines the issues of how that analysis should be incorporated into the strategic marketing decision process through the development of a learning capability and the management of the knowledge gained through rigorous analysis.

This unit signifies a fundamental shift in emphasis in the CIM syllabus, away from a preoccupation with teaching the marketing planning process as a unidimensional linear process that assumes a predetermined sequence of steps, and recognizes that competitive strategy in a large number of organizations is an emergent process of iterative development of learning. This means in studying this unit the CIM candidate has to learn how to apply their learning in a more flexible manner and move away from the idea that the CIM syllabus is simply a matter of getting the process right. A learning outcome of this unit is the ability to appraise competitive strategies and mission statements in the light of the learning capability of an organization. To do that, you will need to develop the ability to question assumptions you may have previously held and critically evaluate the competitive strategies of companies.

Competitive strategy as an emergent learning process

To build superior performance over time, a firm must be able to deliver superior customer value that is unique and difficult to imitate. To do this, firms need to develop the capability to adapt and develop competencies in a changing environment. The strategic marketing decisions made by managers in the process of developing their strategy have their roots in the perceptions of the senior management of their competitive situation. Understanding the relationship between how those perceptions underlie the strategic decisions made is critical to understanding effective strategy implementation. The process that links the two is the company's orientation towards the market and learning. It is the skills developed by the learning in an organization that drive the strategic decisions, which in turn generate competitive advantage. According to Wilson and Gilligan (2004), the three key elements of a customer value-based philosophy that will deliver this capability are a strong market orientation, a process of continuous learning and a commitment to innovation.

Activity 3.1

Identify five companies that you consider to be successful. For each company evaluate to what extent they have a customer-based philosophy.

Question 3.1

Identify what characteristics have to be present in an organization to create a learning environment.

The importance of learning in strategy development

Over time, whatever the industry and whatever the market they may compete in, all firms at some point will go through a period of substantial change, whether driven by customers, competitors or technology suppliers. There is a continuous pressure therefore on businesses to reshape themselves as well as to augment their products and services to maintain or increase their value to customers. It can be argued that firms are only able to sustain their competitiveness by understanding customer needs in a manner that allows superior value to be provided and by being aware of both existing and potential competitor activities so that they are in a position to take appropriate actions to respond to identified opportunities and threats. It is the firms that develop the learning capability to achieve this that are able to reshape themselves and so sustain their competitiveness.

Four organizational values are necessary for a firm to have effective learning capability:

1   A commitment to learning

2   Open-mindedness

3   A shared vision

4   Organizational knowledge sharing.

For a more detailed discussion of these values read Chapter 2 of Doole and Lowe (2005).

The learning capability required to overcome barriers and develop solutions to deal with the ambiguities and challenges encountered is an important part of the strategy development process itself. Firms need to be proactive in the building of knowledge of the marketplace so they are better able to react to environmental changes and defend their competitive positions in their markets. The focus of the strategy then is proactive in developing the knowledge base and building the resources to react and respond to the learning derived from the knowledge gained. According to Hamel and Prahalad (1994), it is the companies that are not able to transfer their learning to the strategy development process that fail to maintain their competitiveness, as depicted in Figure 3.1.

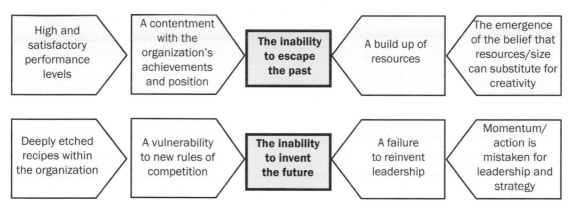

Figure 3.1: Barriers to escaping from the past and building for the future

Source: Adapted from Hamel and Prahalad (1994)

To avoid failure therefore in the making of strategic marketing decisions, there needs to be a process of reflection and examination so that the strategy development process can be developed and clarified over a period of time. The strategy development process itself is an iterative learning process from which the resultant strategy gradually emerges. A firm's long-term strategy tends to be incrementally built as a firm undergoes the process of reflecting on their experiences and responding to the challenges faced.

Insight: Coffee with a conscience

An example of a company with strong organizational values and an effective learning capability is Pollards. Pollards Tea and Coffee is a fifth-generation family business started in Sheffield in 1879 by Joseph Pollard, the great-great-grandfather of the present managing director Simon Bower. During the 1980s and 1990s Sheffield was not a great place to have a business and Bower's parents kept the business going by opening up three cafes and a shop. The company's wholesale trade in coffee and tea was then negligible.

After university, Bower did not join the family business but instead became an insurance loss adjuster, specialising in insurance fraud. Eventually Bower, then 30, grew tired of working for a large organization and this coincided with his parents' decision to retire in five years' time. It was agreed he would join the business after taking a year out, part of which was spent on a coffee plantation in Indonesia. After two years learning about the business Bower bought out his parents.

Now having full control of the business, Bower was able to make his mark. He expanded the coffee roasting side, so that the wholesale business now represents one third of the business. But the major change that Bower has made has been the result of his sincere social conscience developed as a result of his travel experiences and observations of the world around. Pollards now fully embraces the concepts of social responsibility: employing people in his cafes who as Bower would say are 'a bit different' – those who are 'diff'-abled by having learning difficulties; owning tea plantations in India that generate money that is used to support local school and hospital developments; and also helping the homeless in Sheffield. Bower recognizes that some of his and the staff's activities do not always create value in the money and accounting sense but maintains that value is created in other ways – it makes a better place for him and his staff to work. Bower won the Coutts Bank Special Prize for Family Businesses in 2005.

Adapted from: J. Ashworth, Pollards Tea and Coffee, www.coutts.com/familybusiness/prize, accessed on 3 January 2008

Types of learning in strategy development

Two types of learning are important in the strategy development process: *signal learning* and *3R learning*.

Signal learning

Signal learning is concerned with monitoring the environment. A company will carry out learning activities that enable it to generate the knowledge to *signal* the likely challenges and ambiguities in a firm's markets and so ensure that the firm is able to adapt and ensure the appropriateness of the strategic decisions they make. This type of learning is concerned with the traditional activities of the operations of a company. It means a company needs to have an understanding of the key indicators relevant to their products and services so they can monitor their markets and pick the right signals. Hendrix (2003) uses the term *limited visibility* for a situation when companies cannot see their market clearly because they are using the wrong type of indicators. In signal learning, therefore, it is important for companies to clearly articulate the factors they need to monitor to determine critical changes in the market, which may affect their products and services.

Signal learning is also a central component to the firms' ability to control the delivery of their strategies. To assess their performance, companies need to identify their critical success factors to monitor and evaluate how they are performing against the criteria to performance in the markets and the maintenance of their competitive advantage.

Activity 3.2

For your own organization or one of your choice, identify six key indicators that would help it identify potential opportunities and threats in the market in which they operate.

3R learning

3R learning occurs in anticipation of, and in response to, critical events occurring in a firm's markets. It is this type of learning that firms that successfully reinvent themselves undergo in reflecting on the demise of traditional markets. Both Dell Computers and Ryanair are good examples of companies that have undergone such a process. They were able to question long-held assumptions about themselves, their customer base and the strategic focus of their competitors and so developed a new way of competing in their industries. Thus, it is not merely about adaptation, but challenging traditional assumptions, reflecting, evaluating the new learning and responding with newly developed strategic thinking.

Important to this learning process is the ability to acquire knowledge, reflect and then generalize those experiences in the new competitive situation. 3R learning, it is suggested, is the type of learning required by the firm to help it move forward and reduce the frequency and magnitude of the impact of events in a turbulent environment. This type of capability enables firms to develop *advance knowledge* of key events in markets, build the *flexibility* to quickly reconfigure operations and reallocate resources to focus on an emergent opportunity or threat identified and so achieve a *rapid response* to it.

3R learning occurs largely through a firm's interaction with, and its observation of, the environment. Customer demand uncertainty, technological turbulence and competitive uncertainty are crucial environmental factors that demand an innovative capability from a company if they are to survive in such environments. A company that is committed to 3R learning can enhance its innovative capability in a number of ways:

◆ It is more likely to have developed the internal competence to build and market a technological breakthrough.

◆ It has the knowledge and the ability to understand and anticipate latent needs in potential customers and so has the ability to spot opportunities created by emerging market demand.

◆ An organization committed to 3R learning is likely to have a greater innovation capability than its competitors and be much more prepared to learn from its failures as well as its successes.

Both 3R learning and signal learning require a well-managed knowledge capability within an organization. The development of this will be examined in the following sections.

Question 3.2

Critically evaluate the role of 3R learning in the strategic marketing decision-making process.

The role of knowledge management

The task involved in developing a market intelligence system sufficient to provide the knowledge capability necessary to make sound global marketing decisions is enormous. Such a knowledge management system would not only have to identify and analyse potential markets but have the capacity to generate an understanding of the many environmental variables. As such, the role of the market researcher is to provide an assessment of market demand globally, an evaluation of potential markets and of the risks and costs involved in market entries as well as detailed information on which to base effective marketing strategies.

Insight: Canon – the knowledge management company

In Western Europe, Canon is the number one brand in digital cameras. They put down their success to their ability to pioneer new technologies and their ability to move faster than their competitors in this ever-changing sector. Canon has an impressive commitment to R&D. It is committed to spending 8.1 per cent of its global revenues in R&D each year. However, market analysts see one of the core strengths of Canon is its ability to transfer technology developed for the professional market and filter it down into consumer products. To achieve this, they need to have a strong empathy with the consumer markets and an understanding of how technology interfaces with consumers.

Such knowledge capability will incorporate three levels of analysis:

1   Analysis of the macro environment

2   Analysis at an industry/market level

3   Analysis of customers and competitors.

The macro environment

In examining the macro environment a manager needs to evaluate which variables will be the key market drivers in the future. In other words, to evaluate which factors are likely to exert the greatest influence on the market over the next 1–2 years as well as in the longer term. Once these variables have been identified it will be necessary to assess the impact of those factors on the marketing process. The company will need to make an evaluation of what difference the drivers will make (favourable/unfavourable) to their markets/products/brands/customers life cycles over the next few years and what strategic marketing decisions need to be made if the company is to maintain their ability to sustain a competitive advantage. Readers of this coursebook will be familiar with the SLEPT/PEST environmental model used for such an analysis. In Unit 2 we highlighted some of the key drivers in the macro environment that are impacting on the strategic marketing decisions made by companies; it is the drivers that are relevant to the products and services being offered by companies that managers need to build a knowledge capability of. To do this, managers will monitor changes in the political and legal environments, which may impact on their markets. Developments in the economic environment and the changing trends in the sociocultural environment will also need to be analysed as will the impact of technological changes influencing change in the marketing environment.

See CIM SMD Examination June 2006 Q.4

The introduction to this question should include an explanation of the nature of incremental, long-term trends, market changes due to customer, competitor and market structure factor, expected (damage to the environment) and unexpected environmental events and their effect on marketing strategy development and decision making. Careful choice of a destination that has been subject to a variety of environmental factors and events, and is in the process of repositioning its offer to visitors will provide examples to illustrate the impact of environmental events and help identify the strategic marketing options. In discussing strategic marketing decisions, it is important to remember that whilst tourism might be led by one agency many stakeholder organizations have an interest in the decisions and their concerns will always need to be addressed.

Industry/market analysis

The second stage of the external analysis is that of the industry or market. When carrying out such an analysis, the starting point is to formulate a wide definition of a company's market in terms of both the industry and the geographical boundaries. In defining markets by geography a firm needs to ask itself whether it holds the view that the firm is competing in a single global market or a series of separate and national or regional markets, and if so how wide a geographical area would they define their markets as being.

Industry market boundaries are defined by the potential to substitute products and services. An industry is a group of firms, which supplies any given market. Thus in defining its market a firm needs to consider also the boundaries of its industry. On the demand side, a market will be defined by the ability of customers to substitute a firm's product or service for another. Mobile phones can now do many wondrous things including taking pictures, thus redefining the traditional market boundaries of the camera market. On the supply side, the industry boundaries are defined by the ease with which a firm can transfer the products and services to new market segments.

Case study: Obesity eating up the NHS budget

A *British Medical Journal* report said that obesity treatment took up 9 per cent of the National Health Service budget in 2006. However, this is expected to rise considerably following the predicted rise in obese adults from one in five to one in three by 2010. Obesity is linked to a range of diseases and disorders, including heart disease, cancer, depression, back pain, diabetes and skin problems. If the trend continues then obesity could bankrupt the NHS and lead to reduced life expectancies. Unless the UK becomes healthier it has been estimated that spending on the NHS would need to increase by £30 billion over the next 20 years. The World Heath Organization has suggested that in the future 70 per cent of deaths will be due to obesity-related illnesses.

Various quite radical measures have been suggested to increase awareness and to encourage action to address the problem:

- A helpline telephone number could be promoted on labels of clothes with a waist of over 40in (102cm) for men, 37in (94cm) for boys, 35 in (88cm) for women and 31in (80cm) for girls.
- Health checks including waist and weight measurements for school leavers.
- Stricter planning regulations to allow new housing complexes only if sports facilities or green parks are nearby.
- Funding obesity surgery.
- Higher food tax for items high in sugar and salt.
- Allow new urban roads only if they have cycle lanes.

It has been proposed that while individuals have responsibility for their health, other stakeholders from the rest of society have responsibilities too, such as the food industry's in advertising, schools in promoting good diets and lifestyles, training of medical and public health staff, planners and so on.

Adapted from: Obesity could bankrupt the NHS, BBC News Online, 15 December 2006, accessed May 1 2008

Question 3.3

A key challenge is for the government and the NHS to become more proactive to address the problem of obesity. How might learning contribute to a more effective strategy?

Question 3.4

What factors should be taken into account in conducting a detailed analysis of our competitors?

Competitor analysis

A primary objective of competitor analysis is to understand and predict the rivalry or inter-active market behaviour between firms competing in the same market arena.

However, to assess the relative strengths and weaknesses of rivals or track their moves, a firm must be able to identify who their competitors are and from which direction their future competitors are likely to emerge. Managers who simply focus their competitor analysis on their current product/market arena may fail to notice threats that are developing due to the resources and latent capabilities of indirect and potential competitors. How a firm therefore decides to define its market boundaries is a critical decision in how the company then chooses to identify and analyse the competition.

The analysis should therefore include potential suppliers of products/services that consumers view as substitutes as well as those suppliers of related products and services in the arena the company has defined as its potential market. Competitor identification also needs to include an analysis of the degree to which products and services fulfil similar functions and address similar needs in the eyes of the consumer as well as an analysis of the degree to which firms have similar capabilities and benefits.

Having identified competitors it is of course necessary to evaluate their relative capabilities and compare their relative strengths and weaknesses. To predict who in the future is the likely stronger competitor, it is necessary to assess how their capabilities differ and which competitor has the capabilities best suited to the market needs being served. Bergen and P'eteraf (2002) suggest that competitors should be mapped against two criteria as can be seen in Figure 3.2. First is the degree to which the competitors are direct competitors, that is the degree to which they are competing in common markets. This they term *market commonality*. Second, competitors should be mapped as to the degree they are similar in their strengths in serving the needs of the defined market. This they term as *resource similarity*. A firm that scores high on both axes will be identified as a direct competitor while a firm with similar strategic capabilities but not operating in the same market arena will be identified as a potential competitor. Firms scoring low on both axes are viewed as incipient competitors. These firms perhaps need to be monitored to spot any changes in resource capability of market activity that could give them the capability to become direct competitors.

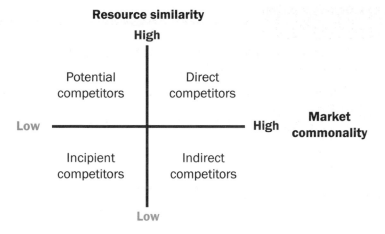

Resource similarity

High

| Potential competitors | Direct competitors |

Low ———————————————|——————————— High

| Incipient competitors | Indirect competitors |

Low

Market commonality

Figure 3.2: Identification of competitors

Source: Adapted from Bergen and P'eteraf (2002)

An outcome of the competitor analysis is to try and predict the strategic marketing decision a competitor will initiate and how the competitor may respond to the marketing decisions made by the firm carrying out the analysis as well as other competitors in the market.

Case study: From brick to video clips

Ten years ago the mobile phone was a brick-like contraption used for talking to people. Now it is a fashion accessory that you can use to e-mail, take videos and photographs, access the Internet and use as a computer.

Worth US$70 billion globally, the market is now being fuelled by the growth in such markets as China and India.

Competitively the mobile phone industry is interesting in that it operates at the intersection of three major industries, communication devices, computers and consumer electronics. In the past the barriers to entry have been high and the global market has been dominated by large vertically integrated firms such as Nokia, Motorola and Ericsson who had a wealth of expertise in high technology, mass production, managing complex supply chains as well as understanding mass consumer markets.

However, now these firms are being challenged. The hardware and software are being commoditized as the giants increasingly outsource manufacturing. Now the original design manufacturers, mainly in China and Taiwan as well as smaller specialist firms in handset design, chip design and software specialists, are starting to chip away and cherry-pick at the market shares of the giants.

At the same time, competitors from other sectors, for example, Apple with its iPhone built on the success of the iPod, are expected to become major players as technologies converge and companies cross new technology boundaries.

Source: Robin Lowe, from various public sources

Question 3.5

Assess the implications of the changing competitive structure of the mobile phone market to either Nokia or Motorola.

Activity 3.3

For your own organization, identify the key competitors and assess the degree to which they are direct, potential or indirect competitors.

Customer analysis

Central to the success of any commercial enterprise is the organization's relationship with its customer. If an organization is to be truly consumer oriented, then the analysis and understanding of their customers is of paramount importance. Without customers, businesses cannot operate. To meet the needs of the customer a company needs to know who their existing and potential customers are and understand their current and emergent needs. Thus the company needs to know:

◆ Who are its customers and what do they buy?

◆ Who is involved in the decision-making unit in making the purchase?

◆ Why and how do they make their purchases?

◆ When, where and how often do they make their purchases?

It is also important to assess the factors that influence customers. These influences tend to fall into three groups:

1 **Social/cultural influences** – such as the culture/sub-culture of the society in which the customer lives, their social status as well as the peer groups and family grouping with which they interact.

2 **Personal influences** – the personal wealth of the customer, their age, occupation and personal circumstances.

3 **Psychological influence** – their attitudes, perceptions and motivations towards the purchase they are making.

Likewise, is it important to have an understanding of the process a company's customers go through in making a purchase. Consumers may go through the stages of the buying process at varying speeds and not necessarily through all the stages in a linear fashion. The start of the buying process is when it is recognized by a potential customer that there is a buying problem to be solved, thus when the customer senses there is a difference between their actual state and desired state. Once a purchasing problem is recognized, it sometimes may stay unsatisfied, in which case it will remain a latent need. However, a consumer may go on from that position to either actively searching for information or simply have a heightened awareness and so be more receptive to external stimuli. In searching for information, particularly on the Internet, the consumer may be faced with a huge number of potential alternative solutions to their buying problem.

Most consumers will not have the time or the energy to make an exhaustive evaluation of these alternatives and so will try to identify specific criteria, either subconsciously or consciously to help them decide among the alternatives on offer. The result of the evaluation stage is the ranking of the alternatives. Potential customers will develop a final shortlist for a more in-depth evaluation to help the formation of the purchase intention. The choice made and the actual decision to purchase is the outcome of the evaluation stage. Sometimes the choice is easy to make if there is a clear alternative or perhaps if it is a simple purchase and so the risk of making a wrong decision is not costly. Customers having made a purchasing decision will seek reassurance after the purchase that the decision made was the correct one and so will make a post-purchase evaluation. Obviously this process will vary enormously depending on the level of risk attached to the purchase, the value of the purchase and the frequency with which the purchase is made. What is important is that managers understand the buying process of their customers and make appropriate strategic marketing decisions that minimize the risks and uncertainties at each stage and so facilitate the smooth passage from problem recognition to a positive purchase decision.

Activity 3.4

For a product or service purchase you have recently made, explain how you completed the different stages of the decision-making process.

B2B versus B2C customers

As readers studying this coursebook will be aware, in principle, there are two main types of customers, the individual/family customers, often referred to as B2C, and organizational customers. However, there are several different types of organizational customers, principally B2B, business to government (B2G), not-for-profit organizations and internal customers. (For a more detailed examination of all these types of customers see Chapter 3 of Doole and Lowe, 2005.) In the context of this coursebook, what is important is that in carrying out a customer analysis to identify who customers are and how and why they buy, the reader needs to be aware that a customer operating in an organizational environment can differ from the individual customer.

Building a knowledge management system

To build the learning capability discussed in the previous sections marketing managers need to ensure they systematically manage the knowledge gained in all the analysis as well as a planned and rigorous approach to the research undertaken. To make effective strategic decisions it is of paramount importance that the knowledge built is trustworthy, credible and verifiable and that it is accessible to all the managers involved in the decision-making process. Earlier in this unit we referred to two types of learning, signal learning and 3R learning. In this section we will examine the type of data-gathering techniques used in the external marketing environment that are useful in building these learning capabilities, and in the following section we will discuss the requirement of an effective learning organization.

Knowledge-gathering activities for signal learning

According to Slater (2001) the type of information-gathering tools that could help develop the capability to recognize the signals of potential problems and opportunities and be responsive are:

◆ Use of focus groups and customer surveys to understand customer wants and perceptions of current products and services

◆ Concept testing and conjoint analysis to guide the development of new products and services

◆ Relationships with customers to gain insights into customer desires

◆ Customer information files to improve segmentation and targeting efforts

◆ Customer satisfaction surveys to improve ways of keeping and maintaining customers.

As said previously, another important role of signal learning is monitoring a company's performance in the marketplace. This topic will be dealt with some depth in Units 11 and 12 of this coursebook.

Knowledge-gathering activities for 3R learning

For 3R learning, companies need to acquire and evaluate market information in a systematic and anticipatory manner so they are able to understand the unexpressed needs of customers and the capabilities and plans of their competitors. To do this, firms need to:

◆ Scan the market broadly

◆ Have a long-term focus to their information-gathering activities

◆ Share knowledge throughout the organization in a coordinated and focused manner.

In this type of learning, companies would combine traditional marketing research techniques with other techniques to uncover customers' unarticulated needs. For 3R learning, therefore, companies would make use of qualitative research to observe customers and to build a picture of how they behave as consumers. They would work closely with lead users in the market and build up a number of different types of knowledge-based relationships to develop an effective flow of information from all the stakeholders in the market. The objective of these relationships would be to gain access to specialist knowledge, either to understand better the most efficient route to market or to obtain advance information of imminent occurrences in the market as well as potential long-term trends. Such relationships enhance the quality of decision-making and help a company to validate the appropriateness of the decisions made to meet the changing dimensions of the market.

An effective learning organization

Garvin (1993, p. 80) considered effective learning organizations as those that become skilled at 'creating, acquiring and transferring knowledge, and at modifying behaviour to reflect new knowledge and insights'. Senge (1992, p. 1), more poetically, described such organizations as:

> organisations where people continually expand their capacity to create the results they truly desire, where new and expansive patterns of thinking are nurtured, where

collective aspiration is set free, and where people are continually learning how to learn together.

However, an organization may well effectively learn, but the learning outcome may itself be misguided and not contribute to the making of strategic marketing decisions that are effective in building customer value. There has to be a link therefore between effective learning and performance improvements. A company can only make such a link if it uses its knowledge management and its learning to build an efficient organizational memory that can be accessed through an effective knowledge management system. Without an effective organizational memory, firms can be caught in a trap where ongoing learning efforts breed long-term dynamism in their marketing programmes but fail to produce long-term market performance improvements.

In creating an effective learning organization a company needs to develop a comprehensive learning strategy for the company that integrates knowledge management and learning. Integrating learning activities with an effective knowledge management is not easy and requires good dialogue and understanding from all parties. Collaboration among functional departments is therefore important. The IT department may be responsible for building the architecture, but it is important in the marketing context that the decision of what is meaningful information and the management of that information is the responsibility of the marketing executives who will be using the information.

Question 3.6

What do you see as the major barriers to the integration of knowledge management and learning activities for strategic marketing decisions? How can these be overcome?

See CIM SMD Examination December 2005 Q.3

The syllabus for SMD emphasiszs the importance of leveraging the knowledge assets of the organization for competitive advantage. Key to this is embedding a learning culture, and processes for effectively managing the wide range of marketing, environmental, technological and internal company information. It is important to emphasize that this question is not simply about customer relationship management, although it might be part of the answer. The main part of the answer should focus on the barriers to developing an effective learning culture, for example, management commitment and recognition of different types of knowledge, and learning and processes for managing the knowledge, for example, how huge amounts of information are collected, analysed and disseminated, and how the lessons of good practice are shared.

The role of Internet-based strategies in developing a sustainable competitive advantage

The Internet has meant huge opportunities for companies of all sizes and has played an important role in helping companies develop a sustainable competitive advantage. It has enabled them to substantially reduce the costs of reaching customers and because of the low-entry costs of the Internet it has permitted firms with low capital resources to become global marketers, in some cases overnight.

Insight: Online shopping growth in Europe

According to eMarketer, e-commerce in Europe will reach 323 billion euros ($407 billion) by 2011. It is anticipated that there will be an average growth rate for the next five years of 25 per cent. Customers see the advantages of e-commerce as being able to shop quickly, to easily find the items, to avoid the hassle of crowded shopping centers and to find good discounts. The UK, Germany and France, account for about 72 per cent of all online sales in Europe and the UK is forecast to see the largest growth.

In 2007, shoppers spent the equivalent of $84 billion, an increase of 39 per cent. While UK consumers spend the most online, there are more online shoppers in Germany (27 million). By comparison France has fewer shoppers (roughly 14 million online shoppers) and spends far less online. Italy, Spain and the Netherlands will grow rapidly too over the period but Eastern European countries like Russia, Poland and the Czech Republic, are not expected to have an impact on online shopping until well into the 2010 decade, according to researchers.

Adapted from: Online shopping forecast: 323 billion euros by 2011, www.bizreport. com, accessed 13 August 2007

Activity 3.5

Consider your own company. In what ways has the company embraced the Internet in developing its competitive marketing strategies? How has this changed the ways in which it approaches its strategic marketing decision-making?

The implications of being able to market goods and services online have been far-reaching. The Internet has led to an explosion of information to the consumer, giving them the potential to source products from the cheapest supplier in the world. This has impacted on the way firms compete globally. The increasing standardization of prices across borders, or at least, to the narrowing of price differentials as consumers become more aware of prices in different countries has meant to build a sustainable competitive advantage, companies have had to rethink the way they compete in the market, the way they segment their markets and the way they build their routes to market.

The Internet, by connecting end-users and producers directly, has reduced the importance of traditional intermediaries (i.e. agents and distributors) as more companies have built the online capability to deal direct with their customers, particularly in B2B marketing. To survive, such intermediaries have begun offering a whole range of new services. The value added of their offering no longer being principally in the physical distribution of goods but rather in the collection, collation, interpretation and dissemination of vast amounts of information. The critical resource possessed by this new breed of 'cybermediary' is information rather than inventory. The Internet has also become a powerful tool for supporting networks both internal and external to the firm. Many global firms have developed supplier intranets through which they source products and services from preferred suppliers who have met certain criteria. It has also become the efficient new medium for building knowledge on the customer base and ensuring an effective learning strategy for the company in the way the Internet enables companies to monitor everything from hits on a website to building detailed profiles of customers and so helping companies build mass-customization strategies.

Thus Internet-based strategies play an important role in helping companies build a sustainable competitive advantage. It has created a fundamental shift in the marketing environment and requires a radically different strategic approach affecting all aspects of the strategic marketing decision process.

Question 3.7

How has the growth of Internet-based strategies by companies impacted on the services offered by intermediaries in the supply chain?

Case study: Tesco – A Fresh and Easy entry to the US but 20 years in the making

Choosing the most appropriate business model for a market is a critical marketing decision and should be based on deep understanding. After studying US shopping habits for 20 years, Tesco, the world's third biggest retailer entered the US market in 2007. Instead of opting to compete with Wal-Mart, the number one retailer, by developing superstores, Tesco decided to focus on small local stores, much smaller than typical US supermarkets, and typically employing between 20 and 30 people.

Tesco has gone to considerable lengths to learn about shopping habits, with researchers living with 60 American families for two weeks to discover what products they bought and what food they ate. A mock outlet was erected in secrecy in a Los Angeles warehouse to test designs for the physical appearance and to train staff. Members of the public were invited along but told they were taking part in a film about supermarkets.

The outlets are branded 'Fresh and Easy' to emphasize its gourmet-style products and all-natural food. Its customers are time-starved shoppers that want fresh, healthy food, including ready meals at affordable prices. The company is promoting environmental awareness, with its new distribution centre in Riverside California having one of the largest solar-panelled roofs in the US. It has had to set up its supply chain and distribution from scratch, in order to achieve its aim of 60 per cent local sourcing. It has chosen western US because of its size and population density, and Tesco aims to locate stores in some of the low income areas, where fresh, healthy, affordable food is not available locally very easily. However, there are many local competitors, such as Vons, Trader Joe's, Ralphs, Albertsons as well as Wal-Mart already entrenched.

Tesco is aiming to succeed where other retailers, such as Marks and Spencer and Sainsbury, failed in the 1980s and early 1990s. Its plans are ambitious as it aims to have 250 stores in California, Arizona and Nevada within its first two years of operation and 800 by 2012.

Adapted from: J Gordon, Tesco makes fresh foray to US, *BBC News Online*, accessed 3 December 2007

Question 3.8

What were the strategic marketing decisions for Tesco?

Question 3.9

Having taken a decision to opt for this retail model, how should Tesco use a 'learning approach' to maintain competitive advantage?

Summary

◆ The values that underlie strategic marketing decisions need to include a strong company orientation towards learning about the market competitors as the strategy development process itself is an iterative learning one.

◆ Firms need to be proactive in the building of knowledge of the market place so they are better able to react to environmental changes and defend their competitive positions in their markets.

◆ Such knowledge capability of a company should incorporate three levels of analysis: analysis of the macro environment, analysis at an industry/market level and an analysis of customers and competitors.

◆ A primary objective of competitor analysis is to understand and predict the rivalry or interactive market behaviour between firms competing in the same market arena.

◆ In an effective learning organization, a company will link the knowledge it has built and the learning it has gained to build an efficient organizational memory that can be accessed through an effective knowledge management system.

◆ For some companies the growth of Internet-based strategies has played a significant role in the way they compete in the marketplace and has impacted on all aspects of the marketing process and the way in which decisions are made. Other companies simply view the Internet as a medium for them to advertise their products and service, in which case the impact of the Internet has been far less.

Further study

Doole, I. and Lowe, R. (2008) *International Marketing Strategy: Analysis, Development and Implementation*, Cengage Learning, 5th Edition, Chapters 2 and 3

Doole, I. and Lowe, R. (2005) *Strategic Marketing Decisions in Global Markets*, Thomson Learning, Chapter 2

Wilson, R.M.S. and Gilligan, C.T. (2004) *Strategic Marketing Management: Planning Implementation and Control*, Butterworth-Heinemann, 3rd edition

Hints and tips

Candidates of the Strategic Marketing Decision syllabus need to be aware of the scope of this module. International Marketing Strategy is no longer taught as a separate module but has been subsumed across all modules. All modules therefore take a global perspective in their scope and orientation. In this module it is expected that the candidate is able to think, analyse and make strategic marketing decisions on a global scale. It is important therefore that you understand the global dimensions of marketing and you collect information on companies that operate globally as well as nationally.

Likewise, it is expected that there will be increasing emphasis on the importance of the Internet in competing globally. References to the Internet and to global markets are incorporated into many of the units of this coursebook. While Internet-based strategies and international marketing are not taught explicitly at Postgraduate Diploma of the CIM syllabus, they are both deeply entrenched into the syllabus and so candidates need to be prepared to answer examination questions where an understanding of the issues involved in these areas is required.

Bibliography

Bergen, M. and P'eteraf, M.A. (2002) Competitor identification and competitor analysis: A broad based managerial approach, *Managerial & Decision Economics*, 23, 160

Doole, I. and Lowe, R. (2005) *Strategic Marketing Decisions in Global Markets*, Thomson Learning

Garvin, D.A. (1993) Building a learning organization, *Harvard Business Review*, July–August, 78–90

Hamel, G. and Prahalad, C.K. (1994) *Competing for the Future*, Boston, MA: Harvard Business School Press

Hendrix, P.E. (2003) Limited visibility, *Marketing Management*, 41–47

Senge, P.M. (1992) *The Fifth Discipline: The Art and Practice of The Learning Organization*, Century Press

Slater, S.F. (2001) Developing a customer value based theory of the firm, *Journal of the Academy of Marketing Science*, 25(2) 162-167

Wilson, R.M.S. and Gilligan, C.T. (2004) *Strategic Marketing Management: Planning, Implementation and Control*, Oxford: Butterworth-Heinemann, 3rd edition

Unit 4 Developing corporate-wide marketing innovation

Learning objectives

The CIM syllabus for Strategic Marketing Decisions requires you to demonstrate an understanding of the impact of innovation throughout the organization's marketing activities.

In studying this unit you will:

2.2 Explain the nature of innovation in marketing and the factors affecting its development in decisions to create competitive advantage and customer preference.

2.3 Evaluate the role of innovation management and risk-taking in achieving competitive advantage.

2.4 Examine the issues in creating an innovative marketing culture within an organization.

2.9 Evaluate the incorporation of customer-led Internet marketing into marketing strategies.

Having completed the unit you will be able to:

◆ Evaluate the role of brands, innovation, integrated marketing communications, alliances, customer relationships and service in decisions for developing a differentiated positioning to create exceptional value for the customer.

◆ Demonstrate the ability to develop innovative and creative marketing solutions to enhance an organization's global competitive position in the context of changing product, market, brand and customer life cycles.

◆ Define and contribute to investment decisions concerning the marketing assets of an organization.

This unit relates to the statements of practice:

Bd.1 Promote a strong market orientation and influence/contribute to strategy formulation and investment decisions.

Cd.1 Promote organization-wide innovation and cooperation in the development of brands.

Ed.1 Promote corporate-wide innovation and cooperation in the development of products and services.

Key definitions

Diffusion curve – is the model of the spread of a new product into the markets, split into customer response segments (innovators, early adopters, early majority, late majority and laggards).

Industry breakpoints – are defined (Strebel, 1996) as a new offering to the market that is so superior in terms of customer value that it disrupts the rules of the competitive game. Two types of breakpoints are discussed. *Divergent breakpoints* are associated with the sharply increasing variety in the competitive offerings and consequently higher value for the customer. *Convergent breakpoints* are the result of improvements in the system and processes resulting in lower delivered costs.

Continuous innovations – cause negligible or slightly disruptive effects upon the purchase and consumption of the product.

Dynamically continuous innovations – have a more disruptive effect on the way that the products and services are used.

Discontinuous innovations – have a highly disruptive effect upon usage and purchasing patterns and require a high level of marketing to explain the benefits and to educate consumers about how the product should be used.

Study guide

This unit is concerned with making strategic marketing decisions that are innovative and, therefore, might challenge the often highly planned, conventional marketing strategies of many organizations. This unit is concerned with examining the ways in which organizations can promote corporate-wide innovation. In doing this it is useful to identify the nature and sources of innovation and the implications of pursuing innovation for marketing management. We examine how technological innovation, such as the Internet, has provided both a threat and an opportunity for firms. Smaller entrepreneurial firms are often at the forefront of innovation, and it is useful to learn from them. Larger firms need to accept that risk is associated with innovation and create a supportive environment that will protect and encourage innovators.

To better understand entrepreneurial marketing and motivate themselves to be more innovative, students should read how entrepreneurs have successfully identified and exploited new opportunities. Students should also familiarize themselves with Internet marketing and e-business. Suggestions for further reading are included in the 'Further study' section at the end of this unit.

The nature and impact of innovation

Innovation is characterized by occasional 'great leaps forward' interspersed with continuous small-scale improvements. Although the most obvious impact of innovation is the launch of an entirely new product or service into a market, in practice, it is possible for organizations to gain improved performance and increase competitive advantage through continual innovation in every aspect of the marketing activity. At the outset it is important to recognize that innovation is not the same as invention. Inventions drive the major technological breakthroughs, but the majority of innovations involve creativity in many different areas, such as design, brand imagery, service development, process improvement, new routes to market and so on.

Continual small-scale innovation throughout the organization is essential. Customers are becoming more demanding and have higher expectations of products, services and process as they are exposed to a greater variety of competitive products. Organizations must respond by continually seeking to improve every aspect of their offerings to retain customer interest and loyalty while they wait for the next great breakthrough.

It is important to recognize too that to be successful in innovation it is not enough to simply have good ideas. It is vital to have an effective process that will lead to commercial success. An innovation is not a success until it is profitably satisfying customer demands.

Technology life cycle

Technology has a major impact on innovation, and there is a technology life cycle. Figure 4.1 shows the nature of the relationship between investment in R&D and the impact on performance in a particular technology. At the top of the S-curve little further improvement in performance is possible, no matter how much further investment is made, as the product (e.g. black and white television technology) has reached the limits of development. At this point a new technology derived from an earlier invention will provide a product (e.g. colour televisions) to satisfy the emerging customer needs. Initially the new technology will provide a basic product with limited performance, but it will be improved over time with further R&D investment.

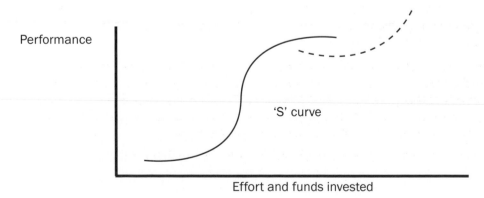

Figure 4.1: R&D investment and performance and discontinuity

Technology both drives change in many market sectors and provides a means of responding to change. As illustrated in Figure 4.2, those firms that are the first to embrace a new technology and find a practical application, for example creating a new product, service or a new route to market, will gain a new source of competitive advantage. However, this might well set new standards for the industry sector, and competitors will have to also achieve those standards if they wish to compete in the future. So all competitors in the sector catch up by embracing the new technology. Consequently, the innovative firm again has to find a new technological advance that allows them to get ahead again.

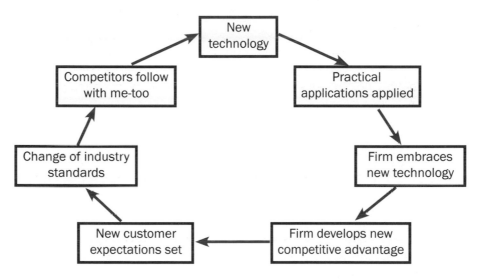

Figure 4.2: Technology and competitive advantage

Source: Doole and Lowe (2005)

Case study: Kodak switching their strategies to digital

The rate of changeover by consumers to digital cameras from traditional film formats has lead to a major opportunity and a massive problem for Kodak, one of the leading players in the field. The industry reached a breakpoint in the S-curve, with sales of film, single-use cameras and other traditional products falling by 20 per cent in 2004. However, Kodak was still able to report higher quarterly profits because digital camera sales increased by 41 per cent in the year.

The major management challenge for Kodak was to restructure its business to cope with the change. It embarked on four years of restructuring work. It had to cut costs in its film manufacturing and processing business, and this has meant a cut in its workforce worldwide of 27,000. After two years of losses the company returned to profit in 2007 with a workforce of 30,000, its lowest since the 1930s.

Adapted from: Kodak to cut an extra 3,000 jobs, *BBC News Online*, accessed 8 February 2007.

Industry breakpoints

Major structural changes occur in markets from time to time, and it is essential that companies are able to anticipate and respond rapidly to them. Breakpoints can be the result of technological breakthrough, but also other factors such as an economic downturn, a new source of supply, changes of government policy or legislation, shifts in customer expectations, changes in distribution channels, declining revenues, new entrants and the identification of new opportunities by one company lead to new responses from competitors.

See CIM SMD Examination June 2005 Q.3

The SMD syllabus deals frequently with companies having to take a new direction because of their being in the mature phase of the life cycle. This question takes one such company and requires the candidate to discuss the different levels of innovation, *incremental and radical*, and evaluate how each may be used in the context given.

The impact of information and communications technology

The developments in information and communications technology, particularly the development of the Internet, illustrate this. The Internet and other associated technologies do not just provide new products and services but also provide the solutions to old marketing process problems, such as how customers in remote locations around the world can contribute to the design of a new global product as much as the customer next door and how a 10-person business can market its products or services to its potential customers in 40 or 50 countries.

Question 4.1

Explain the concepts of technical discontinuities and industry breakpoints. Using examples describe the marketing activity that can be used to successfully exploit the opportunities that result.

New technologies facilitate innovation in many other marketing processes. Technology does not change the elements, challenges and dilemmas associated with the marketing decision-making process but does have a major impact on the nature of the marketing strategy that is used and the solutions that are developed. Most importantly these technologies have speeded up many of the marketing processes and have integrated internal processes with external processes. For example, internal data on sales of an individual product in an individual supermarket can be made available through an extranet to suppliers, who can arrange a delivery to the supermarket against an open order to keep the shelves filled.

Categories of innovation and the marketing implications

There are a number of ways of categorizing innovations. At a fundamental level the types are shown in the Insight.

Insight: The types of innovation

◆ **Product innovation** – Changes in the product and services the organization offers.

◆ **Process innovation** – Changes in the way products and services are created and delivered, for example, online banking.

◆ **Position innovation** – Changes in the context in which products and services are introduced. For example, simplified mobile phones to appeal to older users, who just want to make a telephone call.

◆ **Paradigm innovation** – Changes in the underlying mental models that frame what the organization does.

Source: Utterback (1994).

Innovations can also be placed into one of the three categories – continuous, dynamically continuous and discontinuous – according to the disruption they cause to customer buying and usage patterns. The significance of this is in the nature and cost of marketing activity that is needed to educate customers about the new product and service and explain how it is different from existing ones and persuade them to buy the new one.

Flat screen monitors for computers are continuous innovations and have not changed how customers use them, and so marketing activity focuses on the aesthetics rather than the need to re-educate consumers. As consumers become more knowledgeable, however, there is no guarantee that continuous innovations will be accepted without question. Products that are going to be consumed in the same way but with substantially changed ingredients (e.g. GM ingredients in foods or fluoride in toothpaste) will not always be automatically acceptable to consumers.

A digital camera can fall into both the dynamically continuous and the discontinuous innovation categories. If it is used to take pictures and the memory card is then taken to a photographic shop for processing, it has little effect on the customer's lifestyle, whereas if it is used by the customer in conjunction with a computer or special printer for processing, it has a more disruptive effect on purchasing and usage and customers must be educated as to the benefits. For continuous and dynamically continuous innovations the mass of the market should be easily convinced of the benefits.

The more disruptive the innovation is to the customers' normal purchasing, consumption and disposal patterns the greater the investment that is needed in marketing communications to educate them in respect of why they need the innovation, how they will benefit from it and how they should use it (and not use it). In the early days it will be the innovators of the diffusion curve (Figure 4.3) that will be first to see the benefits of a disruptive innovation. It may take the early adopters and early majority a long time to accept the product. Consequently, the take-up of the product may be slower than expected.

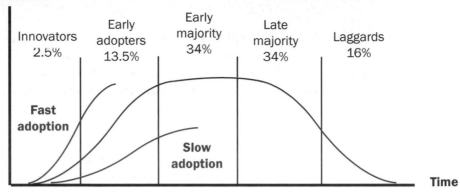

Figure 4.3: The diffusion curve

Major technology change may require a radical change in the firm's management processes such as manufacturing, distribution channel and marketing, and so a re-orientation or even a complete reinvention of the firm's business model might be needed.

Activity 4.1

Assess the innovation capability of your own organization (or one of your choice) and assess the number and quality of successful innovations that the organization produces that reach the market.

Sources of innovation and opportunity identification

While much of our discussion so far has centred on technological breakthroughs, our discussion on industry breakpoints suggests that many breakthroughs are not the result of technology. Other sources of innovation are now highlighted, which have the effect of creating industry breakpoints. We then look at the specific techniques that might be used for identifying opportunities. Many of the innovation opportunities come as a result of major environmental change or unexpected events and create the industry breakpoints.

Opportunity identification

Doole and Lowe (2005) have discussed techniques to identify opportunities. These include:

◆ **Scientific exploration** – that starts with no immediate, obvious application or customer benefit in mind.

◆ **Analysis of current and anticipated customer needs** – is an obvious starting point. Asking customers what they want usually identifies new product and service developments, but it is often difficult for customers to articulate what they do not know is possible.

◆ **Segmenting markets further** – than they have been segmented before is an effective way of developing products and services to meet more precisely the needs of sub-segments of customers.

◆ **Identifying a new emerging segment** – that is born out of changes in the mood, attitudes and expectation of customers and dissatisfaction with current offerings.

◆ **Applying existing techniques in a new sector** – Managers can make connections between seemingly unrelated ideas or apply a technology, process or technique from one business sector to another.

◆ **Vertical integration** – of the supply chain: an organization can eliminate one link in the chain or create a new, better value route to market. A fruit grower in Kent (United Kingdom) vertically integrated the business into jam making (Tiptree Jams).

◆ **Business rationalization** – or mergers often lead to some products and services being no longer required or a customer segment no longer being satisfied.

◆ **Innovation in mature sectors** – The most successful innovations have taken place often in mature sectors by offering customers a quantum leap in value.

Thinking techniques

Creative thinking techniques can be applied by managers in an existing organization to observe trends, understand the underlying causes of common complaints, apply the leading-edge knowledge and expert ideas in the sector and spot market gaps and unfulfilled requirements.

Ignoring the competition and providing a quantum leap

The fast-growth companies do not compete by benchmarking themselves with competitors and trying to match or beat them. They ignore the competition by offering buyers a quantum leap in value, often competing in a quite different way.

Kim and Mabourgne (1997) say that an organization must ask what it would take to win over the mass of buyers without relying on traditional competitive marketing and they propose asking the questions in Table 4.1.

Table 4.1 Giving customers a quantum leap in value

◆ What factors that your industry takes for granted should be eliminated?

◆ What factors that your industry competes on should be reduced well below the standard?

◆ What factors that your industry competes on should be raised well above the standard?

◆ What factors should be created that your industry has never offered?

In doing this the most creative organizations set new standards for their industry. Rarely are these organizations the most powerful market leaders but may become leaders. Recent examples of firms offering a quantum leap in value include the low-cost activities of Amazon and Dell.

Case study

Cirque du Soleil's new act

Cirque du Soleil was created in 1984 by a group of street performers led by its founder, Guy Laliberté, who realized the traditional circus format with the pedestrian animal acts and slapstick comedy routines of the clowns was outdated. Cirque created a new industry sector, by eliminating some of the costly and problematic elements, such as the animals and replaced them with spectacular shows that focused on technology, performance arts and musical theatre. They no longer offered low-priced entertainment targeted at children but instead aimed at adults with premium-priced shows. Cirque now employs 3800 people and has been seen by 50 million people in almost 100 cities.

Source: www.cirquedusoleil.com, accessed March 2008

Question 4.2

What assumptions were challenged in this example?

Activity 4.2

Identify the possible techniques for opportunity identification that could be applied to your own organization or an organization of your choice. Use one of the techniques to identify an opportunity.

Insight: Home and mobile media

People wanting to enjoy a variety of home entertainment media, such as radio, television, music, electronic games and online media, must be prepared to have a roomful of electronic boxes, cables resembling spaghetti and service subscriptions covering a page of a bank statement. If they want on-the-move communications and entertainment, such as telephony, Internet connection, music and radio, they must be prepared to carry pockets or bags full of quickly out-of-date gadgets.

A number of products are emerging to address the confusion, including media PCs, multifunction mobile phones and wireless connectivity, but it is difficult still to predict where the next breakpoints in the sector will occur. Use the techniques discussed to suggest where the next innovations and breakpoints might occur.

Innovation throughout the marketing strategy process

Opportunities for innovation can be initiated by challenging current thinking in every aspect of the marketing strategy development process, and some examples of areas that can be exploited are included in Table 4.2.

Table 4.2 Marketing strategy process innovations

Innovations	Some examples
Environmental changes	Responding to legal changes (e.g. safety or environmental pollution regulations, market derogation)
	Responding to technological advances
Resources and capabilities audit	Exploiting company competencies in a new way (e.g. using e-business)
Strategy	Segmenting the market further than it is at present
	Repositioning to benefit from changes in customer needs and attitudes
Market entry alternatives	Participating in an alliance to redefine the market
The marketing mix	Focusing on interactive rather than mass communications
Supply chain	Finding new value from supply chain contributions
Relationships	Redefining the mix to solution provision rather than selling products and services

The innovation process

The inescapable fact is that the majority of good ideas never become commercial successes. There is a strong possibility that they will fail at every stage of the product development process. For this reason it is vital to have an established, objective and systematic process to:

◆ Increase the number of ideas coming forward

◆ Better manage the process from idea generation to commercialization

◆ Increase the chances of success for the potential winners

◆ Screen out potential losing ideas as early as possible to avoid wasting effort

◆ Minimize the early costs of investigating individual ideas

◆ Tap the organization's creative potential by encouraging everyone in the organization to suggest innovations and improvements

◆ Increase the speed to market to beat the competition

◆ Maximize the value of the innovation to the organization and its customers.

Developing a systematic process for innovation

The familiar process for new product development suggested by Kotler is detailed in Figure 4.4. While it is intended for new product development, the concepts behind the process can be applied to most areas of marketing innovation. The objectives of the NPD process is to delay the largest investment cost, until it has been shown that the new product or service has a high probability of success so that the risk is reduced as far as possible. Carrying out the process as a linear sequence as shown in Figure 4.4 is time consuming, and so many organizations aim to carry out the individual process steps simultaneously, thus reducing the time to market.

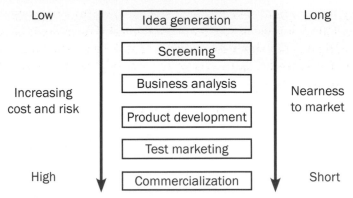

Figure 4.4 The new product development process

Most marketing texts include explanations of how the process should be used, and a fuller discussion is included in Doole and Lowe (2005).

Activity 4.3

Design a process for innovation for your own organization or an organization of your choice, from idea to commercialization. What are the major barriers in the process and how might they be overcome?

Diffusion is key

Achieving a commercial success depends on a number of critical factors in the innovation process including:

◆ Minimizing the early stage costs in the innovation process and only carrying out the high investment at later stages of the process when there is a high probability of success.

◆ Successfully launching the product or service to quickly get a high level of customer first purchases.

◆ Achieving a positive cash flow quickly.

◆ Winning over fast enough a sufficient number of loyal customers who will repeat purchase to generate a sustainable income stream for the product or service.

◆ Using cost-effective market entry methods to build global sales.

◆ Achieving continual improvements after launch through ongoing R&D to keep the product or service fresh.

Research suggests that the reason for failure in innovation is not usually technology failure but more often marketing related. It is ineffective diffusion of the innovation into the market that is the main reason for failure.

Multinational enterprises may need to launch new products and services simultaneously into many markets. Their considerable resources allow them to tolerate large negative outflows over longer periods. By contrast, smaller organizations need to reach the break-even point (Figure 4.5) and generate a positive cash flow as quickly as possible merely to survive. Consequently, they need to keep their R&D investment, marketing and fixed costs as low as possible to quickly recover them through sales revenue. This may mean that their launch and marketing programmes may need to strike a careful balance between creating awareness and interest through a comprehensive promotional programme and incurring unacceptably high costs.

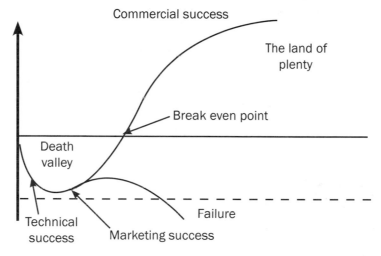

Figure 4.5 Getting to break-even point

Bolton and Thompson (2000) describe the period up to the break-even point shown in Figure 4.5 as 'death valley', which must be crossed before reaching the 'land of plenty'. In the initial commercialization period for any innovation there are two critical points in the new business model, shown in Figure 4.5. The first is whether the new business is a technical success – does it work for the customers and deliver the benefits to them that were set out in the original brief? If it is not a technical success, then the business will fail. The second point is whether the new business is a marketing success – in other words, will sufficient customers from the target segment buy and repeatedly buy to generate the necessary cash flows? If not the business will again fail.

It is worth re-emphasizing that the organization should focus on the opportunity to generate revenue and exploit the market gap rather than stubbornly trying to sell the specific product or service that was originally envisaged. Famously, Honda failed initially to make an impact when it sold large motor cycles in the United States but noticed that people were fascinated by the 50 cc bikes their staff were using. They sold the 50 cc bikes successfully to build up the business and later succeeded with large bikes. They are still the market leader in the United States.

The problem for decision-makers arises when the initial product or service offer fails to generate sufficient revenue. The question becomes how long should it be supported before making a significant revision. A further problem is created if a product or service is successful in some less important country or regional operations but fails in the major markets.

Question 4.3

What do you consider to be the critical success factors in achieving a commercial success?

Risk-taking in bureaucratic and entrepreneurial organizations

There are two certainties associated with innovation: as competition increases, growth and even survival in any market sector will become more difficult without it, and risk-taking is an inevitable part of innovation. Organizations adopt a stance somewhere on a continuum between being risk-averse, characterized by bureaucratic organizations and risk-taking, typically seen in entrepreneurial companies. Over a period of time, an organization must move out of low value-adding areas to higher value-adding areas through innovation. To develop and grow an organization, one must be a risk taker, but for sustainability one must also be a risk manager. An organization should not collapse if one's innovation goes wrong.

Risk-taking in bureaucratic firms

Even the most bureaucratic organizations recognize the need to take risks but fail to put in place a strategy and process to support it. Large firms often ignore the marketing philosophy of meeting customer needs and instead arrogantly believe that they can influence sales through their market power. They believe that timing market entry is less important than getting their launch right, so bureaucratic firms are rarely first movers if there is a significant change.

To become less bureaucratic, firms must recognize that innovators do not follow rules because at its best innovation has no rules. Innovation avoids established patterns, standards and controls that tend to be the central pillars of a bureaucratic firm. There is an inevitable conflict between the entrepreneurs who seek to commercialize innovations and the administrators who seek to apply controls. Stevenson *et al.* (2000) contrasts entrepreneurial and administrative management and emphasizes the differences in strategies, commitment to pursuing opportunity, the commitment and control of resources, management structures and reward systems.

In extreme situations bureaucratic organizations get into a vicious circle of failing to commercialize ideas and so develop a discouraging culture. Innovation paralysis results.

Activity 4.4

As a marketing director of a bureaucratic organization that has a poor record of innovation throughout, prepare a list of actions that you would take to encourage your staff to become more innovative.

Risk-taking in entrepreneurial firms

Referring back to the entrepreneurial styles of management, the lower the fixed asset and cost base of the organization, the faster the entrepreneurial business is likely to enter new markets, albeit initially less intensively. It is likely to be able to withdraw from unpromising areas more quickly too. Entrepreneurs may be risk-takers, but they also have greater scope to be risk managers too. They rely on their ability to be more adaptable, flexible and responsive to manage risk.

Large organizations that are risk-averse ultimately may have to take greater risks because of the need to re-orientate a large fixed asset base. For these reasons in a highly competitive fast-changing market, where development and marketing costs are a high proportion of the selling price, outsourcing and partnering may be lower risk business models than the organization having all the business functions and operations in-house.

Managing innovation and creating the right culture

Creating the right organizational culture is essential, and to this, there is a need for:

◆   A sustained commitment to innovation from top management

◆   A willingness to accept risks

◆   A degree of flexibility

◆   An ability and willingness to commit resources

◆   Individuals to be given more responsibility for new product development

◆   Innovation to be seen as a corporate-wide task.

Organizing for innovation

The organization structure, management style and culture must reflect the commitment to innovation. However, organizing for innovation can cause problems, given that the inno- vation process requires contributions from all functions as well as outside organizations. There can be some dispute as to which department should take overall managerial re- sponsibility for innovation. Consequently, a range of innovation models exist ranging from R&D, brand, marketing and general managers taking responsibility. Many companies be- lieve that the only way to achieve breakthrough innovation is through 'skunk works', which are set up as entirely separate units physically outside their offices to maximize creativity.

See CIM SMD Examination June 2006 Question 2

This requires an explanation of the characteristics of a market leader and market fol- lower in order to demonstrate the change that is needed. It is necessary then to explain the key environmental factors and changes that will demand a response by the firm in the form of developing appropriate strategies, management and an innovative culture to deal with step change and incremental change. In order to provide focus, the answer should highlight the key strategic marketing decision areas that must be addressed.

Customer-led Internet marketing

Much of the early period of Internet-led marketing was characterized by the idea that somehow technology-driven businesses would replace marketing-led businesses run with traditional business models, simply by setting up a website. However, the majority of the companies set up failed to develop a business model that had predictable costs and quan- tifiable and sustainable income streams. Few of the dot-com businesses offered customer value and satisfaction. In practice the (few) winners from the dot-com boom have suc- ceeded by combining good marketing, efficient technology platforms and good business sense. The vast majority of businesses have added Internet marketing onto already suc- cessful traditional formats.

Lower costs

E-commerce can be used to reduce costs, for example, by cutting out non-contributing intermediaries in the supply chain, enabling easier access and management of suppliers and providing better targeting, servicing and management of customers. However, while saving on supply and distribution costs, the e-business model usually requires high initial infrastructure investment and some additional costs of running the business. While e-commerce may still lower costs, this may not be enough to provide customer satisfaction.

Strategy redirection

Rather than seeing e-business simply as providing cost savings, the more astute firms have used e-commerce as the mechanism for redirecting the business, either to exploit the new opportunities or to gain competitive advantage, and so it is essential to decide:

◆ How Internet marketing can be used to further add satisfaction and customer value.

◆ How Internet marketing can be used to better integrate the organization's external and internal processes.

◆ The future role of Internet marketing in the business sector and the changing nature of business models, which is dealt with in Unit 7.

Innovation in Internet marketing

Opportunities for e-business innovation occur at the interface between customers and the internal operation.

The specific characteristics of the Internet that have facilitated the development of Internet marketing are shown in Table 4.3. These characteristics provide the drivers for innovation in Internet marketing.

Table 4.3: The six Is of the Internet

Six Is	Characteristics of the Internet
Interactivity	Customer-initiated contact
	Marketer has 100 per cent customer attention
Intelligence	Can continuously collect and analyse information and make individually focused offers
Individualization	Marketing communications is tailored to meet individual needs so achieving mass customization
Integration	Managing integrated external and internal marketing communications and mixed mode buying
Industry restructuring	Disintermediation involves removing the traditional intermediaries from the distribution channel
	Reintermediation involves gaining a presence on websites that might fulfil the role of intermediary
Independence of location	Reach can be extended into countries where it is not viable to locate a significant sales support activity

Source: Adapted from Deighton (1996)

Question 4.4

A number of technologies have not lived up to their earlier promise. Third-generation mobile phones and consumer purchasing on the Internet have not generated as much revenue as was originally expected. Why do you think this is so?

Case study: The Garden of Eden goes showbiz

The Eden project: showbiz meets science

Among Britain's lottery-funded millennium projects, there were a lot of high-profile flops, including the Dome at Greenwich, Sheffield's rock and pop museum and the Earth Centre in South Yorkshire. But the Eden Project in Cornwall, which opened in March 2001, proved to be a spectacular success. About 645,000 visitors a year were expected, but it attracted 940,000 in its first 6 months alone and now has over 1.5 million visitors each year.

The entrepreneur

Tim Smit, an Anglo-Dutch former pop producer, moved to Cornwall in the late 1980s to set up a recording studio. Next door to the studio was a large, neglected garden, which Smit restored as 'The Lost Gardens of Heligan'. Soon after opening in 1992 it became one of Cornwall's top tourist destinations. Smit's next brainchild was The Eden Project, and his aim was to create a rainforest and other plant 'landscapes' underneath two giant 'biomes' built in a disused china clay pit. His track record gave the lottery's fund commission the confidence to award the project £37.5 million and helped him to attract the private investment that was necessary to match the lottery funding.

The early success of Eden was attributed to the fact that, unlike some of the other lottery-funded projects, it was a good idea looking for money, not money looking for an idea. Many projects of this type appeared to be the result of the determination of cities to get some of the lottery cash, irrespective of how viable the project was. The Eden Project was the vision of one entrepreneur rather than the result of planning by committee. The most notoriously failure – the Dome – was the product of bureaucratic compromise and inappropriate political intervention. After seven years the Dome is only just getting a real role.

The vision

The Lost Gardens of Heligan had proved to Smit that the study of plants could mean good business in the right situation. Smit realized from his former background, however, that an element of showbiz was needed, and his mission was to 'make science sexy'. Science appeals to both children and adults and seems to be good theme-park material. The message of the project was also very serious – that man and plants have co-existed profitably together for centuries and must continue to do so – and this has enabled Eden to make a valuable contribution to education, research, awareness raising of important issues and campaigning. A new £15 million education centre was built in 2005. All the buildings have unique, instantly recognizable designs and are made, where possible, from locally available materials from sustainable sources.

The regional contribution

Eden has a key role and fits in well in the region. There are a number of other garden attractions and so is a 'must' for adults interested in gardening, and given its location in a popular holiday area, it also attracts visitors looking for a day away from the beach. Many lottery-funded visitor attractions seemed to be isolated from other attractions and have no emotional attachment to the area, making it more unlikely that people would visit. Moreover, local people resent money that was intended for charitable purposes being spent on what they regard as pointless projects.

Eden employs over 400 people full-time, 200 seasonal and also has 150 volunteers. It has contributed significantly to the economy of Cornwall, one of the poorest counties in United Kingdom. It claims to have had dealings with 2500 local companies and spends £10 million with local suppliers. 87 per cent of its catering supplies are obtained from Cornwall. It also had a significant impact on the demand for accommodation.

The potential for conflict

Despite the outstanding success of the Eden project, it does face continual challenges, dilemmas and potential conflicts. While it is not expected to pay off its original grants, it does have to continually generate income to pay its way and justify further funding for new projects, some of which will not generate income. The fact that the number of visitors far exceeds the forecast places considerable strain on the facilities and catering – areas where the staff try to avoid compromise and wish to maintain high standards.

Many of its show business activities are high profile and perhaps attract a different type of visitor. The Eden project hosted the 'Africa Calling' concert for 4000 people as part of the 'Make Poverty History' Live 8 campaign in 2005. It was memorable in featuring black artists, answering the criticisms of some of the other concerts. It also creates a giant skating rink as part of its winter event to generate additional income. It has been host to conferences and seminars attended by world experts discussing environmental concerns.

Events such as these create considerable disruption and heartache for the horticulturalists at Eden, whose work is devoted to creating the right conditions for the plants to be at their best. Neither the plants nor the staff take kindly to being trampled on or uprooted by the construction workers and electricians working on the next event, so the management team must try to balance the opposing interests and maintain the motivation of the staff that believed, when they joined, that they were working for a science establishment rather than one they feel is increasingly becoming dedicated to show business. Smit emphasizes that he is not a horticulturalist, and horticulture is not the primary aim of the Eden project.

Source: Robin Lowe, from various public sources

Question 4.5

What do you consider to be the marketing aims of the Eden project and how does this fit with the macro and micro environmental factors?

Question 4.6

How can the marketing decisions address the different stakeholder expectations?

Question 4.7

How might the spirit of building stakeholder value generated by the Eden project be capitalized upon (1) within Cornwall and (2) by the Eden project itself?

Summary

◆ Technology both drives innovation and provides the means of responding to changing customer requirements and expectations.

◆ There are, however, sources other than technology that drive innovation.

◆ There are categories of innovation from 'new to the world breakthroughs' to minor adaptations to products, and these pose different challenges for marketing.

◆ An effective innovation process is essential for managing diffusion of the innovation into the market.

◆ A supportive culture is needed to encourage risk-taking, but innovation also should be carried out within a process that is designed to manage risk too.

◆ In Internet marketing, the website and business model are the platforms for innovation.

◆ The reasons for success and failure in innovation have been well researched, and to be successful, it is vital to learn the lessons of good practice.

Further study

Birley, S. and Muzyka, D.F. (2000) *Mastering Entrepreneurship*, FT Pitman

Bolton, B. and Thompson, J. (2000) *Entrepreneurs, Talent, Temperament, Technique*, Oxford: Butterworth-Heinemann

Doole, I. and Lowe, R (2005) *Strategic Marketing Decisions in Global Markets*, Thomson Learning, Chapter 7.

Hints and tips

In studying this subject and answering questions on innovation it is important to demonstrate that while there are some systematic processes and good practice lessons that are at the heart of innovation, fundamentally it is about being creative, thinking out of the box and taking risks that are proportionate to the opportunity identified.

You should build up examples that illustrate innovation in different areas of the marketing process and you should also build good (and bad) examples of management of the innovation process that can be applied to case studies.

Bibliography

Bolton, B. and Thompson, J. (2000) *Entrepreneurs, Talent, Temperament, Technique*, Oxford: Butterworth-Heinemann

Deighton, J. (1996) The future of interactive marketing, *Harvard Business Review*, Nov–Dec , 151–162

Doole, I. and Lowe, R. (2005) *Strategic Marketing Decisions in Global Markets*, Thomson Learning

Drucker, P.F. (1985) *Innovation and Entrepreneurship*, Oxford: Butterworth-Heinemann

Kim, W.C. and Mabourgne, R. (1997) The strategic logic of high growth, *Harvard Business Review*, 75 (1) Jan-Feb 103-112

Murphy, C. (2003) Innovation masterminds, *Marketing*, 15 May

Stevenson, H.,S. Birley and D.F. Muzyka (2000) Mastering entrepreneurship, *The Six Dimensions of Entrepreneurship*, FT Prentice Hall, pp. 8–13

Strebel, P. (1996) Breakpoint: how to stay in the game in *Mastering Management*, Financial Times, , 13–14, part 17

Utterback J, (1994) *Mastering the Dynamics of Innovation*, Boston MA: Harvard Business School Press

Unit 5
Decisions for a new strategic marketing direction

Learning objectives

The CIM syllabus for Strategic Marketing Decisions requires you to be able to evaluate an organization's current strategy in the light of the context in which it operates and decide whether there is a need for the organization to take a new strategic marketing direction.

In studying this unit you will:

3.2 Evaluate and apply the generic marketing strategies to strategic marketing decision-making in the context of today's competitive environment, including segmentation, targeting and positioning (STP), Porter's three generic strategies.

3.4 Identify and critically evaluate strategic options in relation to shareholder value, using appropriate decision tools. See syllabus section.

3.5 Describe the formulation and evaluation of competitive strategies.

3.3 Critically appraise strategic marketing decisions for pioneers, challengers, followers and niche players.

Having completed this unit you will be able to:

◆ Appraise a range of corporate and business visions, missions and objectives and the processes by which they are formulated, in the light of the changing bases of competitive advantage across geographically diverse markets.

◆ Identify, compare and contrast strategic options and critically evaluate the implications of strategic marketing decisions in relation to the concept of 'shareholder value'.

◆ Demonstrate the ability to re-orientate the formulation and control of cost-effective competitive strategies, appropriate for the objectives and context of an organization operating in a dynamic global environment.

This unit relates to the statements of practice:

Bd.1 Promote a strong market orientation and influence/contribute to strategy formulation and investment decisions.

Bd.2 Specify and direct the strategic marketing planning process.

Key definitions

Five definitions of strategy

Strategies can be intended:

1. **Strategy as a plan** – a consciously intended course of action

2. **Strategy as a ploy** – just a specific manoeuvre to outwit rivals.

Strategies can be realized through behaviour:

3. **Strategy as a pattern** – a stream of consistent behaviours, whether intended or not. It is worth comparing strategic intent with strategic reality. Strategic intent is often only partially realized in the form of a delivered strategy (the reality). There is often an unrealized part of this strategy, which leaves gaps that are often filled by emergent strategies that are not part of the initial intentions.

Strategy can be about external focus:

4. **Strategy as a position** – a unique location for the organization within its environment achieved by matching up the organization (internal context) with the environment (external context).

Strategy can also be an internal focus:

5. **Strategy as a perspective** – an ingrained way of perceiving the world.

Source: Mintzberg *et al.* (2003)

Study guide

This unit is concerned with the ways in which an organization can assess the appropriateness of its current strategy in its current context and design new strategies to exploit opportunities in the global market. We focus upon an evaluation of why strategies fail or wear out. We then go on to identify the key decisions in the formulation of a new strategy, beginning with a redefinition of the business and its markets. An understanding of the success criteria for a strategy is followed by a discussion of the decisions involving the generic strategies, which should be central to the strategy. We have highlighted the Porter generic strategies and STP marketing. We have ended by referring briefly to decisions regarding competitive stance and competitive strategy.

Before starting on the unit, students should familiarize themselves with the planning process by reading one of the recognized texts, such as the *Strategic Marketing Management* coursebook, that are identified in the 'Further study' section.

Strategy evaluation: the reasons for marketing strategy failure and wear-out

Few, if any, marketing strategies can remain the same forever. The evidence for this comes from the fact that from time to time some of the best-known and previously successful organizations go through a period of crisis in which they underperform against the expectations of their customers and other stakeholders, make huge losses or, at worst, fail completely. At these times the marketing strategy that the company has pursued for a long time no longer delivers the required results and needs to be changed. In this section we consider the various reasons for failure, including the organization's inability to respond quickly enough to changes in the market environment. Some other organizations may well have the right marketing strategy for the context in which they are operating, but they fail to implement it effectively because of weaknesses in their management and availability of resources.

The reasons for strategy failure and underperformance

There are many reasons why marketing strategies fail and organizations underperform, and we have grouped these into:

◆   Poor general management and inability to implement an appropriate strategy

◆   An inability to cope with market changes or the strategy taking longer than expected to succeed in the market

◆   Ineffective marketing management

◆   Removal of a protected environment.

Poor management

The most obvious evidence of underperformance comes in the form of poor financial performance or profit warnings made by the management to the City and investment fund managers. While there may be many reasons for underperformance, it is the senior management who are held responsible.

Operational inefficiency and poor cost control leading to uncompetitiveness

The causes of underperformance can include high production costs, poor use of fixed assets such as buildings and facilities, poor customer service, inefficiency in outsourcing and ineffective financial management.

Poor leadership and management

It can be argued that the problems highlighted above are merely symptomatic of indecisive leadership and weak management leading to lack of direction and control.

Lack of investment

Because of a lack of direction and a failure to generate profits, organizations fail to invest in projects to secure the future growth. They fail to invest in facilities, equipment, product and service development, brand development and market development.

Inability to cope with market changes

Firms in crisis often compound the error by making unwise and inappropriate investments as a panic reaction to the situation.

The nature and intensity of change in the sector environment

Different sectors experience change at different rates. For example, change in industries that are driven by high technology, such as computer hardware and software marketing, is likely to be more dramatic than in industries dependent on well-established technology such as specialist engineering. Over time, industries that are regarded as luxuries, experience greater variability in demand than necessities, such as the utilities. The level and patterns of demand in the travel sector are affected by the economic situation and unexpected events, such as war and terrorism.

The problems that can contribute to strategy failure are, therefore, the inability to:

◆ Manage an economic downturn or an industry sector cycle.

◆ Anticipate and plan for legislative and technological changes.

◆ Cope with slower than expected growth in a key segment, country or product.

◆ Cope with slower than expected diffusion of key products and services.

◆ Cope with changes in the route to market and distribution channels.

Ineffective marketing management

There are a number of areas where underperformance in marketing management can lead to strategy failure including:

◆ Ineffective use of marketing tools and resources.

◆ A competitor innovation or the emergence of a new, unexpected competitor.

◆ Overdependence on one key customer. Small firms can become overdependent on one customer, and with the increasing concentration of retailers, distributors and manufacturers even larger suppliers often become increasingly dependent on fewer large customers and a narrow product range, at worst putting them at risk of going out of business, or at best making them targets for takeover.

◆ Overdependence on one major product. Smaller firms and especially those that are new starts with one innovative new product or service tend to be overreliant in the early days on one or two major products. In a highly competitive market, competitors quickly copy new ideas and quickly remove the organization's market lead. Despite their limited resources, they must quickly develop additional or improved products and services to build a sustainable business. Even large businesses that provide one component or service in the supply chain of a global company can become vulnerable to the introduction of alternative products.

Removal of a 'protected' environment

A number of organizations operate in a protected environment, and the strategy for this situation will be inadequate for a new competitive environment.

Imminent end of a monopoly

Governments around the world have privatized state-owned utilities often without fully thinking through the implications for the services, existing organization and its staff. An example of this in the United Kingdom is the privatization of the railways.

Change of customer needs and fashion

The main reason for strategy wear-out, however, is the failure of organizations to respond quickly enough and adapt to changes in the market and, particularly, respond to changes in customer needs and fashion, the emergence of a new competitor or changes in the structure of the market. In looking for one overriding reason for the failure of a marketing strategy, most observers would place the blame firmly on the organization being too internally and not sufficiently externally focused.

Lack of customer and competitor focus

Senior managers often become preoccupied with managing staff, internal systems, structures and processes rather than using the resources that are available or could be accessed to add customer value. Efforts should be made to concentrate on the activities that yield the best results for all stakeholders and avoid the activities that simply maintain the current position or at worst drain resources from more value-adding activities to try to save dying products and services.

Question 5.1

If you look in the business press for a few days, you will find reports of underperformance of a major global organization. Choose one organization to study. Using newspaper reports and the checklist of reasons highlighted in this section analyse the cause of the underperformance in the organization.

Activity 5.1

Strategic wear-out usually follows a quite long period of good performance. Often the signs of strategic wear-out are there, but the management fail to respond. Assess the vulnerability to strategic wear-out of the marketing strategy of your own organization or an organization of your choice. Where is the greatest risk?

Redefining the business

Having considered the possible reasons for marketing strategy failure we now consider what preventive action should be taken. First the organization should have in place an effective marketing information system for collecting and monitoring information. Organizations that might be affected by this type of market environment change must decide whether they need to make major changes to the nature of the business and its place within its chosen market sector. In doing this it is necessary to ask a number of questions. To ensure the sustainability of its business model, does the organization need to:

1 Stay in its current business and make only incremental changes to the marketing strategy, by broadly maintaining its current position in the market, focusing on its current contribution to the value chain, relying on its current source of competitive advantage and targeting its current and closely related market segments?

2 Make some major modifications to its role and contribution in the current market; perhaps through new product or market development initiatives, further differentiation of its products and services, increasing value added in the supply chain and enhance the source of competitive advantage?

3 Carry out some significant restructuring, perhaps by vertical integration or by outsourcing, redefining the basis of competitive advantage or moving into another market?

4 Completely reinvent its role and contribution through diversifying into a completely new sector?

Some examples of the above might include the following:

◆ Public sector organizations and organizations that have very specific responsibilities enshrined in law do make incremental changes but have little room to change their fundamental business model. Professional organizations, such as law firms, accountants and health care organizations, do experience substantial changes and initiate innovations but essentially they stay in the same business.

◆ Supermarkets also essentially stay in the same business of retailing but the successful ones continually innovate in order to stay ahead of the competition, introduce new products and services and enter new product categories. They have always outsourced products but are constantly finding new ways of adding customer value, often through supply-chain developments.

◆ A number of businesses, including banks, airlines, telecommunications and manufacturing businesses, have found it necessary to embark on major restructuring by outsourcing activities to lower-cost suppliers. They are concentrating more on their knowledge assets including market, customer, process technology, R&D capability rather than on operations.

◆ A number of businesses have reinvented themselves, with varying degrees of success. GEC was a large and highly profitable manufacturer of electrical engineering and communications products, and during the dot-com era it reinvented itself as Marconi in order to exploit the emerging IT market. The gamble (which it was) failed, the company only just avoided bankruptcy and years after is still struggling to regain a sustainable position.

Insight: Defining the business model

It may be necessary to redefine the business, and to do so this, it is useful to address the questions that will help redefine the business model. The key factors in the business model are:

◆ What the organization will do and what tasks it will carry out.

◆ How the organization will connect with the market.

◆ What the offer is, how it is positioned and communicated to the customers.

◆ What the income streams will be.

◆ How the organization arranges its resources and what the cost streams will be.

◆ The organization's role within the value chain.

◆ How surpluses will be generated for further investment.

Selecting target markets

Before considering in detail the segmentation, targeting and positioning strategy it is necessary to decide where the market focus should be. Hooley *et al.* (2004) discuss market attractiveness and the competitive position of the company in each market to distinguish between core, peripheral, illusion and dead-end business.

Case study: A new direction for IBM

Periodically an organization must review its strategy and decide whether it is still pursuing a direction that will continue to generate value for its stakeholders. In 1981 IBM introduced the first personal computer (PC) to the market and was essentially responsible for turning computing into a mass market. However, very quickly, competitors started to sell 'IBM compatible' copies and over time IBM has been unable to stop the PC hardware becoming a commodity. It is now a highly competitive market in which only very focused, specialist companies are able to compete.

Perhaps the biggest mistake that IBM made, however, was failing to realize that the profits from the industry would be made from the software. Unfortunately it allowed Microsoft, at that stage a fledgling business, to provide the software that would control its PC.

Eventually IBM had little competitive advantage and realized that it could no longer operate on the slender profit margins in the PC industry, against competitors such as Dell. In 2004 IBM sold its PC hardware division to the Chinese firm Lenovo (formerly known as Legend) for $1.75 billion. About 10,000 IBM staff transferred to the new company, which moved its HQ from Beijing to upstate New York.

Despite these apparent setbacks IBM has always responded by setting out in a new direction. From being a business machine manufacturer and computer hardware supplier it added IT software and IT solutions provider to its list of capabilities. Now it realizes that these markets are dwarfed by the potential market in providing IT and business process outsourcing services to client firms. But this is a business which requires highly educated but inexpensive labour, and to achieve this it must transfer many operations to India and China. Moreover, redefining its business, customer base and brand continually sets new marketing communications challenges.

Source: Robin Lowe, from various publicly available sources

Question 5.2

Identify the benefits, threats and future challenges for IBM and Lenovo for this radical step.

Turnaround strategies

The most urgent need for a redefinition of the business occurs when the underperformance in the organization is so acute that its very survival is at risk. A turnaround strategy is needed to reverse the underperformance and put the firm back on a more secure path. Usually the poor performance is accompanied by a lethargic or 'blame' culture, lack of leadership and teamworking, demoralized staff and management not focused on results. Often there is conflict between top managers on what needs to be done to improve the situation, and this often leads to changes of personnel. The action usually taken focuses largely on cost cutting as a short-term measure to improve efficiency and competitiveness and ensure survival. However, for the turnaround strategy to deliver long-term improvement it is necessary to take action to address the more fundamental causes of poor performance such as redefining the segmentation, targeting and positioning strategy, rationalizing the portfolio, making customer service and satisfaction a priority, improving channel effectives and obtaining better value from marketing communications.

Insight: Breakthroughs in business models

By using creativity in STP approaches and combining this with innovation in the business proposition it is possible to create 'breakthrough' business models. Examples include

Business models	Examples
Bait and hook	Low margin basic product with high margin refill, for example razor and blades, mobile phone and air time, computer printer and cartridges
'No frills'	Yield management processes to maximize revenue by using flexible pricing, at South West Air, easyjet and Ryanair
Online retailing	Easy purchasing on line with customized recommendations at Amazon
Online auctions	Organizer takes percentage from advertiser and completed deal, for example eBay and Betfair

Source: Http://digitalenterprise.org/models/models.html, accessed March 2008

Generic decisions for a successful strategy

While it is not our intention to discuss in detail the marketing strategy and planning process, you should refer to the particular coursebook to remind yourself of the key decision points, such as objective setting and strategy evaluation criteria and the key models that help in setting the criteria by which the key strategic decisions should be made. We have highlighted here some important criteria for a successful strategy and the Porter generic strategies before considering STP.

Criteria for a successful strategy

The starting point in this section is to emphasize that in making strategic marketing decisions it is vital, first, that organizations are quite clear about the purpose of the strategy. Mintzberg *et al.* (2003) suggest that a strategy is needed when the potential aims or responses of intelligent opponents can seriously affect the endeavour's desired outcome. A strategy comprises patterns from the past and plans for the future and comprises a set of objectives, policies and plans that taken together define the scope of the enterprise and its approach to survival and success. The criteria for a successful strategy should include as a minimum:

◆ **Clear decisive objectives** – although subordinate goals may change in the heat of the campaign or competition, the overriding goals must remain clear and understood.

◆ **Maintaining the initiative** – it must allow freedom of action, enhance commitment and maintain the pace and determine the course of events, rather than reacting to them.

◆ **Concentration** – it must be capable of concentrating superior power at a particular place and time to be decisive.

◆ **Flexibility** – it must keep in reserve resources and capabilities in order to allow flexibility and manoeuvrability.

◆ **Co-ordinated and committed leadership** – leaders must be appointed for each of the goals, and their interests and ambitions must match the needs of their roles.

◆ **Surprise** – it must make use of speed, secrecy and intelligence to attack unprepared competitors.

◆ **Security** – it must secure resources to support the actions.

Activity 5.2

How would you define the strategy of your own organization or an organization of your choice in Mintzberg's terms and how does it score on Mintzberg's criteria for success? What steps are needed to ensure better levels of future success?

Porter's three competitive strategies

To compete effectively, Porter proposed that organizations need to select one from the following three generic competitive strategies and pursue it consistently:

1 **Cost leadership** – involves proactively seeking to lower costs in each element of the supply chain with the intention of outperforming rivals.

2 **Focus strategy** – involves creating a strong, specialist reputation in a very small number of customer segments.

3 **Differentiation strategy** – involves the delivery of superior customer value in one or more activities supported by a strong brand.

Wilson and Gilligan (2004) discuss the ways in which the strategy can be achieved, the benefits and the possible problems of each, and the danger of not pursuing any of the three and so being 'stuck in the middle'. It should be pointed out that a low-cost strategy does not necessarily mean a low-price strategy too, and many organizations following a focus or differentiation strategy work hard to achieve low costs too.

Activity 5.3

Which of Porter's three generic strategies are being pursued by the strategic business units of your own organization or an organization of your choice? Is there any evidence of the strategic business units being stuck in the middle?

STP decisions

The fundamental process in marketing strategy development is segmentation, targeting and positioning, and this should be at the core of all marketing strategies. Consequently, these are the areas where the key decision-making occurs. Before we do that, it is worth emphasizing the key areas of decision-making identified in Table 5.1.

Table 5.1: Key decisions in the STP process

Stages	Key decisions
1. Segmentation	
Choose the variables upon which the segmentation will be based	Build a deep understanding of the customer requirements and purchasing behaviour and reflect this in the variables used
	Avoid simple, single segmentation variables that do not achieve precision in targeting and positioning
Create segments for the whole market	Ensure the segments are measurable, substantial, accessible, stable and useful (Dibb, 2003)
Profile the segments and understand their needs and expectations	Ensure the profile is an accurate reflection of the key elements of customer attitudes, values and behaviour
2. Targeting	
Devise a targeting strategy	Determine the criteria for selecting the target segments, based on a deep understanding of the customers and company capability
Prioritize the segments and decide how many to serve	Apply criteria that will enable selection decisions to be made on the basis of the segments the organization is best able to serve or will be the most profitable
	Only target the number of segments that can be effectively resourced
3. Positioning	
Understand the target segment perceptions	Understand the customers' perceptions of the organization, brand or products and where they diverge from the organization's intended image and value proposition

Create a positioning approach that meets the target segment perceptions and expectations	Decide on a value proposition that emphasizes to the customers the tangible and intangible benefits offered and how they are differentiated from competitor offerings
	Determine whether repositioning is needed, and if so, whether the necessary investment could be recouped
Design or redesign the marketing mix to meet the segment perceptions and expectations	Assess the contribution of each element of the marketing mix in delivering the value proposition to the customer groups

Source: Doole and Lowe (2005)

Segmentation hierarchies

Fundamental to the STP process is the need for the organization to obtain a deep understanding of the customers. Customers all have different expectations of the products and services that they receive, and segmentation identifies groups that have similar needs and make similar decisions in the purchasing process. The typical consumer base variables that are used for segmentation are listed in Table 5.2. The choice of variables is key as it represents not only what is common among the individual customers that make up the segment but what is also distinctive from other segments. Segmentation variables based on characteristics that are relatively easy to collect, such as age, gender or income, may provide an approximation to predicted purchasing behaviour, but it will be far from precise. Behavioural segmentation will be more predictive of purchasing behaviour and customer satisfaction criteria, but in most circumstances the information needed about customers for behavioural segmentation will be much more difficult and expensive to collect.

Table 5.2 Consumer segmentation base variables

Demographic – sex, age, income level, social class and educational factors

Psychological – lifestyle factors: activities, interests and opinions

Behavioural – patterns of consumption, loyalty to product category and brand

Faced with this obstacle Dibb (2003) emphasizes the need to choose the base variables that will truly discriminate between customer needs and buyer behaviour and avoid a segmentation approach that is simple to apply but does not really provide the benefits of directing the marketing strategy. The implication of this is that a single variable approach is unlikely to add real value.

Using multiple variables, a hierarchy of segmentation can be created to form the basis for a marketing strategy, in which further segmentation or subsegmentation will achieve an even better match between customer needs and the specific elements of the marketing mix, such as promotion and distribution channels.

In international marketing, a hierarchy of segmentation variables provides the basis for an international strategy that balances the need for standardization of the marketing activity, where possible, but facilitates adaptation to meet customer needs more precisely, where necessary. For example, a global segment of wealthy customers need and want similar luxury products worldwide, and the producers of such products will be able to obtain some economies of scale by developing and producing standardized products that have appeal worldwide. However, advertising may need to make different appeals according to the culture of customers of the region, and different languages may be needed for the packaging of products that are going to be sold in specific countries. Too often it is assumed that the appeal will be the same in all markets, but managers need to consider self-reference criteria and overcome their preconceived ideas of the perceived benefits, which at one level may be similar, but at another different for different cultures. For example, a perfume may have a worldwide appeal, but a sexy provocative advertisement may be unacceptable in some cultures.

For a full discussion of the segmentation of B2B and B2C markets read Hooley *et al.*, 2004.

Question 5.3

How can better methods of segmentation assist in decision-making in global markets?

Targeting the most profitable customers

A number of texts identify the criteria for assessing segment attractiveness and offer processes for a systematic approach to segment selection in some detail. However, following the theme of this unit it is essential to regularly review the targeting criteria and process, because of changes that impact on segment attractiveness.

◆   Companies change as markets develop and so their views change about the attractiveness of segments.

◆   Markets change, for example the next generation of consumers have different views about preferred products.

◆   Competitors change. Dyson quickly took 58 per cent of the market in the high end of the vacuum cleaner market against established competition.

◆   Market reinvention takes place, for example Amazon reinvented book selling.

◆   Market boundaries change. Supermarkets have rapidly increased their share of petrol sales and entered the financial services market.

Positioning and repositioning

The concept of positioning can be applied to companies, brands, products and services. The key points of positioning are:

◆   The positioning must be as distinctive as possible and must clearly differentiate the organization's position from that of the competition. It is the customers' perception of positioning that is important and perceptual mapping is useful for positioning research.

◆   The organization's image is projected through all its activities, not just marketing but also such things as staff recruitment and working conditions. All of these influences must converge with the customer's perception of the company, brand or product.

Increasingly it is through the imagery rather than the product specification, quality or pricing that the organization confirms the positioning. In doing this it must make choices. Organizations put a value proposition to one customer segment that makes promises about the quality of the products and level of service that might be expected. The positioning might suggest that customers like the one in the segment (with the same demographic, lifestyle or behavioural characteristics or aspirations) are likely to buy the organization's products and services. By inference, the organization might also be saying that customers who do not have these characteristics or aspirations probably do not buy this product or service.

In cross-cultural marketing either in the domestic or in the international market, organizations must take care with this type of positioning. Particular problems exist where the imagery is created for one target market segment but is unacceptable to another segment with a different culture.

Repositioning

Organizational underperformance can be associated with a failure to appeal in sufficient volume to the target segment resulting in insufficient sales as the organization comes under increasing attack from competitors. Alternatively the target segments are simply not large enough to sustain a growing business. As a result it may be necessary for the organization to reposition. This decision should not be taken lightly as the investment and commitment necessary to carry it through effectively can be huge. Effective positioning is achieving a convergence between customer perceptions and the organization's positioning delivered through the marketing mix, and this is difficult enough. Effective repositioning requires the organization to reformulate every aspect of its marketing mix, neutralize the old customer perceptions and recreate and influence new perceptions by actions and communications. Changing well-entrenched customer perceptions is a very lengthy process, and subtle repositioning communicated through promotional messages is unlikely to be understood by many customers who do not have high involvement in the organization, brand or product. While some repositionings, such as Lucozade and Guinness, have been very successful, many others have left customers confused.

The use of STP and segments of one

The determination and capability of organizations to gain greater customer insights and to manage customer data allows ever-smaller subsegments to be profiled, targeted and served as niche markets. In the limit the subsegment size can be one, giving rise to one-to-one marketing.

Question 5.4

Select a B2B organization whose products and services you are familiar with. Write down the criteria that might be a meaningful basis for segmentation of the customers in its overall market sector. Identify the criteria that appear to have been used by the company as its target segment. Finally evaluate the market mix that it uses and decide whether it communicates clear and distinctive positioning to its customers.

Growth strategies and decisions

Other generic strategies that are important in decision-making relate to the alternative growth options identified by Ansoff (1957). The strategic options tend to increase in terms of the investment cost and risk of achieving success in the following order: penetration, market development, product development and diversification. The market leaders must simultaneously pursue all the first three options. However, many organizations do not have sufficient financial and management resources to proactively and aggressively pursue more than two of these options at the same time.

The decisions on which growth option to pursue will be influenced by the macro-environment, market changes (customer and competitor factors) and the organization's capability, ambitions, choice of marketing approach and competitive stance, which now follow.

Alternative marketing approaches

As part of the fundamental review of the business the firm should consider its approach to marketing.

Approaches to marketing

◆ **Product push marketing** – is an approach that concentrates on persuading customers to buy the products and services that the firm can produce, deliver and further develop easily, largely using their existing realm of knowledge and resources.

◆ **Customer-led marketing** – is typified by those organizations that do everything they can to satisfy customer needs. Some organizations have taken this to extremes and set out to deliver customer needs almost irrespective of cost.

◆ **Resource-based marketing** – is considered to be a balanced strategy between meeting the market requirements and exploiting the organization's capabilities to serve the market. Resource-based marketing takes into account the competitive situation, the full range of assets, skills and competencies of the organization and aims to exploit the organization's role within the supply chain.

◆ **Entrepreneurial marketing** – entrepreneurs tend to focus on the opportunity or market gap, irrespective of whether or not this will make use of existing assets and resources. Entrepreneurial marketing usually takes the form of a new business start or a new spin out from within an existing firm. Increasingly, large firms realize that it is difficult to develop a breakthrough innovation within the firm and resort to managing diversification by setting up separate entities.

◆ **Network marketing** – is becoming increasingly significant as organizations, desperate for growth, use connections through alliances, partnerships and equity participation in other organizations to exploit opportunities that are not deliverable through their directly owned assets. The rationale for network marketing is that in conjunction with partners, an organization can increase the overall size of the potential market that can be served by the two or more companies.

In practice the appropriateness of the choice of approach depends on the context of the organization and its market.

Question 5.5

Using appropriate examples, explain the different marketing approaches of firms and how they might build competitive advantage in these areas.

Case study: Apple goes for the low-price market

Apple, led by its charismatic, entrepreneurial founder, Steve Jobs, has traditionally produced products that have focused on design and ease of use rather than price. The result has been a niche marketer selling to purchasers that are probably better described as fans and devotees rather than customers. Apple's main products, the iMac and iPod, have achieved almost iconic status.

For many potential customers the price of Apple products has prevented them buying and so, in an effort to attract a mass market, in 2005, Jobs announced that the company was going to offer low-price versions of its key products to convert users to Apple products. The cheapest Mac mini went on sale for $499 (without monitor, keyboard and mouse) and the cheapest iPod Shuffle, which holds about 120 songs, went on sale for $99.

Although many saw this change of direction as one of the most courageous moves the company had made, it very quickly proved successful, adding significantly to Apple's profitability. In 2007 Apple's profits increased from $542m to $904m with its sales of computers up by the fourth quarter to 2.2 million to add to its sales of 10.2 million iPods. As Apple announced sales of 1.12 million of its new iPhone, the share price had doubled in the year.

Adapted from public sources

Question 5.6

Explain the risks to Apple of targeting a customer segment for cheaper products and the potential benefits. What are the critical success factors?

Adopting the right competitive stance

Against the background of the assessment made earlier in this unit there are a number of alternative competitive stances that organizations might adopt, and these are discussed in the marketing strategy texts by Wilson and Gilligan (2004). The main competitive strategies are:

◆ **Leaders** – keep ahead of the field by developing an ever-stronger selling proposition and competitive advantage to build customer loyalty, discouraging other possible market entrants.

◆ **Challengers** – develop a strong alternative proposition and challenge the leaders' weaknesses continually, often by aggressive pricing.

◆ **Followers** – imitate the other competitors at lower cost. They look for unexploited opportunities.

See CIM SMD Examination June 2005 Q.2

This question examines the value disciplines of Treacy and Wiersema (See Unit 1 and Chapter 3 of Doole and Lowe, 2005). In this question you have to critically evaluate the three-value discipline. The question is specific in nature and requires the candidate to apply conceptual knowledge to best practice examples in these disciplines that are developed in this and previous units.

While these are the main competitive stances, there are also specialist strategies too that do not necessarily fall into the above categories.

◆ **Pioneers** – are innovators and tend to be the first into new opportunities. Some may also be market leaders but others may not maintain a consistent strategy and may fail to consolidate their pioneering efforts and build their business.

◆ **Market nichers** – survive and grow through specializing in a part of the market that is too small to be attractive to larger firms or in a market niche that they define and create themselves. With globalization, some market nichers have built substantial businesses through creating a global niche.

Companies must decide whether their current competitive stance is appropriate for the present and the future. Clearly, if the organization redefines its business, it must also decide whether it should attempt to change its competitive stance and adopt new competitive strategies. The competitive strategies that are adopted to attack and defend are usually described in terms of planning military campaigns, and Wilson and Gilligan (2004) and Hooley et al. (2004) discuss the alternatives in some detail.

It is useful to have an understanding of these strategies as they help to articulate a proposed strategy, and there are a number of examples in the texts of their use by leading companies. Their appropriateness fo r a particular situation requires considerable analysis and is therefore beyond the scope of this coursebook.

Activity 5.4

How would you characterize your organization or an organization of your choice? Is it a market leader, challenger, follower or nicher? Is it also a market pioneer? What competitive strategy is it pursuing?

Case study: Does eBay need to find a new direction?

In October 2007 eBay reported a 30 per cent increase in quarterly revenues to $1.89 billion but posted a loss for the first time in eight years. eBay was forced to admit that it had overpaid for Skype, the internet telephony group that it had bought two years earlier for $2.6 billion. It wrote down the value of Skype by $900 million after failing to generate sufficient profits from the business. It also paid an additional $500 million to the founders of Skype under an earn-out agreement it made at the time of the purchase.

Skype enables users to make free calls over the Web but it seems that eBay have not yet really worked out how revenues from Skype can be grown. The service only generated

$400 million of business in 2007. eBay is continuing to encourage people to use Skype for communications but is not trying hard to link the service with the auction site, even though it was seen as a way of reducing fraud.

There are threats to eBay's current business. Meg Whitman, president and CEO of eBay warned that a slowdown in retail spending would hit the company's revenues even before the full extent of the global credit squeeze became known. New users are not being recruited so fast but eBay claims that their focus is now on generating more business from existing users.

Social networking sites, such as Facebook, could start to compete with eBay but Whitman believes that if such sites moved to running a commercial rather than a social operation, users may well migrate to other sites. She even goes as far as suggesting that the social network business model may not last if new communication models emerge. Google's OpenSocial initiative is one such new model but, again, eBay is not really able to integrate with this because of legal obligations, because of its need to hold confidential financial information about customers.

More important for eBay perhaps is whether it can be successful in Asia. So far it has not performed well, especially in China, where its website did not appeal to locals. Even though the site was translated into Chinese, local users complained about the layout of pages, the user's flow through the site and how it was read. An overhaul undertaken by a local firm has led to an increase in users.

Adapted from: J Richards, eBay chief bids to regain momentum, *The Times*, 3 January 2008.

Question 5.7

What are the key issues that needed to be considered by eBay?

Question 5.8

What marketing competencies are needed ensure the further success of eBay?

Summary

◆ There are a number of reasons for organization underperformance and strategy wear-out. Whilst external factors, such as changes in the market, customer requirements and competition, might be the cause, it is the management of the organization that must anticipate and respond to likely changes.

◆ From time to time, therefore, it is necessary to redefine the organization's role in its chosen market sector and decide on an appropriate approach to the market.

◆ Generic strategic approaches are essential in determining the organization's competitive approach (Porter), its customer targets, positioning and marketing activity (STP).

◆ Increasingly organizations need to develop a hierarchy approach to segmentation especially in international marketing.

◆ Having assessed their competitive capability organizations must then adopt an appropriate competitive stance that will secure their position in the market.

Further study

Doole, I. and Lowe, R. (2005) *Strategic Marketing Decisions in Global Markets*, Thomson Learning, Chapters 5 and 6

You should ensure that you have a full understanding of marketing strategy and planning process by studying the following texts:

Hooley, G., Saunders, J. and Piercy, N. (2004) *Marketing Strategy and Competitive Positioning*, FT Prentice Hall, 3rd edition

Wilson, R.M.S. and Gilligan, C. (2004) *Strategic Marketing Management: Planning, Implementation and Control*, Oxford: Elsevier Butterworth-Heinemann, 3rd edition

Hints and tips

Build a collection of examples that illustrate to you the diversity of strategic decisions that companies make together with a brief explanation of the reasons. Try to find examples from different industries from those that you are most familiar with, as this will help to broaden your experience and possible management solutions for your own situation. It will also help you to recall examples in the examination.

As STP marketing is central to the marketing process, ensure that you have a full understanding of the key decision areas in the STP process.

Bibliography

Ansoff, I. (1957) Strategies for Diversification, *Harvard Business Review*, Vol. 35 Issue 5, Sep-Oct, pp.113-124

Dibb, S. (2003) Marketing segmentation: changes and challenges, in S. Hart (ed.), *Marketing Changes*, London: Thomson Learning

Doole, I. and Lowe, R. (2005) *Strategic Marketing Decisions in Global Markets*, Thomson Learning

Hooley, G., Saunders, J. and Piercy, N. (2004) *Marketing Strategy and Competitive Positioning*, FT Prentice Hall, 3rd edition

Mintzberg, H., Lampel, J., Quinn, J.B. and Ghoshall, S. (2003) *Strategies The Strategy Process, Concepts, Contexts, Cases*, Pearson Education 2–29

Wilson, R.M.S. and Gilligan, C. (2004) *Strategic Marketing Management: Planning, Implementation and Control*, Oxford: Elsevier Butterworth-Heinemann, 3rd edition

Unit 6
Strategic decisions for global development

Learning objectives

The CIM syllabus for Strategic Marketing Decisions expects you to have an appreciation of the different contexts for marketing decisions. While it is important to recognize that international marketing should be considered throughout the syllabus, this unit focuses on the strategic decisions that international players must take.

In studying this unit you will:

3.1 Examine the issues of decisions to build competitive capability and approaches to leveraging capability to create advantage across geographically diverse markets.

3.10 Leverage individual and corporate learning across geographically diverse markets for competitive advantage.

3.6 Determine the lessons of best practice from strategic decisions made by successful global companies.

Having completed this unit you will be able to:

- Appraise a range of corporate and business visions, missions and objectives and the processes by which they are formulated, in the light of the changing bases of competitive advantage across geographically diverse markets.

- Demonstrate the ability to develop innovative and creative marketing solutions to enhance an organization's global competitive position in the context of changing product, market and brand and customer life cycles.

- Define and contribute to investment decisions concerning the marketing assets of an organization.

- Demonstrate the ability to re-orientate the formulation and control of cost-effective competitive strategies, appropriate for the objectives and context of an organization operating in a dynamic global environment.

This unit relates to the statements of practice:

Bd.1 Promote a strong market orientation and influence/contribute to strategy formulation and investment decisions.

Bd.2 Specify and direct the strategic marketing planning process.

Cd.1 Promote organization-wide innovation and cooperation in the development of brands.

Key definitions

Export marketing – the marketing of goods and/or services across national/political boundaries.

Multinational marketing – the marketing activities of an organization that has activities, interests or operations in more than one country and where there is some kind of influence or control of marketing activities from outside the country in which the goods or services will actually be sold, but where the global markets are primarily perceived to be independent markets and profit centres in their own right.

Global marketing – where the whole organization focuses on the selection and exploitation of global marketing opportunities and marshalls resources around the globe with the objective of achieving a global competitive advantage.

Study guide

This unit is concerned with making strategic marketing decisions in the global context to exploit new opportunities in the global market through leveraging capability and sharing learning. Organizations adopt different approaches depending on their resources, ambition and market context. Understanding the factors that have contributed to globalization is essential in understanding how the very largest firms grow. It is important too to recognize the times when activities can be standardized or should be adapted for local markets. Smaller firms also succeed in global markets provided that they take appropriate decisions on strategic approaches for their situation, for example niche marketing. In both large and small firms we also emphasize the importance of corporate learning to ensure that the lessons learned in the market can be shared as widely as possible.

Many students are unfamiliar with international marketing, and therefore before starting on the unit, students should familiarize themselves with this aspect of marketing by reading one of the recognized texts that are identified in the 'Further study' section.

Building competitive advantage through globalization

International marketing

Companies develop international marketing strategies to improve corporate performance through growth and strengthening their competitive advantage. The strategies are driven by the increasing trend to globalization. However, companies differ in their approach to international marketing strategy development and the speed and progress they make in achieving an international presence.

International marketing is often defined largely in terms of the level of involvement of the company in the global marketplace, and three levels are considered: export, multinational and global marketing.

Exporting is the simplest form of international marketing activity and is the preferred approach for many firms. However, the latter definitions are more complex and more formal. They indicate a revised attitude to international marketing and suggest fundamental changes in the basic philosophy.

Global marketing

Over the last few years the importance of international marketing has increased as globalization has increased the range of possible opportunities for proactive organizations with aggressive growth strategies. The downside of globalization, of course, is that reactive companies are now much more likely to be attacked in their home market. While some domestic businesses might be able to stay unaffected, the majority of businesses are experiencing direct or indirect international competition. In this section, therefore, we focus on how the globalization of markets is affecting the strategic decisions of both large and small firms. Doole and Lowe (2008) explain the themes that are leading to globalization and thus are important considerations in the development of international strategies.

Exploiting the globalization drivers

The most successful global businesses are aggressively building their global strategies around the following themes:

◆ Increased market access because of the opening up of markets in China and Central and Eastern Europe.

◆ Increased market opportunities because of the deregulation of many markets, such as the financial market and privatization of state-owned utilities.

◆ Greater uniformity of industry standards, encouraged, for example, by the EU.

◆ Sourcing of products and components initially, but more recently services, too, from a wider range of countries, particularly those emerging markets with a high ratio of skills to cost.

◆ More globally standardized products and services, particularly in areas of new technology, but increasingly in more culturally sensitive product areas, such as food.

◆ Common technology used in many more markets, particularly in areas of information technology, bioscience and pharmaceuticals, where there is a high cost of R&D that must be recovered through sales in many countries.

◆ Similar customer requirements leading to transnational customer segments, resulting from increased communication and travel.

◆ Competition from the same organizations in each major market and thus interdependence of markets

◆ Cooperation between organizations from different parts of the world, leading to companies competing with each other and cooperating with each other in different niches of the same market.

◆ Worldwide or regional organization of distribution, ignoring country boundaries.

◆ Communication generated and received almost anywhere in the world.

◆ Global organization strategies that increasingly treat the world as one market.

Insight: Marketing to the poor

Many marketers assume that the world's poor are of no interest. For many sophisticated products designed for western consumers this may be so, but Prahalad and Hart (2002) explain that for the right products there is substantial global demand:

	Global population (millions)	Purchasing power ($)
The wealthy	800	$15 000
The emerging middle class	1500	$1500–15 000
Low-income markets	4000	<$1500

Adapted from: Prahalad, C. K. and Hart, S. L. (2002)

Activity 6.1

For your organization or an organization of your choice, assess the current and future impact of the globalization drivers on the business.

The benefits and challenges of developing strategies for globally diverse markets

The benefits to organizations of increased globalization are increased profit through market growth and a reduced cost base because of economies of scale and the experience effect (the more times you do the same operation the more efficient you become). There are intangible benefits too from a much more visible brand and its associated imagery, achieved through the sheer volume and consistency of communications and extensive distribution.

Associated with globalization is the increasing presence of global companies as they enter more country markets and achieve greater worldwide reach through communications, alliances and distribution partnerships. External factors too, such as the increase in regional trading blocks creating greater interdependence of marketing, enable global firms to increase their power, influence and competitiveness.

There are significant challenges too in developing a worldwide strategy, and these can be addressed in terms of the firm's response to three fundamental questions.

1   In what circumstances is it best to adopt a standardized approach (the same marketing actions in as many markets as possible) or a highly adapted approach (different marketing actions for each country market)?

2   How can a firm achieve regional or worldwide exposure of products and marketing messages with large but finite resources?

3   What is likely to be the basis of future global competitiveness in the sector?

In answering these three questions the first involves the choice for a company between a global, regional or multi-domestic strategy and these different approaches are defined below. The answer to the second question involves considering a number of options for responding to market opportunities through the marketing mix and other marketing activities. An important issue, however, is concerned with market and product coverage, and the decision the firm makes must also take into account the strategies of their competitors and particularly their power within the market sector. The third question is about the nature of future global competitive advantage and, for example, how important it will be for the major players to have a large fast-growing home market or a low-operational cost base to order to be competitive in global markets.

See CIM SMD Examination June 2005 Q.1

This case study question enables you to prepare for examination questions on the global competitiveness of larger companies. It looks at the changing dimensions of the global market in which Dyson operate and how their market position has been threatened by the changing competitive landscape and new entrants into the market from China.

Strategy alternatives for global firms

While we have emphasized the potential benefits for multinational enterprises (MNEs) of standardizing the marketing strategy and actions, a worldwide strategy does not necessarily lead to globally standardized marketing. Instead it could mean developing a separate strategy for each international market. The conditions in the international trading environment are an important factor in this decision and influence the choice of strategies for both large and smaller firms.

The concepts of global, multi-domestic and regional strategies (Figure 6.1) reflect the different approaches. Global strategies assume that there is one global segment to be served. In contrast the multi-domestic strategy assumes that market conditions are so different in each market that a different strategy is required for each. Regional strategies recognize the emergence of regional trading blocks as essentially 'home markets'. You should familiarize yourself with these concepts as they underpin international strategies.

In practice, the very largest and most complex organizations have business units, brands, joint ventures, products and services that are at different stages of market development, so it is unlikely that a global or multi-domestic strategy will be appropriate for every part of the organization. The corporate brand identity and products may be globally standardized, but the services may need to be adapted for each country and so the services brand manager may be pursuing a multi-domestic strategy. Such composite strategies are referred to as 'transnational strategies'.

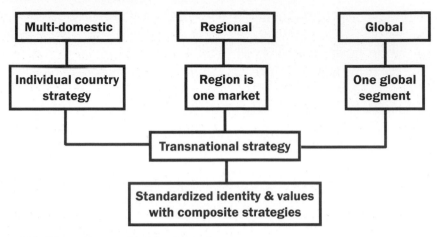

Figure 6.1: Alternative worldwide strategies

Source: Doole and Lowe (2008)

Leveraging capability in global markets

Clearly the benefits for a firm are increasing its scale of operations through increased global activity. They include:

◆ Better knowledge of the requirements and expectations of customers worldwide.

◆ The economies associated with increased scale of operations and R&D.

◆ Improving efficiency and effectiveness through repeating programmes and processes and as a result.

◆ Building the capability and knowledge of the organization that can be applied to new business and marketing initiatives.

Insight: China invests in Africa

Governments can play a key role in supporting the internationalization of its firms. A key factor is recognizing that globalization involves integrated inward and outward bound activity, trade and investment working together. China requires oil, raw materials and other resources in order to continue to fuel its spectacular growth and almost every corner of Africa offers something that could be valuable. In just about every country China sees opportunities for trading and investment. As well as the opportunity to mine copper in Zambia, to extract iron ore in Gabon and to refine oil in Angola, Chinese firms are exploiting the opportunities to build the infrastructure in Africa: roads, school buildings, computer networks, telecom systems and power generation.

Chinese firms win bids because of their very low costs, but China also offers 'no strings' aid, in contrast to Western donors, who impose conditions usually relating to human rights issues. Critics suggest that China's approach enables unsavoury and corrupt governments to ignore Western calls for reform, knowing that they can be bankrolled by China. Sudan is the leading recipient of Chinese investment and some suggest that this is a major reason for the government maintaining its stance in the ongoing Darfur crisis.

The Chinese government maintains that it continues to seek a 'harmonious world' and would prefer to coax African countries down the path to development, rather than imposing its will on them. In November 2006, 48 heads of government attended a forum in Beijing with the purpose of building strategic partnerships. China's initiative is not without its cost, however. Nine Chinese oil workers were killed by rebels in Ethiopia and there have been stories of anti-Chinese unrest in Zambia.

Adapted from A. Blenford, China in Africa, *BBC News Online*, accessed 26 November 2007

The lessons of best (and worst) practice in global firms

In Activity 6.1 we suggested that you might consider the concept of globalization and its implications for strategy development. One key issue in globalization is to what extent it is possible and desirable to standardize products and services in response to the globalization push and pull factors.

Standardization gives the potential benefits of economies of scale and the effects of the experience curve, but the disadvantage of supplying products that may not have local appeal. The question then facing firms is whether it is better to standardize and attempt to 'educate' consumers to accepting the new product or whether it is better to supply an equivalent to the traditional local product.

The issue of standardization has absorbed many writers over the last decade, but the truly globally standardized brand or product – a highly desirable objective for some firms – is still rare. An indication is given of the elements of global marketing that are relatively easy to standardize in Doole and Lowe (2008).

There are many reasons why it might be necessary to adapt elements of the marketing mix including legal, cultural differences and usage conditions. Consequently a product might need to be modified for different markets because of different safety standards, its packaging and advertising because of legal requirements, and language differences and culture may dictate that certain colours, symbols and brand names would have the wrong meaning. Distribution tends to be difficult to standardize because companies must make use of the traditional distribution channels that are often very slow to change. Prices are almost impossible to standardize because of the fluctuating currency exchange rates and the differing stages of economic development of countries, leaving customers with differing abilities to pay the same price.

Achieving uniform positioning of a product or service, too, is extremely difficult. Countries are at different stages of economic development, and few firms practise truly effective global segmentation, so a product may be an everyday purchase in one country and a luxury in another.

Programme and process standardization

In practice, it is useful to distinguish between programme and process standardization. By 'marketing programme' we are referring to using exactly the same new product launch programme or advertising campaign, for example, across all the countries in Europe and by 'marketing process' we are referring to taking the same steps, but the nature of the steps may be adapted to the local situation. For example, a market research study might be made in a number of countries to achieve the same objectives, but it would be necessary to change some aspects of the study, because of differences in culture. It may be appropriate to adopt the same overall process for an advertising campaign but adapt the creative elements to local requirements and media to what is available and preferred in each country. So while it might be possible to save money by standardizing the programme, it may not be advisable as the standard product or campaign may not be successful in all the countries. However, using the same process may facilitate corporate learning of good practice and make savings on such things as setting up evaluation procedures.

Question 6.1

What do you consider to be the benefits of standardization? Explain why it is difficult to find a truly standardized product.

International marketing challenges

Throughout the international marketing process there are pitfalls and challenges, some of which are detailed below. These give rise to creating the lessons of good and bad practice. Good and bad practice are discussed in greater detail in Doole and Lowe (2008).

Opportunity analysis and marketing research – are essential to decide which countries are most commercially attractive, offer the most potential and can most effectively be served by the company. However, emerging markets carry risks, first those associated with unstable environments and second from the unreliability and difficulty in obtaining information.

Sensitivity to different cultures – is essential throughout the process, including customer research, product and service development and communications. There are many examples of organizations offending customers and underperforming because of their cultural insensitivity.

Transnational segmentation – Over-focus on country characteristics segmentation rather than transnational benefit segmentation can seriously curtail global development because of the failure to benefit from scale economies. Good practice requires a hierarchy approach starting with transnational segmentation followed then by country-based segmentation, but, typically, few managers have the vision to carry out transnational segmentation effectively.

Market entry strategies – Arguably the most critical decision for organizations is deciding which market entry strategy to adopt. Choosing between the options, such as using agents or distributors, licensing or acquiring a local company, requires an appropriate balance to be struck between the organization's desire for host market involvement and control and the level of investment and risk it is prepared to take.

Marketing mix – As we have already indicated, there are a series of decisions needed: about the marketing mix: the level of standardization that is possible: and adaptation to local market needs. Decisions are required on the product portfolio, new product development, distribution, communications and pricing strategy, and each of these is critical. Each decision could well be influenced by different factors, including the stage of economic development, cultural demands, legal controls, usage conditions and ethical considerations.

Insight: The size of the informal economy

For marketers selling to less-developed countries, what is known as the informal economy, which frequently involves covert and often illegal activities, seriously distorts the apparent market size. In Africa it makes up 42 per cent of GDP and is as high as 58–59 per cent in Zimbabwe, Tanzania and Nigeria. In Latin America the informal economy in Bolivia is 67 per cent compared with that in Chile is 20 per cent. In Asia, Thailand's informal economy is 53 per cent compared with Japan's 11 per cent. In the United Kingdom it is estimated to be 13 per cent.

While much of the informal economy comprises criminal activity, such as stolen goods, drug dealing, prostitution and smuggling, it also includes tax evasion and tax avoidance associated with legal business activity. This often occurs because the local government is corrupt or overly bureaucratic for small business owners that might be too poorly educated to follow complex procedures. All these activities present problems for legitimate marketers seeking to do business in these markets.

Adapted from: F. Schneider, Size and measurement of the informal economy in 110 countries around the world, www.worldbank.org, accessed on 2 January 2008

Question 6.2

Outline the market entry methods and the levels of involvement associated with the development of a company's globalization process from initial exporting through to becoming a global corporation. Specify what you consider to be the important criteria in deciding the appropriate entry method.

Activity 6.2

For a small to medium sized business, carry out an audit of its international marketing mix elements (the 7Ps plus market entry). To what degree are they standardized? How much scope is there for more standardization and what benefits would you expect?

Choices and investment decisions

For relatively simple niche marketing organizations that target one segment, offer a relatively limited range of products and services, it is possible to develop a relatively straightforward STP strategy based on largely standardized marketing processes throughout the operation. It m ay be possible to develop some standardized programmes too, for example, in marketing research, R&D of new products and even communications across a region. Even for these organizations, investment decisions are complex, because the profit impact of product or market development and supply-chain choices may be significantly different in the short and long term. Moreover, the barriers to implementation and level of success will be significantly affected by the turbulent international environment.

The largest and most complex businesses operate in most countries and are subject to a myriad of often conflicting influences. They target multiple segments with large product and service portfolios and must motivate and galvanize their workforces into taking appropriate action. The decisions they make must reinforce the global corporate strategy, standards and values and must be logical, justifiable and understandable to their staff. At the same time they need to be sensitive to local and national situations and deliver stake-holder value in both the short and the long term.

International planning and organization

Having just given a flavour to the sheer diversity of problems in managing the marketing strategy implementation it is also important to recognize the problems organizations have in planning and managing the organization. The problems arise from misunderstandings about the different environments, miscommunications, lack of cultural sensitivity, lack of a planning culture and the difficulty of maintaining meaningful controls.

Organization structure for global firms

The establishment of a suitable organization structure should reflect the firm's wishes to integrate individual activities to ensure effective communication, planning and implementation. Small firms can simply decide whether to set up a special department to handle exports or include exports within the general management of the firm. As the business develops, so different market requirements and internal pressures force changes in the organizational structure.

The organization structure must respond as the roles of managers are constantly adjusted to meet new marketing challenges and seek to maximize the contributions from individual managers, no matter where they are located. It must also seek to avoid duplication and bureaucracy and instead constantly seek to encourage innovation. The complexity of these organization issues is greater in transnational companies, where the organization structure has taken on an entirely new meaning with advanced forms of networking and matrix structures.

The organization structure can either help or hinder the firm in delivering its objectives and can contribute to the international marketing problems identified.

Question 6.3

Marketing environments are changing faster and more dramatically. This makes the planning and control activity difficult to manage across global markets. What is causing the faster change, what are the implications of this, and how can planners attempt to improve the process?

Skill and capability development

In thinking about learning it is useful to revisit the sequence of decisions in international marketing strategy and the three broad issues that managers need to address:

1   The identification, analysis and evaluation of opportunities.

2   The establishment of a strategic perspective and development of a global marketing strategy.

3   The approach to be used in the implementation and operation of the global strategy.

It is these issues that form the base of the management process that underpins the development of a global marketing strategy, and so these are the key areas for knowledge, skill and capability development. To be successful in international markets, firms must have managers that have the ability to *think*, *analyse* and *plan* on an international scale. To operate effectively, a global marketing manager needs:

◆ Proactive marketing skills

◆ A global outlook and positive attitude to the international arena

◆ A broad knowledge of the global marketplace.

It is necessary to develop the management skills to manipulate the interface between the marketing mix and the complex environmental factors. However, it is difficult for individual managers to take the local country approach at the same time as a regional/global view.

Leveraging corporate learning across geographically diverse markets

Markets around the world are subject to many influences. While it is possible to identify those that are common to many country markets, the real difficulty lies in understanding the specific nature and importance of influences within markets. Understanding the apparently conflicting nature of these influences is essential to develop appropriate strategies.

This is particularly problematic in the largest and most complex companies, which are referred to as 'transnational companies'. They aim to standardize some elements of the marketing activity and adapt others and so end up with composite strategies. These transnational companies aim to achieve superior performance by pursuing three strategic aims:

1 Global-scale efficiency and competitiveness

2 National level responsibilities and flexibility

3 Cross-market capacity to leverage learning on a worldwide basis.

The strategies that transnational firms develop to achieve global competitive advantage need to accommodate some or all the following:

◆ Simple and complex individual product and market policies, which may be independent or interdependent in different parts of the organization.

◆ Customer segments that may be specific and unique to a specific market or transnational and valid across borders.

◆ Cooperative relationships with firms that might also be customers, suppliers and competitors at the same time, while simultaneously ensuring that the distinctive values and positioning of the company are maintained by building meaningful value-added relationships in the supply chain.

Question 6.4

Explain the concept of transnational strategies and what competencies transnational organizations must have to succeed.

ment in the quality of Chinese education, there is less justification for financing students abroad. Second, the Chinese currency is linked to the depreciating US dollar. This has meant that the cost of tuition fees and accommodation has increased by more than 40 per cent in two years. Third, the UK authorities have made entry more difficult as they have tightened up on the granting of student visas, as evidence has emerged of organized crime taking advantage of a more relaxed approach to granting student visas. The international competitive situation is also changing with other countries including the United States, Canada, Australia and other EU countries competing strongly in providing English-taught degrees.

Some observers comment, however, that another reason for the current decline in applications from Chinese students is that the UK universities and colleges are failing to provide the experience that Chinese students are looking for. Often the students are placed on courses that have few students from other nationalities and so are unable to mix with students from other cultures. They are given inadequate pastoral care, insufficient support in learning English and do not get sufficient chance to gain social and work experience.

Question 6.5

How might universities address the situation described in the case study above.

The geographic development of SMEs

Given the different patterns of internationalization identified earlier, it is inevitable that the geographic development can be significantly different (Doole and Lowe, 2008). It is worth reflecting on the alternatives (Figure 6.2) between, first, market spreading by the traditional expansion and concentration methods and, second, internationalization through networking, which is driven by the nature of the firm's family and business contacts, and, third, through the new market development of the firm's supply chain.

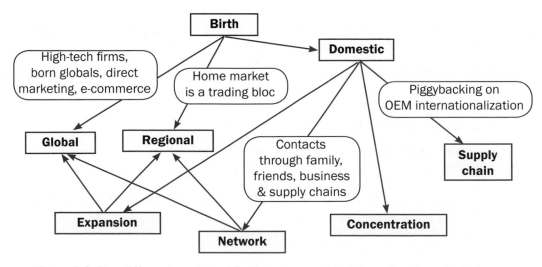

Figure 6.2: The different models of SME involvement in international marketing

The most significant development in the internationalization of SMEs is the phenomenon of the Born Global in which the new firms consider their market to be the world rather than one or two countries. There are two factors driving the Born Global firms. The first is market pull because in new technology markets the firms' customers and competitors will tend to be global and the firm must find a global niche in which to operate. The second is that information and telecommunications technology are enabling firms to communicate instantly and do business around the world using e-commerce.

The importance of niche marketing

Activity 6.3

Using Table 6.1, assess an organization of your choice in terms of it being an exporter or a niche international marketer.

Table 6.1: Difference between exporting and niche marketing

	Exporting	International niche marketing
Marketing strategy	Selling production capacity	Meeting customer needs
Financial objective	To amortize overheads	To add value
Segmentation	Usually by country and customer characteristics	By identifying common international customer benefit
Pricing	Cost based	Market or customer based
Management focus	Efficiency in operations	Meeting market requirements
Distribution	Using existing agents or distributors	Managing the supply chain
Market information	Relying on agent or distributor feedback	Analysing the market situation and customer needs
Customer relationship	Working through intermediaries	Building multiple-level relationships

Source: Doole and Lowe (2008)

Building and sustaining the niche

To sustain and develop the niche, the firm must:

- ◆ Have good information about the segment needs
- ◆ Have a clear understanding of the important segmentation criteria
- ◆ Understand the value of the product niche to the targeted segment(s)
- ◆ Provide high levels of service
- ◆ Carry out small-scale innovations
- ◆ Seek cost efficiency in the supply chain

♦ Maintain a separate focus, perhaps, by being content to remain relatively small

♦ Concentrate on profit rather than market share and evaluate and apply appropriate market entry and marketing mix strategies to build market share in each country in which they wish to become involved.

Leveraging learning in SMEs

SMEs can be characterized by their proactivity in international marketing typically and categorized as passive, reactive, experimental, proactive or world-class international marketers as shown in Figure 6.3.

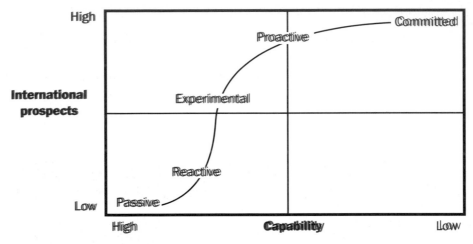

Figure 6.3: Levels of internationalization

Successful SME international marketers share with their larger counterparts the characteristics of being very customer-oriented and having a strong international competitive focus. However, their small size and lack of resources means that they build success in international markets in other ways too. They learn by developing very effective relationships, often personal, with customers, suppliers, contacts and experts that can bypass more lengthy ways of collecting information.

They also develop a culture of learning throughout the firm, invest in skills development, share experiences and knowledge, and this allows them to be very flexible in their international market development. Staff invest high levels of emotional energy in the firm and are usually very innovative.

Activity 6.4

Thinking about your own organization or one of your choice (large or small). How would you categorize the firm in terms of international marketing (passive, reactive, experimental, proactive and committed)? What evidence do you have to justify this categorization? How does the organization learn from its international marketing activity?

Summary

◆ Companies adopt different approaches to international marketing depending on the way they view international markets, how they organize themselves to exploit the opportunities and how they expand internationally.

◆ The very largest firms are exploiting the globalization drivers to develop the customer appeal of the business on a worldwide basis, but they decide on different strategic approaches, depending on their situation.

◆ A key challenge is improving global efficiency and competitiveness, local responsiveness and leveraging corporate learning across their global operation.

◆ The most successful international small firms focus on developing a global niche that they can defend and exploit.

◆ To be successful, it is necessary to get the worldwide operations to take and 'buy into' a planned approach but not one that is inappropriately standardized and centralized, so that local staff have little scope for innovation and decision-making.

Further study

For further reading on this unit you should refer to:

Doole, I. and Lowe, R. (2005) *Strategic Marketing Decisions in Global Markets*, Thomson Learning, Chapter 6

Before starting this unit you should familiarize yourself with international marketing by reading the following recognized text:

Doole, I. and Lowe, R. (2008) *International Marketing Strategy*, Cengage Learning, 5th Edition.

Hints and tips

The unit assumes that you have built up a good understanding of the global environment, trends and issues and you should also make sure that you understand cultural issues and know how they impact on strategic marketing decisions.

Bibliography

Doole, I. and Lowe, R. (2008) *International Marketing Strategy: Analysis, Development and Implementation*, Cengage Learning, 5th Edition,

Doole, I. and Lowe, R. (2008) *International Marketing Strategy*, Cengage Learning, 5th Edition

Prahalad, C. K. and Hart, S. L. (2002) The fortune at the bottom of the pyramid, *Strategy and Business*, 26 (54), 67

Unit 7
Developing innovative strategies to achieve global fast growth

Learning objectives

The CIM syllabus for Strategic Marketing Decisions requires you to be able to suggest specific strategies that will achieve fast growth, by developing innovative marketing approaches, for example, to the delivery of service and by using e-business.

In studying this unit you will:

3.8 Critically appraise innovative marketing strategies in small and large companies operating on global markets.

3.7 Evaluate the use of e-technology to build and exploit competitive advantage.

Having completed this unit you will be able to:

◆ Appraise a range of corporate and business visions, missions and objectives and the processes by which they are formulated, in the light of the changing bases of competitive advantage across geographically diverse markets.

◆ Identify, compare and contrast strategic options and critically evaluate the implications of strategic marketing decisions in relation to the concept of 'shareholder value'.

◆ Demonstrate the ability to develop innovative and creative marketing solutions to enhance an organization's global competitive position in the context of changing product, market and brand and customer life cycles.

This unit relates to the statements of practice:

Bd.1 Promote a strong market orientation and influence/contribute to strategy formulation and investment decisions.

Cd.1 Promote organization-wide innovation and cooperation in the development of brands.

Ed.1 Promote corporate-wide innovation and cooperation in the development of products and services.

Gd.1 Select and monitor channel criteria to meet the organization's needs in a changing environment.

> ## Key definitions
>
> **Assets** – are the 'things' that the organization possesses, including the physical facilities, the customer database and brand.
>
> **Competencies** – are skills that exist within the organization's staff, including brand management, IT and supply chain.
>
> **Core competencies** – are the skills that pervade the organization and are those areas and activities in which the firm has a very high-developed ability.

Study guide

In this unit we focus particularly upon the development of innovative marketing strategies in small and large firms and the strategies that lead to fast growth in global markets. Over the last few years much of the fastest growth appears to have been driven by technology and particularly e-commerce developments. However, in developed markets many products have reached commodity status. Competition comes increasingly from countries with a lower cost base for production and services. To survive and grow, organizations are increasingly building their competitive advantage around superior knowledge of their customers and markets and customer service enhancement through efficient and effective management.

This unit is concerned with making decisions that are innovative and, therefore, might challenge the often highly planned, conventional marketing strategies of many organizations. To better understand entrepreneurial marketing and motivate themselves to be more innovative, students should read how entrepreneurs have successfully identified and exploited new opportunities. Suggestions for further reading are included at the end of this unit.

Entrepreneurial and fast-growth strategies

There are a number of firms that manage to achieve above-average performance and grow even during periods of economic recession, and in this unit we explore how this can be done. At the end of this section you may conclude that there are no secrets to achieving fast growth and that entrepreneurial or fast-growth strategies are largely founded on common sense and good management. The problem is that common sense is not always common, and as managers spend so much time in dealing with daily crises, the mundane activities and routine marketing, they lose focus and do not have time to apply common sense and innovation. This section is therefore intended to reinforce some fundamental principles in the context of fast growth.

Proactivity and hypergrowth

Typically within a market, firms usually adopt one of four stances in their approach to market innovation.

'Pioneers' are the entrepreneurial marketing firms that endeavour to be first in. 'Second-in' firms tend to follow the pioneers in innovation but improve on their initial offering. The 'imitators' are those firms that copy the product and service innovations but try to offer

It is essential, therefore, to build a total customer value proposition and not rely simply on the performance of the core product or service. Central to this is managing the complete customer interaction and, as far as possible, customer experiences in dealing with the firm.

Implementation – the drivers of entrepreneurial companies

Much is written about the growth sectors; particularly those relating to major technological leaps forward, and we discuss this in other units. However, many firms are involved in markets that are in the mature phase. These provide the greatest challenge for entrepreneurial companies that wish to grow fast without the need for product invention. However, even in these markets some important decisions need to be made about allocating resources to what is important and this is shown in Figure 7.1.

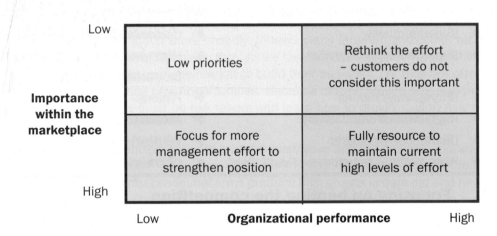

Figure 7.1: Resource allocation in mature markets

Customer management

These fast-growth businesses focus on high levels of customer management:

◆ Segmentation and sub-segmentation to better satisfy more specialized customer needs leading ultimately to one-to-one marketing.

◆ Understanding the lifetime value of customers and the need to build customer loyalty.

◆ Exploiting the opportunities for cross-selling, when the level of trust of customers in the company is high.

◆ Managing customers through the entire process of information search, purchasing and consuming the product or service and post-purchase customer service, to ensure a satisfactory experience.

◆ Building appropriate relationships with all the stakeholders that might influence purchasing decisions.

◆ Focusing on providing the very highest levels of service at the customer interface throughout the purchasing process.

Improving the process

As companies increasingly offer similar products and services it becomes harder to differentiate products and services on the core attributes. Consequently, achieving fast growth becomes a more difficult challenge and there are few options for increasing market share. One remaining differentiator is providing superior customer satisfaction and service at each point of the customer–supplier interface.

Activity 7.2

Carry out an audit of the customer management process of your organization or one that you have dealt with. Is there a clearly stated and implemented customer service strategy? Is the strategy designed to provide competitive advantage? You may wish to refer to Table 7.2.

Table 7.2: Areas for customer management process improvements

Quality	Being right
Speed	Being fast
Dependability	Being on time
Flexibility	Being able to change
Cost	Being productive

Question 7.1

What do you consider to be the characteristics of a fast-growth organization? What prevents many large organizations achieving above-average growth performance?

Strategy decisions for a new direction

Going beyond customer-led: taking customers in a new direction

The conventional marketing approach is that it is essential to be customer-led, and we use the term periodically in this coursebook. However, in Unit 4 we discussed discontinuities in technology and industry breakpoints and observed that it is innovative businesses, often new to the sector, rather than the existing firms that exploit the opportunities. They take the market in a new direction by anticipating what might be important to customers in the future instead of carrying out research to find out what they want and need. Customers rarely have a detailed vision of what they would like in the future and do not know what is possible. Products such as the Sony Walkman would not have been developed, if Sony had relied on customer research.

An innovative organization should therefore exploit the areas of opportunity that go beyond defined customer needs as shown in Figure 7.2.

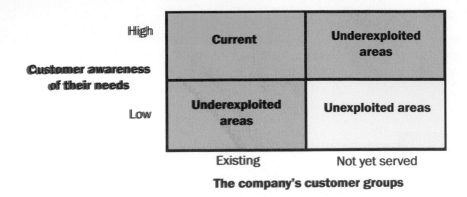

Figure 7.2: Identifying new market opportunity

Building and sustaining the strategy

Bolton and Thompson (2000) have clarified the steps, from having the initial idea through to developing a sustainable business (Figure 7.3). Having the idea and spotting the market gap are not enough. Skills, knowledge and competence must be applied to achieve distinctive positioning in the market. The positioning must be unique to offer customers a 'quantum leap' in benefits. The firm must build competitive advantage and increase the barriers to the entry of competitors. For example a new product can be quickly copied but if its positioning is distinctive because of its design and image, and if it has been launched and marketed well, then there will be a lead time before it comes under serious attack from the competitors. By then it could have established a secure position in the supply chain.

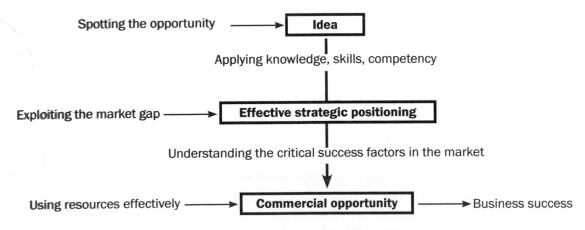

Figure 7.3: The development stages for a new business

However, the entire firm's resources and capabilities must be mobilized to achieve the result. As Figure 7.4 shows, the firm must be capable of recognizing the opportunity and be willing to change and apply competencies and resources in new ways to achieve this strategic positioning.

Figure 7.4: Entrepreneurial management and strategic positioning

After establishing an initial market position through a visionary leap forward too many firms sit back instead of building a sustainable business and reinforcing the competitive advantage and strategic positioning through continuous small-scale innovations. Furthermore, to reduce its risk exposure the firm must improve management effectiveness and learn good practice by reflecting on successes and failures.

There are many challenges in the early stages of a new business or innovation within an existing business. Doole and Lowe (2005) discuss this in greater detail.

Question 7.2

A significant number of organizations achieve fast growth for short periods, especially after start up, but many of them fail to maintain the growth rates. Why do you think this is?

Case study: Playstation losing to Wii

Being 'second' into a new market can allow established firms to learn about the market and use their resources to grow fast when they finally do decide to enter. Before Sony's Playstation entered the market in 1994, Nintendo, Sega and Atari were the main players. However, Sony made its 100 millionth Playstation sale in 2004.

Sony is credited with achieving spectacular growth because it targeted a new segment, adults, by changing gaming from being a child's toy played in the bedroom to an all-family entertainment gadget that sits alongside the Hi-Fi and DVD recorder in the main family room. The Playstation created a media star, Laura Croft, that became part of mass popular culture but also managed to maintain the technological interest. By appealing to grown-ups too, Sony's strategy aimed to ensure that its young devotees would continue to play into adulthood.

However, at the next cycle of console launches Sony's lead position was gone. By August 2007 only 5.5 million PlayStation 3 consoles had been shipped worldwide, compared with more than 10 million each of the Nintendo Wii and Microsoft's Xbox 360, a later market entrant. The success of Nintendo's Wii was particularly impressive as it was mainly due to broadening the range of customer segments of gamers. The Wii was less technologically advanced than the Playstation and Xbox but benefited from good games and a system that allowed players to control characters on the screen by waving a tennis bat, sword or gun. Like many fast-growth successes, however, the demand for the Wii outstripped supply and many customers had to wait to receive their games.

Robin Lowe, from various publicly available sources

Question 7.3

What have been the critical success factors for the fast growth of games consoles and what are they likely to be in the future?

Search for greater competitiveness

What is clear from the re-evaluation of the organizations' activities is that they will have to find new ways of competing in the future. The basis of competitiveness in many market sectors is changing rapidly, and this was the subject of the book on competing for the future (Hamel and Prahalad, 1994). Subsequently, much has been written on the subject by other authors, but some of the main conclusions about how to achieve future competitiveness are:

◆ **Dropping losers and backing the winners** – Perhaps one of the great fallacies in marketing management is that more products or business units should be retained because they make a contribution to the overall costs of the operation, even though they are not particularly profitable. In practice, unprofitable areas can be a huge (often hidden) drain on resources and management time, so their realistic costs, can be much higher than reported. There are additional costs too – the opportunity cost of not putting resources into areas of greater future profitability, and the damage to the brand of not using resources to build future value for it.

◆ **Business restructuring for flexibility** – Backing winners not losers can be applied to all aspects of the business. So it is not just the product portfolio that should be restructured, but the decision might be made to move out of lower productivity business areas. Also outsourcing might be used for certain activities, the workforce might be reduced to make the company more flexible, adaptable and more sharply focused.

◆ **Continuous improvement in quality and service** – Redesigning business and customer management processes is essential to make the organization better and faster and to give the customer ever-better value and experiences.

◆ **Organization and sector reinvention** – Many market sectors could be (and are being) reinvented, and the organizations with the best industry insights will take the lead in determining the future.

◆ **Increasing globalization** – Greater globalization means that the future opportunities for organizations lie in global market development, leveraging the current value-adding, highly productive competencies and assets into new markets and reducing resources applied to lower productivity activities, by outsourcing manufacturing.

The consequences of these are that the most valuable future organization capabilities are to be able to instigate, manage and capitalize on change. At the heart of this is having a clear idea about what assets and competencies will be required in the future. The most valuable organizational competencies and assets are those that can be leveraged into the future business processes, and the worthless competencies and assets are those that are locked into the business models of the past.

Activity 7.3

Classify your organization's products and services into:

◆ Yesterday's successes and money generators

◆ Today's successes and money generators

◆ Tomorrow's successes and money generators

◆ The also-rans

◆ The failures.

What implications does this have for redefining the organization's source of competitive advantage in terms of superior, more effectively applied knowledge, capabilities and assets?

Insight: Open innovation

The idea of getting external contributions to an organization's innovation process has been around for a long time but the concept of open innovation was articulated in the book by Chesbrough (2003). Organizations such as Philips and IBM are committed to accessing ideas from individuals outside their organizations rather than just relying on those of their own staff. Often external facilitators help with the process. One example of collaboration is that between the McLaren Formula 1 racing team, who have worked with St Thomas' Hospital, London accident and emergency team to study whether the processes used in managing racing car pitstops might be transferred to the hospital.

Unilever use collaboration with external partners in order to innovate throughout the organization, whether it is improving the spray system on a deodorant, working with Philips to develop a capsule system on an iron that will deliver treatments to the clothes being ironed, to the application of the company's brand Dove to spa treatments. Chief executive Patrick Cescau sums it up by saying 'Unilever would rather work with some-one who has the answer today rather than hoping that the company's internal development team will find the answer some time in the future'.

Source: Robin Lowe, from publicly available sources

Knowledge management

The process of identifying and effectively managing competencies and assets (knowledge management) will therefore become increasingly important.

The areas of knowledge that might provide the organization with competitive advantage are very context-specific but might include:

◆ Detailed understanding of customer needs and future expectations

◆ Customer databases and the ability to analyse them

◆ Key contacts and knowledge of the market

◆ Supply-chain management and partner relationship

◆ Process technology

◆ Research capability

◆ Intellectual property creation and protection

◆ Brand value creation

◆ Cost and price dynamics.

Question 7.4

How will the innovative organizations compete and win in their chosen sector in the future? Choosing one industry sector, explain what the future critical success factors will be.

See CIM SMD Examination December 2004 Q.3

Strategy development can take different forms depending on whether it is being developed in a large or small organization. This question allows you to explore some of those differences and helps you prepare for the varying organizational contexts that are presented in the examination.

E-business innovations

During the late 1990s e-business innovations were expected to create a new generation of fast-growth businesses, eliminate many firms with traditional business models and change forever the way in which business is done. In practice this is all happening, but not at the same pace and on the same scale in all market sectors as was predicted. Some of the most significant e-business innovations have been in improving the customer management process in mature sectors, such as the purchase of travel, books, music and financial products. By defining new routes to the market some innovative companies in the sector have managed to provide a quantum leap in value for customers.

We have discussed the drivers of Internet marketing in Unit 4 and concluded that innovations must be customer-led, with technology playing a supporting, enabling role. It is essential to maximize the value contribution of the technology advances (systems, processes, etc.) to customers and the organization through innovative website design and new business models.

Innovation in website development

Table 7.3 summarizes four main categories of websites. In thinking about their purpose it is possible to see how their value contribution can be enhanced by linking the external website with internal business processes and databases, to provide better customer service (e.g. faster, more relevant and complete information, simpler processes and interactions) and organization cost savings (e.g. in customer management, staff time devoted to service delivery, and eliminating duplicated and unnecessary processes).

For a fuller discussion of this topic, refer to Chapter 8 of Doole and Lowe (2005).

Table 7.3: Four categories of websites

Website type	Purpose of the website
Site to provide organization information (e.g. www.Philips.com)	◆ Explains the origins, business mission and areas of activity, standards and values, brands, financial performance, job opportunities and contact points ◆ Information about products and their applications
Site to provide service online (e.g. www.bloomberg.com and www.fedex.com)	◆ Puts customers in control of their accounts and enables them to track inventories, orders, transactions and deliveries from anywhere in the world ◆ Provides real-time information, for example, on travel and share prices
Site to provide information online (e.g. www.bbc.co.uk)	◆ Provides access to current and archived past files of news, data and images ◆ Media organizations can maintain and build relationships with their consumers beyond the scheduled content and provide content to areas where it is not accessible by traditional communication methods
Site to carry out business transactions (e.g. www.expedia.com)	◆ Facilitates fast, convenient, interactive online transactions through a variety of business models (see below)

Further enhancing the website

Once the purpose of the website within the overall company strategy has been decided there are considerable opportunities for innovation to ensure that the website is further developed to increase the value added. Chaffey *et al.* (2003) define the characteristics of successful marketing-led websites that will appeal to customers. While basic website requirements, ease of navigation, attractiveness, interactivity, and usefulness such as reliability and security, are fundamental, others, such as multi-language options, sensitivity to local cultures and knowledge of local laws, are essential for global development.

Activity 7.4

A number of texts discuss good website design (e.g. Chaffey *et al.*, 2003). List the characteristics of good websites and use them to assess three that you regularly use. Apply these and critically evaluate your own organization's website. How could innovation in website design be used to significantly improve the customer management process (refer to Table 7.12)?

Internet business models

In moving beyond information provision to business transactions online, the main e-business models are Business-to-Consumer (B2C) and Business-to-Business (B2B) models. However, Chaffey *et al.* (2003) note that eleven different models have been developed, and these are shown in Table 7.4. Of these, the two most significant developments are Customer to Customer (C2C) and Customer to Business (C2B), and we discuss these later.

Table 7.4: Eleven types of e-business models

1	E-shop
2	E-procurement
3	E-mails
4	E-auctions
5	Virtual communities
6	Collaborative platforms
7	Third-party marketplace (hubs)
8	Value chain integrators
9	Value chain service providers
10	Information brokerage
11	Trust and other services

Source: Chaffey *et al.* (2003)

Business-to-consumer

Many customers are prepared to use the Internet to carry out their information search on companies, products and services but are still unwilling to pay for products and services online because of fears about the security of online payment and the potential for fraud. It is useful to be able to refer potential customers to telephone sales or a physical store to make their purchase and collection. A key challenge for firms is to ensure that their website address is prominent when search engines are used for keyword searches. This has led to innovative communication strategies by many firms, and this is discussed in Unit 9.

A key decision for firms is the degree to which their products and services lend themselves to online retailing perhaps because they:

◆ Require low customer involvement in the purchasing process

◆ Can be delivered online (e.g. software and financial services)

◆ Are sold on the basis of proven design or quality of manufacture

◆ Do not involve considerable negotiation between supplier and purchaser

◆ Are neither large nor perishable which may give fulfilment (physical delivery) problems.

The boundaries between what can and cannot be sold online are becoming less clear as innovation in websites and business models develop. Stores with physical and online retailing are integrating their activities. However, some organizations still try to keep their physical and online stores separate, frustrating customers in the process. There are still many challenges for online and integrated stores. For example, setting prices that are appropriate to both the physical and the global virtual markets but still different, inevitably leads to comparisons being made. Often the disparities in pricing simply cannot be explained to customers.

Business-to-business

The transactions in the B2B virtual marketplace differ from the B2C marketplace:

◆ B2B transactions are typically more complex and the developments in B2B business models reflect the changing process needs of the participants.

◆ Some B2B transactions are relatively routine repurchases or reorders often of commodity items.

◆ For many of the participants, the driver of the B2B market is the need to match supply and demand in real time, usually because of the inflexibility of product capacity.

◆ Interactions involve the exchange of significant amounts of information between the seller and customer before, during and after any transaction, and it must be shared between many departments. The information includes such things as specifications, designs and drawings, purchase contracts, manufacturing and delivery schedules, inventory control, negotiation of price and delivery.

◆ Some of these purchases will be core to the business, such as raw materials and essential maintenance services, and others will be occasional or peripheral, such as facilities management or purchase of office equipment.

The Internet enables a far wider range of data to be exchanged without restriction on the number of participant organizations. Web portals are the means by which the exchanges take place and business can be transacted through them. There are the 'hubs' where all the interested participants congregate. Typically there are two types of hubs:

◆ Industry specific hubs, such as automobile or aerospace manufacturing

◆ Function specific hubs, such as advertising or human resource management.

Using e-hubs, firms improve the efficiency of the processes of transactions and thereby ensure lower costs. The hubs can reduce the transaction cost by bringing together all the purchasing requirements of many hundreds of customers worldwide. E-hubs also attract buyers who are able to negotiate bulk discounts on behalf of a range of smaller individual buyers.

Transacting business through hubs has a significant effect not just on the way that business is done but also on the way that the company must be organized to respond more quickly to business opportunities. It also affects the culture that must be developed throughout the organization.

Question 7.5

What do you consider to be the advantages and disadvantages of business transactions in the B2B market through e-hubs? Explain the characteristics of organizations that you would expect to be successful.

Other models

Online auctions (C2C) have become extremely popular, and eBay is the most success-ful site for trading between individuals who buy and sell antiques, collectible items and memorabilia, by virtual bidding. eBay provides the website at www.ebay.com and takes a fee to insert advertisements and a further fee based on the final value. C2B works in reverse to the normal type of auction as consumers join together to reduce the prices they pay through bulk buying. A final date is set, and the price falls as more customers join the buying group. One example is Letsbuyit.com. Priceline.com is similar but provides a mechanism for consumers to say what they are prepared to pay for an airline ticket. Sup-pliers decide whether they are prepared to accept the offer.

It is increasingly recognized that, while online retailing has many benefits as a route to market for international development, a combination of virtual and physical routes to mar-ket might deliver the best results for many businesses.

Further value-adding activities using communications and infor-mation technology innovation

The interactivity of the Internet allows service delivery and product promotion offers to be made closer to the point at which customers might be prepared to buy, for example, through product placement in films, on television and on websites.

The technologies are being further integrated, albeit at a rather slower speed than might have been expected when the 3G licences were bought by the telephone network compa-nies, to enable services to be supplied to hand-held devices. Innovations in mobile phone technology are enabling still and moving images, data and audioclips to be transferred to mobile phones resulting in e-business service delivery, and sales promotions and commu-nications being used in a much wider range of situations. Further opportunities come from tracking customer movements using global positioning systems and offering products and services in their new location.

Permission marketing

Many e-business innovations will increase the targeted marketing messages directed to individual customers, and it is unlikely that traditional marketing will be phased out. Godin (2002) has suggested that customers in future will see up to 3000 messages per day, the majority of which will come using the new communications technologies. Because very few of these messages are requested, Godin calls this 'interruption marketing'. Godin has introduced the term 'permission marketing' to suggest that the communications will be more effective if customers agree to receive communications from a particular firm, be-cause it will develop the ongoing relationship.

It is suggested that the opt-in approach, in which firms would need to seek permission from recipients before sending e-mail, is preferable to an opt-out approach in which the customer would have to take the initiative in asking a firm *not* to send messages that were of no interest, as this would be more difficult to implement, would not help 'policing' and would be unlikely to reduce the unwanted mail to a sufficient degree. Implementing the opt-in approach could be a first step in controlling spam – the unwanted messages that are blocking up the Internet. Of course it would prevent customers receiving a wide range of information.

Viral marketing takes this one stage further by encouraging people to pass along an electronic marketing message to a friend. A high pass rate from person to person will result in a 'snowball' effect, but a message will soon fizzle out if there is a low pass rate. Hotmail achieved great success with viral marketing, but there have been few campaigns since that have achieved outstanding success.

Case study: Competition or co-operation to win in technology

Technology firms can adopt one of two approaches to competition and co-operation. They can adopt either a totally closed approach in which they aim to dominate their sector by locking in customers to their total portfolio of products and services and making it extremely difficult for offerings from other suppliers or competitors to interface with their own. Or they can provide an open platform that allows any company to provide complementary products and services. When the 'locking out' is carried to what the lawmakers consider to be extremes then it is considered as anti-competitive. Microsoft was found by the EU to have abused its monopoly power and fined in 2004.

In 2007 Apple introduced its iPhone in an exclusive distribution agreement with the service provider, O_2, leaving many potential customers frustrated with the restrictions placed on the use of the product. Having a small market share meant that the iPhone strategy did not come to the attention of the authorities at least in its early days.

However, with its iPod, Apple has a much larger market share but its strategy has been the same. Customers are locked into the 'Apple world' as they must buy iTunes from the iTunes Music Store and purchase only Apple certified iPod accessories.

There are obvious benefits in adopting this type of strategy but if the organization becomes too successful, as Microsoft did, then it comes to the attention of the regulatory authorities. Whilst the resulting fine (in Microsoft's case €497 million by the EU) may not be too significant in terms of affecting the company's profitability, the organization may suffer damage to its reputation and brand, and also find it much harder to get innovations accepted by the authorities, who will be suspicious that the company is simply further exploiting its position.

Adapted from: B. Thompson, Time for Apple to face the music, *BBC News Online*, 19 September 2007

Question 7.6

What are the arguments for and against co-operation? How can an organization maintain competitive advantage whilst pursuing a co-operation strategy?

Summary

◆ Organizations adopt different levels of innovation proactivity in the market, and the strategies that they choose to pursue must reflect this.

◆ When compared with average performers the characteristics of the fastest growth organizations show differences in ambition, attitudes to business, management style, awareness of customer value and approaches to dealing with competition.

◆ Critical to early-stage fast growth is the need to orientate the organization to achieving initial growth but then rapidly building distinctive positioning and a management approach that will build a sustainable future.

◆ It is harder to achieve fast growth and rapidly increase market share in larger businesses in mature markets. Critical for success is better customer management processes to give exceptional service and satisfaction.

◆ Future competitiveness will depend on picking winners and dropping losers and focusing on opportunities for adding greater value. Knowledge, competencies and assets will provide the basis of competitive advantage, and routine operations will be outsourced.

◆ E-business provides the mechanism to exploit many of these knowledge assets ultimately to provide personalized marketing. There are, however, a number of obstacles to overcome.

Further study

For a more detailed discussion of the topics in this unit you should refer to:

Doole, I. and Lowe, R. (2005) *Strategic Marketing Decisions in Global Markets*, Thomson Learning, Chapter 8

For further treatment of strategic marketing you should refer to:

Wilson, R.M.S. and Gilligan, C. (2004) *Strategic Marketing Management: Planning Implementation and Control*, Oxford: Butterworth-Heinemann.

and Internet marketing to:

Chaffey, D., Mayer, R., Johnston, K. and Ellis-Chadwick, F. (2003) *Internet Marketing: Strategy, Implementation and Practice*, FT Prentice Hall

Bibliography

Bolton, B. and Thompson, J. (2000) *Entrepreneurs, Talent, Temperament, Technique*, Butterworth-Heinemann

Chaffey, D., Mayer, R., Johnston, K. and Ellis-Chadwick, F. (2003) *Internet Marketing: Strategy, Implementation and Practice*, FT Prentice Hall

Chesbrough, H. (2003) *Open Innovation: The New Imperative for Creating and Profiting from Technology*, Boston: Harvard Business School Press

Doole, I. and Lowe, R. (2005) *Strategic Marketing Decisions in Global Markets*, Thomson Learning

Godin, S. (2002) *Permission Marketing: Turning Strangers into Friends and Friends into Customers*, Free Press

Hamel, G. and Prahalad, C.K. (1994) *Competing for the Future: Breakthrough Strategies for Seizing Control of your Industry and Creating the Markets of Tomorrow*, Harvard Business School Press

Roure, J. (2000) Ten myths about entrepreneurs, in S. Birely and D.F. Muzyka (eds), *Mastering Entrepreneurship*, FT Prentice Hall

Wilson, R.M.S. and Gilligan, C. (2004) *Strategic Marketing Management: Planning Implementation and Control*, Oxford: Butterworth-Heinemann, 3rd edition

Unit 8

Building portfolio value: branding, products and services

Learning objectives

The CIM syllabus for Strategic Marketing Decisions includes the requirement to understand the decisions that are required to build the revenue streams that come from a strong portfolio of products and services. However, stakeholder value is also generated through its intangible assets and principally, the brand.

In studying this unit you will:

4.2 Assess the nature and dimensions of branding/brand decisions, their role in the development of advantage and their significance in global markets.

4.3 Examine product strategies and the role of new product development (NPD) in competitive strategy.

Having completed this unit you will be able to:

◆ Evaluate the role of brands, innovation, integrated marketing communications, alliances, customer relationships and service in decisions for developing a differentiated positioning to create exceptional value for the customer.

◆ Demonstrate the ability to develop innovative and creative marketing solutions to enhance an organization's global competitive position in the context of changing product, market, and brand and customer life cycles.

◆ Define and contribute to investment decisions concerning the marketing assets of an organization.

This unit relates to the statements of practice:

Cd.1 Promote organization-wide innovation and cooperation in the development of brands.

Ed.1 Promote corporate-wide innovation and cooperation in the development of products and services.

Study guide

This unit is concerned with making strategic marketing decisions that add value for the organization and its stakeholders, principally customers, through portfolio development. We start by explaining the importance of integrating all the marketing mix activities, supply-chain developments and relationships with customers and other companies in the process of adding value. You should, therefore, keep in mind the links between the subjects considered in this unit with those in Units 9 (communications and relationship building) and 10 (pricing, supply-chain and partnership development) to fully understand the value benefits of integrating the marketing mix.

In this unit we focus on portfolio management, maintenance and development and specifically on the decisions that are made on branding, both at a strategic level to increase brand awareness, impact and equity and at an operational level, in the application of branding to products and services. We then turn to the management of the portfolio of products and services and focus on the management decisions of maintaining and building the portfolio, where necessary, carrying out rationalization, NPD and service enhancement.

Before starting this unit, students should familiarize themselves with the issues of branding, product and service, and NPD concepts, using the reading mentioned in the 'Further study' section.

Key definitions

A successful brand – is an identifiable product, service or place augmented in such a way that the buyer or user perceives relevant, unique, sustainable added values that match their needs most closely (de Chernatony, 2001).

Product portfolio – is the collection of products and services that are managed together rather than as individual products.

Brand equity – is the net present value of the future cash flow attributable to the brand name.

Intangible assets – non-material assets such as technical expertise, brands or patents.

Adding value through branding

Previously in this coursebook we have emphasized that for many global companies today it is their intangible assets that provide their most significant source of future competitive advantage. Of these intangible assets the brand is the most significant. For example, the brand equity of the Coca-Cola brand was estimated by Interbrand to be worth $70 billion in 2006. The brand has been created through sustained marketing investment in advertising and promoting a consistent message for over 100 years.

At the outset, therefore, it is possible to categorize firms according to their approach to branding:

◆ Those firms for which the brand is pivotal to their strategies and investing in, protecting and building the brand is (almost) the most critical activity.

◆ Those firms that use their existing and already established brands as an asset to be used to promote additional products and services but do not have a strategy to invest and develop them.

◆ Those firms that merely 'name' products, fail to manage and support the name through focused marketing activity and so do not create a brand that has future value.

Most of the world's most valuable brands have received heavy and sustained investment over decades in every aspect of their marketing strategy, from customer research, segmentation and positioning through to every aspect of marketing mix activity. Usually the investment includes a large commitment to advertising but other factors, such as totally consistent quality, reliability and continuous innovation, are just as important to achieve widespread customer loyalty and referrals.

Careful consideration should be given to whether a new or improved product, line extension or modification will enhance the overall brand as well as helping with the initial sales of the product. In many less sophisticated organizations, managers use the name or brand on new products, line extensions or modifications without any real thought to whether the name will enhance or erode the value of either the product or the firm's overall reputation. Their purpose is often very short term. They simply want customers to buy a product or service presented under the brand name. These kinds of decisions at best do little to enhance the brand and at worst devalue the brand by confusing customers as to what it stands for. Even with well-known brands there are many examples of inappropriate brand extensions, product modifications and failed repositionings.

The purpose of brands

The purpose of brands is to create value for customers by helping them to make purchasing choices from the increasing range of competitive offerings available and help to reduce the risk of choosing the wrong product or service.

Customers expect brands to be a 'guarantee' of satisfaction right through the purchase decision-making process, from obtaining information through to delivery and post-purchase support. In some sectors, customers do not differentiate between the brand owner and the brand distributor, so it is essential to manage the brand throughout the supply chain.

While organizations try to create a distinctive positive image in consumers' minds through their marketing activities, ultimately customers make up their own minds and build their own individual perception of the brand. Different customer segments may build up different perceptions of the brand because of their different demands and expectations. The organization needs a sufficient volume of customers to be prepared to pay a price premium to offset the investment that is made in the brand.

The real question and the subject for the remainder of this section is how can the brand be leveraged to add value for customers and the organization in the future and how can erosion of value be avoided.

Customer brand perception

The customers' positive perception of the brand is built from various sources:

◆ **Experience** – of previous use of the product and satisfaction with its performance.

◆ **Personal referral** – from friends and acquaintances; peer pressure, such as wearing the 'cool' brand, can be critical.

◆ **Editorial and other public sources** – such as the media, consumer reports and endorsement by experts or fashion gurus.

◆ **Communications** – by the organization, both through interactions between its staff and customers and through the promotion mix.

The organization must make strategic marketing decisions that influence customer perceptions and reinforce a positive image.

Categories of brands

Brands (Doyle, 2000) can be categorized as follows:

◆ **Attribute brands** – that build confidence among customers where the functional attributes such as quality and performance are important but are difficult for consumers to assess.

◆ **Aspirational brands** – that convey to customers images about the type of people who purchase the brand. Such brands do not simply deliver the customers' functional requirements of the products and services but also deliver status, recognition and esteem.

◆ **Experience brands** – focus on a shared philosophy between the customer and brand.

The choice of approach is dependent upon the context and particularly whether customers are able to distinguish between the product attributes and how 'involved' they are with the product purchase and use.

For example, in global markets some cultures place more importance on the attributes, functionality and specification, whereas in other cultures aspirational branding might be more appealing. Where appropriate, organizations must be prepared to modify their approach.

Insight: Car branding issues

Branding is central to much of the promotion communication work carried out, and it is possible to see some of the dilemmas faced by brand managers simply by watching and reflecting on the nature of their advertising and the messages being put out – and then thinking about the implications for brand management. Renault, for example, has been very successful in building the Clio brand through successive television commercials. For many existing and potential customers the Clio brand is more recognizable than the Renault brand. While this might be good for Clio sales it may not help in the promotion of other models.

Money spent on promoting a small car, especially when it has such a strong sub brand, may not allow brand equity to be leveraged for the benefit of niche products, such as the Renault Espace, the sales of which will not justify mass promotion methods.

Renault has been very successful in designing and engineering their cars to high safety standards confirmed in official safety tests. The question is how can Renault achieved the maximum impact in its promotion and differentiation from its competitors from safety, something that consumers either take for granted or would prefer not to think about.

Source: Robin Lowe, from publicly available sources

Country of origin effect

Brands give confidence to the buyers in situations where the buyers' knowledge about the product and its design and manufacture is limited, for example, because they are not able to assess the quality of the technology. In such situations the country-of-origin perceptions can influence their buying decisions by creating trust in the particular expertise of firms and workers from that country. Increasingly, of course, the MNE's headquarters, the brand's perceived 'home', the location of product design and places of manufacture and service centres may all be in different countries as the supply chain is developed. However, consumers are becoming much more aware of these differences and are making increasingly sophisticated decisions based on country of origin (COO) perceptions.

Global branding

Strategically global branding offers the opportunity for the organization to benefit from economies of scale and the experience effect and is the response to targeting a global customer segment. To build and maintain a strong global brand requires every decision throughout the marketing process to be consistent with the brand standards and values. The decisions range from the need to gain deep insights into customer brand perception through to careful selection of celebrity endorsers that might be used to personify the brand.

The difficulty in global branding is to maintain consistency through standardization, where possible, but also be able to make adaptations to the mix, where necessary, for cultural, legal or usage reasons without distorting the brand identity.

Specific benefits to the organization

Well-managed brands have the potential to add value to the organization by providing the following benefits (Doyle, 2000):

◆ **Price premium** – Branded products should allow higher prices to be charged than for products that have an equivalent specification but no brand.

◆ **Higher volumes** – Alternatively, branded products can generate higher volumes than non-branded products if they are priced at market rates, rather than at a premium.

◆ **Lower costs** – High volumes should lead to cost reduction because of the economies of scale and the experience effect.

◆ **Better utilization of assets** – The predictably high level of sales should lead brand managers to make more effective use of assets, such as equipment, the supply chain and distribution channels.

Question 8.1

What are the benefits to customers and the organization of having a high profile, distinctive brand?

Factors contributing to brand value erosion

Over the last two decades, brands have come under increasing pressure. Some have been devalued, and others have been discontinued. We have categorized the factors that have contributed to brand value erosion as external ones outside the organization's control, including unexpected events, and internal ones as poor brand management.

External factors

Private branding

As the major retailers have become more powerful and improved the quality of their own label products, so the private brand share of the market has increased significantly, as consumers perceive private brands to provide better value for money. The key decision for branded product producers is whether or not they should also manufacture for private label brands too.

Brand forgery

Brand forgery not only reduces the revenues for brands through lost sales, but customers also sometimes associate poor quality of the forged brand product with the legitimate brand. Reducing or eliminating forgery is costly and time-consuming for governments and companies. It is widespread and in some product areas, such as CDs and software copying, is very mobile and difficult to close down.

Negative brand associations

As part of the strategy to explain the brand attributes to customers, firms make associations with the personalities, who encapsulate the standards, values and beliefs of the brand. For some brand, associations are made with the owners, such as Richard Branson and Bill Gates, and for others it is sports and media celebrities. While these are generally positive, the brand can be damaged if the personalities are associated with inappropriate behaviour.

Product or corporate brands can also become too closely associated with sponsored events that disappoint visitors or are badly organized. Public relations activity that is designed to achieve a better relationship with governments and politicians can backfire if they are shown later to be corrupt, and high-profile alliances with organizations that fail can also have a negative impact.

Insight: Endorsing skin whitening – improving self confidence or turning back the clock?

As celebrity endorsement becomes ever more important in the promotion of products that involve personal image it is inevitable that there will be controversy. The skin lightening industry is worth at least £100 million in India, but some would suggest that this is a relic of the past and a 5000 year old culture that thought that high ideals, nobility and high caste were associated with fair skin. Some would say that in today's enlightened society there is no place for such products. So a 40-second advertisement in India, also seen in the UK via YouTube, might be considered controversial. It shows one of the biggest Bollywood heart throbs, Shahrukh Khan, in a song and dance extravaganza handing over a whitening product from the Fair-and-Handsome-for-Men range to an unfortunate dark-skinned young man. Within a few weeks he has turned lighter skinned and more confident, and is now surrounded by girls chanting 'Hi handsome'.

For human rights activist, Kiran Kaur, this is a step back in time as it confirms the condescending attitude that many Indians have towards dark-coloured skin. It is made worse because of the endorsement from a star, whose every move is followed by adoring fans on websites around the world. A distributor for Fair and Handsome, Manish Shah, says that the product and advertising is justified because 'everyone wants to look good'. The product is not bad for skin and can help people that have an inferiority complex because of their skin colour.

Adapted from: N Puri, Beyond the pale, *BBC News Online*, 25 September 2007

Unacceptable business practices

A number of brands have been associated with unethical business practices such as environmental pollution, exploiting child labour and misleading customers. Often this is due to malpractice by contractors who must be very carefully policed. The problem in this area is that what is acceptable and unacceptable is often a very personal view and is affected by different stakeholder values, culture, affluence levels and understanding of business practices.

Unexpected crises

High-profile brands are vulnerable to unexpected crises that occur from time to time. These events are often outside the organization's control, for example tampering with products, attacks on IT systems and anti-company propaganda through protests and websites, and accidents such as airline crashes.

Customers expect (sometimes unreasonably) to have systems in place that will prevent many of these events. Even with those that are unavoidable and where no blame is attributed to the firm, the brand can still suffer from being associated with negative publicity. It is vital that the organization has in place an effective strategy for responding fast to any crises and managing them effectively.

Grey marketing

Branded products that reach the market through unauthorized channels are often sold at much lower prices than the authorized channels and can lead to customers believing that they have been 'ripped off'. There are three types of grey marketing: parallel importing, reimporting and lateral importing, and for a fuller discussion read Doole and Lowe (2008).

Activity 8.1

For your own organization or an organization of your choice carry out a critical evaluation of the company's brands and the value they contribute to customers and the organization.

Insight: Luxury brands – class or mass?

Luxury used to mean 'beautifully crafted, hideously expensive and unashamedly elitist', only available to those with class – not just wealth. Now luxury is no longer reserved for the rich, but increasingly is for the global middle class on an ego trip. Luxury houses such as Dior, Cartier and Chanel have grown rapidly as they have extended their product lines to appeal to these aspirations. The $220 billion global industry is built on exclusive brands but, having doubled in size in the last ten years, will the brands continue to stretch and still retain their cachet? Armani sells chocolates and Prada has a mobile phone. Gucci claims to be in the business of selling dreams, not handbags, but for $80 it is also possible to purchase a pack of Gucci playing cards! Similarly Louis Vuitton sunglasses sell for $275. But the luxury brands are extending upwards as well as downwards. The Louis Vuitton Tambour Tourbillon watch sells for $220,000 and Hennesey is selling a limited edition of 100 bottles of cognac for $200,000 per bottle, the packaging for which comprises a case surmounted by exclusive, hand crafted, Venetian glass pearls.

For their part too, mass marketers are also looking for a share of the luxury market, albeit through association. The mass clothing retailer, H&M, regularly works with big name fashion designers, such as Karl Lagerfeld and Stella McCartney, whose brand is part of the Gucci group. The question is, can luxury brands continue to stretch at both ends of the scale?

Adapted from: P Gumbel, Luxury goes mass market, *Fortune*, 6 September 2007

Brand building and management

At the start of the section we distinguished between brands as assets to be built or brands as names to be used with products and services. It is essential to develop a strategy to create future brand value for the organization and customers.

Brand strategy – There are a number of brand strategies that you should be familiar with, including corporate umbrella branding, range branding and individual brand names. The use of these differs according to the context and company approach.

Brand portfolio management

A number of actions can be taken to improve the portfolio:

◆ **Brand building** – Building knowledge of customer perceptions through research is used to strengthen the brand essence and identity and thus reinforce brand value in customers' minds through effective brand communications.

◆ **Brand positioning or repositioning** – Customer insights are needed to define brand positioning more clearly or for repositioning to avoid customers being unclear what the brand stands for.

◆ **Brand extension** – Brand names with positive appeal can be applied to new products and services, but it is important to ensure that they fit with customer perceptions, otherwise they will be devalued.

◆ **Brand rationalization** – To be successful, brands require substantial and sustained marketing support. Companies that have acquired many new brands or have carried out regular brand extension find that the portfolio can become unfocused and action is required to delete products. However, the decision to delete old products can be risky if they offend too many loyal customers.

◆ **Brand innovation** – and NPD are essential to keep the brand fresh in customers' minds through continual innovation and occasional new developments.

◆ **Global branding** – offers the chance to provide support on a much higher level and creates the expectation that considerable additional sales will result. Of course, as we have mentioned earlier, the global success of the brand depends on consistency of image and customer appeal, but customers from different cultures may have different expectations and beliefs about the brand that might make consistent positioning difficult.

Brand management

Over the last decade, there has been increasing evidence that many brands have come under pressure, as it has become more difficult to charge premium prices. Khashani (1995) identified the customer and competitor factors that have increased the pressure on brands and listed the actions that must be taken to address the problems. One of the main problems identified was a failure of management to invest in and build the brand.

See CIM SMD Examination December 2004 Q.1

Branding is an important issue in the SMD syllabus and arises in varying guises in different types of questions. You need to ensure you understand the important characteristics of building a global brand and should be able to assess the strategic implications of a company's branding strategy and how it could be improved. It is this issue which is examined in the Lego case study in this examination.

Business-to-business branding

So far the discussion has focused largely on global consumer branding, but branding is increasingly important in business-to-business marketing too. The rationale for the existence of brands in business-to-business marketing is the same as in consumer goods marketing – to clearly communicate the attributes, values and standards of the company, product or service and to resist the decline into commoditization of products, which leads to decisions being based only on price.

Branding is a focus for building relationships. Purchasers and users value the commitment of suppliers to the product and service and benefit from the added value from dealing with a firm with strong brands. In some situations there may be benefits for low-profile brands from an association with globally recognized branded components (e.g. Intel microprocessors in computers or Lycra in garments). This trend is becoming increasingly important as consumers become more influential in the supply chain and demand products which contain branded components.

Branding in the not-for-profit sector

As with many aspects of marketing branding is becoming increasingly important in the not-for-profit sector, as the brand provides a 'short cut' in explaining the promised customer experience. There are many examples of the need for branding decisions in the not-for-profit-sector to assist in improving stakeholder communications. In destination marketing the violent image of New York of a decade ago no longer detracts from the positive aspects of the promised experience. By contrast the positive image of Prague has been eroded recently by stories of badly behaved young visitors, attracted by low alcohol prices and low-cost airline tickets. The name Great Ormond Street Hospital in London is associated with the very highest standards of care for sick children and the hospital and its staff want to maintain that positioning.

Activity 8.2

Choose a brand from your own organization or an organization of your choice. Explain the appeal of the brand to customers and how effectively it adds intangible benefits. In what areas of brand management is there scope for increasing added value through the intangible benefits?

Product and service portfolio decisions

Much of what has gone earlier in the study guide has focused on the company's situation, capabilities, resources, markets, customers and competition and how this can drive the strategic direction, growth and thus lead to successful performance.

However, it is the products and services of the company that generate the income streams on which the company's performance is judged. Efficient distribution and memorable communications are important in adding value but cannot make a success of an unwanted product or service. For this reason proactive product and service management is critical.

Product and service analysis

There are many concepts and techniques, such as product life cycle and portfolio analysis that are referred to in the pre-reading that are used to analyse the product and service portfolio. Answers are required for a number of questions, including:

◆　Which products and services are performing well or badly, in terms of volume, value contribution to overheads and profitability?

◆　Which phase of the life cycle and cell of the portfolio matrices is each product and service in and what implications has this for future investment and revenue generation?

◆　Which market segments, including geographic segments, are best for generating demand for existing and new products and services?

◆　Which products and services generate the greatest volume, value and profitability through the various customer segments and distribution channels?

◆　How successful are the introduction of new products and services measured by the diffusion rates?

◆　Which product and service areas are there the best opportunities for new development?

Answering these questions will enable managers to reach conclusions about the strategies that should be adopted for each individual product and category of product and service both globally and in specific market segments. The implications of this might be that decisions will be required about which products need to be eliminated, reinvigorated or replaced with a new development. Some alternative strategies follow:

Rationalization of product range

There are a number of reasons for the rationalization of products within the portfolio and these include:

◆ When products and services have reached the end of the life cycle and support instead should be given to growth products.

◆ When the marketing budget is limited and cannot effectively support all the products in the portfolio.

◆ When there is a need to standardize products, for example in international markets, to reduce costs through scale economies.

◆ When there is a need to reduce inventory and product line changeover time in manufacturing.

Retention of poorly performing products

There may be reasons why poorly performing or unprofitable products should be retained. A low-volume sales product might be an essential part of a range. It might be a loss leader and leverage sales of complementary, higher volume or value products. The product might be what everyone remembers the brand for, and therefore to discontinue it could lead to brand damage. Not choosing to discontinue the product might be important in retaining some residual customer loyalty until a replacement is developed and introduced. In other cases, keeping the product might ensure the production line, skills and knowledge are retained until the next big order materializes. This is often necessary in sectors such as shipbuilding, aircraft manufacture or defence equipment manufacture.

Decisions need to be taken about whether contributing to overheads is sufficient reason to retain a product. It is worthwhile remembering that discontinuing a product that contributes to overheads will result in the remaining products having to share an additional overhead burden that could lead to them becoming loss making as a result.

Question 8.2

What might be the reasons for rationalizing the product/service range in the portfolio? What factors should be taken into account when deciding which products and services to delete from the range?

See CIM SMD Examination December 2005 Q.2

The SMD syllabus deals frequently with companies having to take a new direction because of their being in the mature phase of the life cycle. This question does not require a detailed explanation of the plc but does require the focus to be on developing possible strategies for products and services in the mature stage of the life cycle. Using examples it is possible to show how many organizations have built competitive advantage in this situation by keeping the offer fresh through small-scale innovations throughout the marketing process, but particularly in the provision of exceptionally high levels of service and intangible benefit associated with brand image.

The downward spiral into commoditization

Having been around for a long time many products in widespread use have reached the mature phase of the life cycle. The product and services are well known and are often taken for granted by the customers, and the organization may see very little opportunity for innovation or product development. It becomes increasingly difficult for some organizations to continue to differentiate their product and add customer value and, in desperation, they resort to price cutting. Competition often remains intense as firms attempt to hang on to market share. This problem is compounded by e-commerce which has increased price transparency, allowing customers to more easily compare prices and buy from the lowest-priced supplier, forcing the higher-priced alternatives to lower their prices or risk going out of business.

As supermarkets become more powerful they are able to apply pressure to suppliers to force them into offering volume discounts. This is made worse as they put further pressure on branded goods suppliers by offering own label products across an ever-broader range.

Becoming the lowest-cost supplier of commodities

Firms that supply commodities have no alternative but to aggressively and continuously reduce costs throughout their supply chain and be prepared to source components and services from the lowest-cost supplier no matter what the location is. For many years the textile and garment-making industry has been driven by cost advantage to source from emerging countries. Banks and insurance companies are lowering their costs by making staff redundant in high-cost locations and relocating their service operations to low-cost countries. As we have seen earlier, e-hubs will further increase the pressure towards commoditization in the B2B sector.

Differentiation by adding value

It is easy for a firm to be drawn into believing that they are in the business of selling a specific product or service made to a specific design with the inevitable consequence of trying to achieve ever-lower prices. But some of the most successful firms have been able to manage customer perceptions of lower prices while differentiating products and adding value. For example, Tesco has grown from being the 'pile it high, sell it cheap' food retailer of the late 1960s to become the leading UK food retailer. It has achieved this through continually differentiating the relatively mundane activity of food shopping by adding customer value through a whole range of successful, often small initiatives. However, it is also building a value brand designed to give customers every-day low prices (EDLP).

Activity 8.3

For your own organization or an organization of your choice carry out a critical assessment of the value added throughout the portfolio. Which are the areas where the portfolio is underperforming?

The global portfolio

We have discussed earlier some product portfolio issues in making international marketing decisions, and it is worth returning to them at this point:

◆ Global standardization/local adaptation product and service decisions taken, for example, for cultural, legal and usage reasons, in different countries.

◆ The fact that the products may be at different stages of the life cycle in different countries. This adds an additional complication for NPD and portfolio rationalization decisions because the global perspective must be considered. In some countries it may be desirable to cut the old product and replace it with a new development, while in other markets it may be preferable to promote the existing product.

◆ Emerging markets may require a more basic version of the product compared to more technologically advanced countries.

◆ In emerging markets it may be possible to 'leapfrog' one technology completely as is happening with mobile phone technology.

New product and service developments (NPD)

In Unit 4 we introduced the NPD process as a framework for the innovation process and the various elements contained within it. The idea is that the process is linear and a series of single gateways at which decisions are made. As a linear process the next stage is not begun until the previous one is completed, assessed and the decision taken to proceed, usually by senior management. While in concept this provides the necessary discipline, cost containment and control, it can be a lengthy process, particularly if decision-making in the company is slow and bureaucratic. Often the time to market launch is critical because of:

◆ The importance of being first mover in a market to set the new basis for competing.

◆ The speed at which information and intelligence about new developments spreads through markets.

◆ The speed with which competitors copy and introduce new product and services.

◆ The demands of customers and their dissatisfaction with old products.

Some companies do not have these pressures, and so the linear process is appropriate. However, an increasing number of firms must undertake the various stages in the NPD process simultaneously to reduce the time to market, so marketing launch and commercialization plans might be needed in concept at early stages. It may be that the company is committed to a new product launch, but the final product features may depend on differentiating the product from competitor products that are introduced to the market during the period up to the firm's launch. The packaging design concepts may be produced at the same time that the product features are being finally developed.

New product development categories

There are a number of categories of new products, and these are shown in Table 8.1. These reflect the fact that the majority of new developments made by companies are needed to update and refresh the portfolio through incremental improvements. In fact new-to-the-world products are not too common, so the firms that wait for the next big R&D breakthrough to improve their fortunes are likely to be disappointed.

Table 8.1: New product categories

Category	Contribution (%)
New to the world	10
New product lines	20
Additions to product lines	26
Revisions/improvements	26
Cost reductions	11
Repositionings	7

Aligning NPD to the marketing strategy

A key task in developing new products is ensuring that the time and resources spent on new developments are aligned with the marketing strategy. It is therefore necessary to answer a number of questions, and these are highlighted in Table 8.2.

Table 8.2: Aligning NPD to the marketing strategy

Fit with mission	Will all stakeholders understand the new idea?
Fit with product/market scope	Can the ideas be contained within an identified and easily communicated area?
Match between growth strategies and resources	Are the resources being used effectively within the growth options?
Delivery of competitive advantage	Is the advantage tangible or in the mind of the innovator?
Synergy between firm and target market	Will this add value to the current customer segment?
Fit with positioning	Does this reinforce or enhance the current positioning? Does it fit with the brand image?
Market entry alternatives	Could the idea be better exploited by alternative collaboration to reduce risks?
Is the timing right?	Should the product be launched now or should the firm wait for others to create the demand?

Question 8.3

In marketing international services, the elements of the extended marketing mix 'physical evidence', process and people provide the basis for adding value for customers. As a consultant to a global bank explain how these should be used within the marketing mix to build competitive advantage.

Service enhancement

There is considerable difficulty and uncertainty in the development of new products, and we have already emphasized in Unit 7 that many fast-growth businesses are successful through adding very high levels of customer service into their product and service offer, but this is an area where organizations often fail to maximize the use of their assets and competencies. Services can either be regarded as 'add-ons' to a product offering or a service offering alone. Services also involve the process management of information (e.g. financial services), people (airlines) and physical objects (e.g. laundry). As we have indicated with the examples, the balance between each of these varies according to the context.

However, what is quite clear is that the quality of service is becoming ever more important as the differentiator between product offerings and between competing service offerings. Many organizations are focusing on the customer 'experience', and this is where portfolio enhancement can be increased. While it would seem relatively straightforward to enhance service delivery, in practice the cost of improving processes, systems and staff training to achieve the required levels can be extremely high.

Success and failure in NPD

The problem with NPD is the high risk of failure. Griffin (1997) found that although failure rates had been reduced during the mid-1980s and mid-1990s, only one in five ideas made it through to success.

Griffin suggests that products and services are often abandoned during the NPD process because of:

◆   A lack of available technology

◆   A change in the firm's strategy

◆   A competitor pre-emptive new product launch

◆   Market information suggesting that the new product or service will not meet customer needs or expectations.

However, 55 per cent of products and services that are launched also fail. The reasons for this include:

◆   The size of the market is frequently overestimated and the adoption curve misunderstood.

◆   The product fails to perform.

◆   Competitors prove to be too firmly entrenched.

◆   The product is poorly positioned, inadequately promoted or priced at too high a level.

◆   Distributors lack commitment.

◆   The new product is pushed through despite market research findings.

Case study: Children benefiting from laptop development

The organisation One Laptop per Child (OLPC) was set up by Nicholas Negroponte to provide durable, low cost and simple-to-use laptop computers to children in the developing world. The machine has no moving parts, can be powered by solar, foot pump or pull-string powered chargers, is housed in a waterproof case and can be read in sunlight. The price has recently increased from $176 to $188 but the eventual aim is to sell the machines for $100. Governments in less developed countries can buy the machines in lots of 250,000. In July 2007, suppliers were given the go ahead to increase production of components, suggesting that OLPC had the three million orders necessary for viable production. In November 2007 OLPC launched on a trial basis another scheme 'Give One, Get One' (G1G1) in which US residents could purchase two machines for $399, one which would be sent to the buyer and the other sent to a child in a developing country. The first countries to benefit from donated laptops were Cambodia, Afghanistan, Rwanda and Haiti, the least developed countries that could not afford to buy the product.

The G1G1 scheme however also may reflect the fact that whilst OLPC have obtained promises to buy from leaders in developing countries these have not always led to firm orders and cash. The G1G1 scheme does however have additional benefits. Extending the scheme to developed countries could have the benefit of encouraging more people to develop content, software development and support.

Adapted from: J Fildes $100 laptop to sell to public, *BBC News Online*, 24 September 2007

Question 8.4

Why do some new product developments, such as the one discussed in the case, which appear to offer value to stakeholders, not always succeed in the way that is expected?

Achieving success in NPD

The key to success is an effective NPD strategy which will create a flow of new products that might vary in market impact but will include some high revenue or high margin generators. This approach is preferable to trying to spot one blockbuster new product.

To do this Griffin suggests three fundamental requirements of the process:

◆ Uncover unmet needs and problems

◆ Develop a competitively advantaged product

◆ Shepherd the products through the firm.

Activity 8.4

For your own organization or an organization of your choice, assess the effectiveness of NPD in the company. Where in the process do you believe there is scope for improvement and why?

NPD, platforms and 1:1 marketing

We have discussed the need for 1:1 marketing and customization, and advances in technology makes this increasingly possible. The challenge for organizations in the future is to be able to create common product platforms and a computer-aided, modular approach to building the final product for the individual customer. The modular approach ensures cost efficiency but also allows a high degree of customization, especially when applied along with other marketing mix elements.

Question 8.5

You have a consultancy contract to provide advice to a medium-sized specialist engineering company that supplies equipment to the energy generation business. The business is efficiently run but is losing money and needs to reassess its ageing portfolio. Prepare, with justification, a list of actions and areas of investigation that you would undertake.

Case study: Unilever's global brands

In 2004, Niall Fitzgerald, the then Chairman of Unilever, was the main architect of a five-year growth strategy which focused on achieving growth through 400 leading brands. The strategy has involved disposal of many minor local country brands and non-core activity. Although the strategy had hit 11 out of 12 targets for margins, cost savings and debt reduction, the firm has failed to meet its target of 5–6 per cent growth from its leading brands, which include Magnum, Ben and Jerry's and Hellmann's mayonnaise.

As a result of this the company announced that it would switch its focus to increasing shareholder returns through share buy-backs and dividend increases. Although some brands such as Knorr soups, Lipton tea and Dove soap had achieved their growth forecast, other brands had performed less well, so that in fact the top 400 brands only achieved 2.5 per cent growth overall in 2003. The main underperforming brands were Slim Fast, Calvin Klein fragrances, Cif and Domestos household range and frozen foods.

Unilever replaced Fitzgerald in 2005 with Patrick Cescau and by 2007 the performance of Unilever was back on course with sales growth up 3.8 per cent and profits up 7 per cent. The turnaround was achieved by focusing resources on those products with the most potential for growth, including its care brands, such as Dove and Lifebuoy, its vitality brands that encourage healthy living, such as Knorr, Vie, Flora and Blue Band, as well as emerging market opportunities. Whilst Unilever had previously encouraged quite a high degree of decentralization and entrepreneurship at a local country level Cescau's strategy was set up global teams to drive product innovation, leaving the country operations to 'get things done' and implement the strategies, particularly focusing on managing the relationships with the biggest customers – the major retailers.

Source: Robin Lowe, from public available sources

Question 8.6

The Unilever strategy is based on concentrating resources on the development of global brands. What do you consider to be the arguments for and against this strategy?

Question 8.7

What should Unilever do now?

Summary

◆ Brands are a major means of differentiation of one product or service from those from the competition.

◆ It is the customers' perception of the brand that ultimately determines the true brand value. This is the reason why the brand becomes a valuable intangible asset of the organization.

◆ Every aspect of the marketing mix must be managed effectively to build the brand, and this requires continual investment, consistent communications, innovation and service enhancement to create exceptional value for the customer.

◆ It is essential to have a product and service portfolio strategy and use appropriate criteria for making portfolio decisions that involve rationalization and new development.

◆ In international markets, the challenge is to maximize company performance by developing a portfolio that is balanced between globally standardized products and services and locally adapted ones.

◆ NPD and service enhancement should be a continual process to which the organization is committed. A high proportion of products fail and so it is essential for organizations to have an effective NPD process.

Further study

de Chernatony, L. (2001) *From Brand Vision to Brand Evaluation*, Butterworth-Heinemann, for more on branding and brand management

Doole, I. and Lowe, R. (2005) *Strategic Marketing Decisions in Global Markets*, Thomson Learning, Chapter 9

Wilson, R. and Gilligan, C. (2004) *Strategic Marketing Management: Planning, Implementation and Control*, Oxford: Butterworth-Heinemann, 3rd edition, provides a fuller discussion of product and service management.

Key definitions

Integrated marketing communications – Shimp (2003) provides a definition of IMC which focuses on five features:

1 Start with the customer or prospect.

2 Use any form of relevant contact.

3 Achieve synergy through consistency across the communication elements.

4 Build relationships.

5 Affect behaviour.

Relationship marketing – is creating and building mutually beneficial relationships by bringing together the necessary stakeholders and resources to deliver the best possible perceived value proposition for the customer.

Study guide

This unit is concerned with the ways in which an organization builds competitive advantage by developing an integrated strategy for communications and relationship building with all its stakeholders. In doing this we consider the challenge of increasing the effectiveness of communications by recognizing the need to be aware of the positive and negative messages that are received by customers and appreciating how planning and using the right communication methods, can achieve success. We then focus on taking decisions in relationship marketing that can be used, where appropriate, to build customer loyalty.

The purpose of communications

The purpose of communications is for the organization to present and exchange information with its various stakeholders (individuals and organizations), according to its defined objectives and to deliver specific results. This means not only that recipients must accurately receive and understand the information conveyed but also that they may be subject to some persuasion too. This aspect of communications is the traditional promotion P (promoting to external stakeholders) of the marketing mix and includes advertising, personal selling, PR and sales promotion.

The communications role goes further, however, as it implies the need for a two-way dialogue with customers. This has led to the concept of relationship marketing with the objective of building interactive relationships with the most profitable and valuable customers and other influential stakeholders. Because all staff of the organization will have a direct or indirect role in communicating and building relationships with stakeholders it is vital that they work towards the organization's overall objectives and always meet the standards and values of the organization in all their interactions.

Whilst relationship marketing has become key to successful business to business marketing, in many sectors consumer marketing has also become more interactive, but in a different way. It has become dominated by the Internet as an increasing source of purchasing and usage information for consumers and has become ever more influenced by informal communications, typically on social networking websites, such as Youtube and Facebook.

Insight: The power of social networking

It is widely accepted that the Internet has changed the behaviour of consumers in searching for information about products and services they may wish to buy. Research by Yahoo showed that 77 per cent of consumers are influenced by internet research, typically spending 12 hours researching a potential online purchase.

Increasingly social networking sites provide the source of information. They can be very powerful. A remark by a Sony senior executive dismissing a rival product Wii as an 'impulse buy' prompted comments from bloggers criticizing Sony for being arrogant. A blogger and media commentator, Jeff Jarvis, complained about Dell, triggering an avalanche of adverse comments from others, leading to a drop in Dell's share price. The problem for firms is that these networking sites provide a focus for critical comment.

Of course marketing managers can use these sites to exploit grass roots marketing by providing 'seed' stories or even manipulate satisfaction ratings but this can be dangerous if consumers find out.

Source: Robin Lowe from various public sources

Internal, interactive and external marketing

Figure 9.1 shows the importance of considering three dimensions in communications: external, internal and interactive or relationship marketing.

Internal marketing
Communicating to the staff the mission, values, objectives, priorities and procedures

The company

External marketing
Ensuring that the range of services, pricing structure, promotional effort and location meet external stakeholder expectations

Customer groups

Staff

Interactive marketing
The effectiveness with which staff deal with each of the customer groups

Figure 9.1: External, internal and interactive marketing

Internal marketing ensures that all staff employed in its business units, and supply-chain partnerships, are aware of the strategies, tactics, priorities and procedures to achieve the firm's mission and objectives. This is particularly important for staff, who are in different worldwide locations and often subject to cultural and language boundaries in the same way that external audiences may misunderstand the firm's external communications.

Interactive marketing ensures that every contact between staff and customers is consistent with the organization's service standards and values and that the decisions taken by individual members of staff are consistent with the organization's strategy.

External marketing is the traditional role of communications with external stakeholders and can be summarized by the DRIP factors (Fill, 1999).

◆ **D**ifferentiate products and services

◆ **R**emind and reassure customers and potential customers

◆ **I**nform

◆ **P**ersuade targets to think or act in a certain way.

Four levels of communications and relationship building

Communications and relationship building activities in the organization embrace four distinct strategic elements and these are shown in Figure 9.2. Distribution will be discussed in Unit 10.

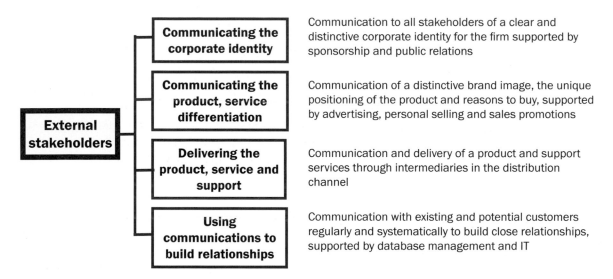

Figure 9.2: The dimensions of external marketing communications

Activity 9.1

Carry out an audit of communications in your organization under the headings of external, internal and interactive marketing. How consistent are the communications and where could improvements be made to improve their effectiveness?

The integration of communications

Stakeholders receive messages, both intended and unintended, from every part of the organization's activities, from the clothes that customer-facing staff wear, the packaging design, the delays in answering the telephone at the call centre to stories in the newspaper about the chief executive's extravagant partying habit.

The ways of communicating

Davidson (2002) explains that an organization communicates in eight ways:

1   Actions – what it does?

2   Behaviour – how things are done?

3   Face-to-face by management – through talks, visits and meetings it shows what the management thinks is important.

4   Signals – from the organization's actions, facilities and objects, including executive bonuses, dress and buildings.

5   Product and services – and particularly their quality.

6   Intended communications – such as advertising, which is not always received as the organization expects.

7   Word of mouth and word of Web (including e-mail).

8   Comment by other organizations – such as pressure groups, competitors and the media.

As the number of communications have increased dramatically and customers have become more critical and sceptical, the importance of IMC has been emphasized to avoid conflicting messages and instead communicate consistent and mutually supporting messages. Kotler (2003) says that 'companies need to orchestrate a consistent set of impressions from its personnel, facilities and actions that deliver the company's brand meaning and promise to its various audiences'.

Activity 9.2

Thinking about a company with which you have communicated recently, list the areas that you received negative and mixed messages. What could have been done to improve the experience?

The areas of integration

Corporate strategy – It is essential to communicate the standards and values, objectives, strategies and performance of the organization to external and internal stakeholders, including shareholders and staff.

The management style, the organization culture, human resources and recruitment policies convey important messages, such as openness, integrity or creativity to a variety of stakeholders.

Brand strategies – It is vital to clearly convey to customers what the brand stands for and reinforce this by ensuring that all brand activities communicate a consistent message. Communications often go further and define the direction of the brand strategy. For example, the success of many of the world's greatest brands can be attributed to consistent promotion sustained by investment over decades.

Global integration – As organizations operate more internationally, travel and communications become more global because of the Internet and satellite television, so the consistency of communications across borders becomes essential. This means that organizations must standardize some elements of their communications programmes and processes. However, Doole and Lowe (2008) explain that there are many disadvantages and pitfalls associated with overstandardization of communications across borders.

Marketing mix integration – Customers continually receive communications from every element of the marketing mix, such as product specification, leaflets and advertising, service centre efficiency and friendliness, the appearance of a distributor's delivery driver. Some are intended, and some are unintentional.

It is important to remember that non-verbal communication in many markets has greater impact than verbal communications, and inconsistencies may be culture based. For example, the colours and styles used in creative work communicate non-verbally with the customers, reinforcing the positive or negative images and customer perceptions. Customers pick up small errors in colour, matching the corporate colours and design, and in different cultures the significance of colours, symbols and numbers is so great that they alone could deter customers from buying a product.

Question 9.1

Explain the concept of integrated marketing communications, and using examples of good and bad practice show how value can be added or removed.

Success and failure in marketing communications

All forms of marketing communication have a fundamental purpose, which is to ensure that the intended messages (those which are part of the firm's strategy) are conveyed accurately between the sender and the receiver and that the impact of unintentional messages (those which are likely to have an adverse effect on the firm's market performance and reputation) are kept to a minimum. Noise might devalue or discredit the intended message or simply cause it to be lost in the volume of communications.

International marketing communications are particularly difficult. Mistakes in the use of language, particularly using messages which do not translate or are mistranslated, are a particular problem, but more serious is a lack of sensitivity to different cultures among international communicators. Failures of high-profile firms are highly visible and can show them to be incompetent, insensitive or arrogant.

The problems that prevent effective communications can be within or outside the organization's control.

Within the organization's control:

◆ Inconsistency in the messages conveyed to customers by staff at different levels, in different locations.

◆ Different styles of presentation of corporate identity, brand and product image can leave customers confused.

◆ A lack of co-ordination of messages, such as press releases, advertising campaigns and changes in product specification or pricing.

◆ Failure to appreciate the differences in the fields of perception (the way the message is understood) of the sender and receiver.

◆ Ignoring the needs of different audiences.

◆ Achieving little impact from a single message.

◆ Lack of synergy and reinforcement from multiple communications.

◆ More than one message communicated together, so confusing the recipient.

◆ Setting unclear objectives.

◆ Trying to achieve too much with one communication to justify the high cost.

◆ Inconsistency within the distribution channel.

◆ Advertising agencies focusing on their creative work rather than selling the product.

Some problems outside the organization's control include:

◆ Counterfeiting or other infringements of patents or copyright causes the firm to lose revenue and suffer damage to its image if consumers believe the low-quality goods supplied by the counterfeiter are genuine.

◆ Grey marketing, which is distribution through channels that are not authorized by the organization, communicates contradictory messages that damage the brand and confuse consumers, often because prices undercut the official channel.

◆ Competitors, governments or pressure groups attack the standards and values of organizations by alleging, fairly or unfairly, bad business practice.

Marketing communications planning

The framework for communications planning is shown in Table 9.1. Situation analysis should establish a clear, current and desired future position for the organization within its market environment context. The analysis should also confirm the organization's current communications capability within its market. It should be possible to establish from this the organization's ability to influence and persuade its stakeholders through its integrated communications strategy.

Table 9.1: The marketing communications plan

Situation analysis	Environment market: stakeholders, competition, customers and structure
Objectives	The short- and long-term objectives
Messages	Target audiences and messages
Communications	The media, the promotions mix and integration of the channels
Budgets	Basis of allocation
Control	Measurement, evaluation and correct deviations

It will also enable decisions to be made about the communications objectives and budgets to be set (as these must be different from the overall marketing strategy objectives), the target audience, the tools and media and the measurements made to evaluate progress.

Audiences

Profiles of all stakeholder audiences need to be prepared. A clear understanding of the target buyers, their background, experience, preferred information sources, purchasing behaviour and processes will help in the creation of the message and selection of appropriate marketing tools and media. In B2B markets, organizational purchasing is a more formal process and involves a buying centre as shown in Table 9.2. Each member of staff has a separate responsibility and motivation for buying and therefore requires a different message.

Table 9.2: The B2B Buying centre

Users	Often initiate the purchase and define the specification
Influencers	Help define the product and evaluate the alternatives
Deciders	Decide product requirements and suppliers
Approvers	Authorize the proposals of deciders and buyers
Buyers	Have the formal authority for selecting suppliers and negotiating terms
Gatekeepers	Can stop the sellers reaching the buying centre

Question 9.2

Identify the key decisions that would be needed when developing an outline communications plan for the launch of a new low-cost airline and what factors would be key when making the decisions.

Insight: Will advertising continue to finance the Internet

Internet users have come to expect free Internet content as of right but the vast amount of information and other material does not come for free. It is financed almost totally by advertising in one form or another. ZenithOptimedia estimates worldwide Internet advertising in 2007 to be $448 billion. Internet advertising generates revenue through placement designed to increase awareness and 'click through' to encourage action on the part of potential purchasers. The revenues of Google have been generated by click-through fees, 'one nickel at a time' as journalist John Batelle puts it, whilst providing the search facility, which is the foundation of Internet use. Through innovation and investment in services to support this primary activity, Google has grown its revenues from less than $500 million in 2002 to $10.5 billion in 2006. 99 per cent of its sales come from fees charged to advertisers for using its network to access Internet users.

The question, of course, is how sustainable is this model of financing the Internet. Downturns in the global economy always result in reduced advertising expenditure, but there is a more fundamental question. How cost-effective is Internet advertising? Whilst Internet use and e-commerce is growing fast, awareness-raising is important for firms, particularly being on the first page of the results of Internet searches. But for many, Internet ads are at best 'invisible' and at worst irritating and intrusive. Furthermore, a survey carried out by AOL into US web behaviour suggested that only 0.2 per cent of users are heavy clickers and are untypical as they are usually older, mostly female and probably from 'lower economic and social capital groups'.

Adapted from: B. Thompson, The writing is on the wall for ads, *BBC NewsOnline*, 4 December 2007 and N. G. Carr, The Google Enigma, Strategy and Business, www. strategy-business.com, accessed May 1 2008

Question 9.3

What do you consider to be the competitive advantage of Google and what challenges does it face in the future?

Communication tools and media

The key decisions in media planning are the choice of media:

◆ **Reach** – is the percentage of the target audience exposed to the message at least once during the relevant period.

◆ **Coverage** – is the size of the potential audience that might be exposed to a particular medium vehicle.

◆ **Frequency** – is the repetition level of the communication.

◆ **Gross Rating Point (GRP)** – is the reach multiplied by the frequency and is a measure of the total number of exposures of the communication.

◆ **Efficiency** is a further key dimension of decision-making, given the need to reach as many potential customers as possible, given a constant budget.

Decisions on media planning involve a trade-off between reach, frequency and the impact, and different buying situations require different patterns of advertising.

◆ **Recency** – The concept of recency suggests that it is important to plan the communication to reach potential customers that are ready to buy. Some suggest that the main stimuli to purchase is running out of the product, and so there may be little point in advertising at other times.

The communication tools

It is essential to be familiar with the main communication tools and have an understanding of their use, and for a fuller discussion read Doole and Lowe (2005). In practice, the choice of tools will be determined by the specific communications context and the following four selection criteria: cost, communication effectiveness, credibility and control.

Advertising – The role of advertising is to inform, persuade, remind and reinforce. It has been the mass communication method for consumer products and services and has been used to build brands over decades, but it is a one-way communication. It is more difficult to target effectively than more interactive communications tools, such as Internet marketing. Television is the main advertisement medium, but audiences are becoming more fragmented due to the increase in number of television channels, advertisements are typically becoming shorter, placed together and there are more of them, and it has become easier for viewers to switch between channels, so reducing their impact. Kotler (2003) suggests that few advertisements are likely to cover their costs in increased sales and should not be expected to deliver the sales targets of inferior products.

Sales promotion – Kotler maintains that sales promotion is concerned with transaction marketing, not building relationships as it is a short-term trigger to act, and builds current sales rather than the brand. Indeed sales might be increased short term but in the long run, profitability will be hit. Sales promotions are typically used with weaker brands and attract brand switchers. Firms must decide whether frequent sales promotions are either necessary or useful in growing sales, because they will not help to build the brand.

PR – is perceived by customers as 'news', more authoritative and believable than advertising. PR is underused and undervalued by many firms and has a variety of uses. While it is apparently 'free' to place, it requires long-term relationships to be built, for example with editors. The disadvantage of PR for firms is that it is difficult to control. For example, a story can be published rather differently from how it was intended.

One of the key roles of PR is managing crises that might adversely affect the company or brand value from time to time, for example product contamination, lapses in quality control and design faults.

Sponsorship – Many firms sponsor events or individuals, and the key decision is whether it will be regarded as a cost or investment. Sponsorship (Shimp, 2003) consists of the event exchange, which is the fee paid to be associated with the event and the marketing of the association by the sponsor. To obtain the maximum benefit a sum two or three times the cost of the sponsorship is needed for pre-event and follow-up activity. Overall success is likely to be greater if there is a match between the event audience and the firm's target customers. Sponsorship of sports and media celebrities can backfire if they engage in inappropriate behaviour.

Insight: For Sunseeker 'The World is Not Enough'

Product placement in films and television programmes is becoming an increasingly important promotion tool.

In 1968, Robert Braithwaite founded his boat building company, Sunseeker, with a team of seven. Despite many setbacks they kept trying but without real success. Then Braithwaite made an important strategic marketing decision. He decided to focus on power boats, rather than sailing boats and invested in innovation, technology and design.

Braithwaite recognized the importance of building the brand and his ambition was to make Sunseeker the 'Hoover' of the luxury powerboat industry. This seemed to have been fully achieved when, in the opening sequence of the film 'The World is Not Enough', James Bond churned up the Thames in front of the familiar London sites in his Sunseeker boat as he pursed an attractive female assassin.

The harbour area in Poole, its home, seems to be dominated by Sunseeker boats worth up to £5 million each awaiting delivery to millionaires, world rulers, sports stars and successful marketing directors(?). Ninety-nine per cent of the boats are exported. It now employs 2100 employees, has a turnover of £240 million and in 2007 announced plans to create a further 500 jobs over four years.

Source: Robin Lowe, from publicly available sources

Personal selling – Personal selling is necessary where complex negotiation and persuasion are needed and where there is sufficient margin to cover the four or five visits that might be needed to make the sale. It is, however, becoming ever more expensive and organizations have other ways of communicating with customers to collect orders, such as telephone selling, sales agents, and direct and e-marketing. Consequently personal selling is being used more selectively and is usually managed better with emphasis given to salesperson motivation, direction and control.

Direct marketing – Direct marketing traditionally took the form of direct mailing and telephone selling, supported by database management of the information, but the major change has come from e-business development. For many firms their direct marketing strategy means using a combination of direct marketing techniques (traditional and e-business), different routes to market and Web-based promotion, integrating the initiatives and responses through CRM.

B2B – For most B2B communications decisions there is a small target audience, and so the mass market tools, such as advertising (apart from trade press advertising) and sales promotions, would not normally be used. Direct marketing, PR and personal selling are likely to be more effective methods.

Constraints – It is important to re-emphasize that there are a number of constraints in the use of communications, particularly in international marketing, including cultural, political, infrastructure and legal issues which affect the availability, acceptability and usage of media.

The tools are widening all the time with promotion through websites, e-mail and text messaging. Global positioning systems (GPS) coupled with mobile telephony offer further possibilities.

Question 9.4

Choose two communications tools. Explain for what purposes they are most useful and, using examples, show when they are most effective.

Messages

Most messages in the B2C market must be simple, and Kotler (2003) suggests, where possible, they should be based on a single benefit or story or a character that the customers know and can associate strongly with the proposition. Customers need to be taken through a number of stages during the purchasing process.

To achieve the best effect, different messages, marketing communication tools and contributions from the whole marketing mix might be required at different stages in this purchasing process. In a B2B situation, even a different member of the buying centre might need to be targeted at each of these stages. There are a range of communications models (see Fill, 1999; Shimp, 2003), including 'AIDA' (Awareness, Interest, Desire, Action).

It is suggested that such rational and detailed customer decision-making models are often difficult to apply and may be only appropriate for high-involvement decisions, such as the purchase of a car, but not for low-involvement decisions, where impulse buying replaces the measured process.

Budgets

Wilson and Gilligan (2004) identify the various approaches to budgeting:

◆ What the organization can afford

◆ Matching competitors' spend or the norms for the industry

◆ A fixed percentage of past sales

◆ A fixed percentage of past profit

◆ A fixed amount to carry out a specific objective or task.

The decision about which approach to take is determined by the organizational context and often reflects the company's view about the marketing communications budget and whether it is regarded as a cost or an investment.

Measuring the effectiveness of marketing communications is difficult, because many of the tools do not precisely target specific customers nor can the effect of the single tool be isolated. In consequence the budgets of many firms are decided in a rather ad hoc way often leading to internal battles about priorities.

See CIM SMD Examination June 2005 Q.4

This question allows you to show you to practise in an applied manner the implications of a company moving from a traditional promotional strategy to one that is a more innovative Web-based strategy, discussed in Unit 7.

Measurement and control

The difficulty of measuring effectiveness

Organizations that are driven by measurement often overcompensate for this difficulty by selecting the marketing communications tools that can most easily be measured. In consumer markets, sales promotions have an obvious short-term impact that can be measured and so often tend to be overused, and as a result premium price positioning and brand value can be wasted.

Tools, such as advertising or PR, that offer the most valuable long-term effects, such as awareness raising and brand-value enhancement, are usually more difficult to measure. Internet-based interactive communication is becoming an increasingly important tool that responds quickly to changing consumer attitudes, information search, purchasing behaviour and product and service usage.

Control

Despite some reservations about their inappropriate use, a variety of measurement methods shown below are used for decision-making:

◆ Regular auditing

◆ Pre-activity research and measurement

◆ Ongoing research and measurement

◆ Post-activity research and measurement

◆ Tracking research

◆ Benchmarking.

Measurement

The measurements can involve internal staff, customers and other outside agencies and experts. It is worthwhile emphasizing a number of points about decisions on marketing ommunications evaluation.

◆   There should be a strong link between measurement and objectives, and in areas such as brand-value enhancement this might mean that measurements should relate to the holistic benefit that is gained from integrated communications, rather than the impact of just one tool.

◆   The main purpose of evaluation might be considered to be control to correct short-term deviations from the intended performance, but more importantly it should be to inform strategy development.

◆   The most beneficial dimension of evaluation should be to learn from mistakes and good practice, and this should be shared with colleagues through knowledge management processes.

Activity 9.3

Carry out an evaluation of a recent promotion campaign. What lessons can be learned from this and how could the campaign have been improved?

Developing profitable long-term marketing relationships

The key to relationship marketing is developing and maintaining mutual advantageous relationships between supplier and customer. It is particularly relevant for B2B relationships between firms in a supply chain that might use their combined capability and resources to deliver the maximum added value for the ultimate customer. Firms increasingly realize that it is less costly if they can persuade customers to stay loyal rather than lose them to a competitor and face the cost of winning them over again.

Customer retention is particularly important for B2B marketing, where the number of opportunities to bid for and win over new customers may be very limited and the loss of a major customer could have a disastrous effect on the firm. Relationship marketing focuses on the lifetime value of the customer to the supplier but also recognizes that the cost of the customer changing to a new supplier can be considerable too. Both supplier and customer have something to gain from the relationship marketing concept which is based on the idea of achieving a 'win–win'.

Throughout the firm the objectives of relationship marketing are to:

◆   Maintain and build existing customers by offering more tailored and cost effective business solutions.

◆   Use existing relationships to obtain referral to business units and other supply chain members.

◆   Increase the revenue from customers by offering solutions that are a combination of products and services.

◆ Reduce the operational and communications cost of servicing the customers, including the work prior to a trading relationship.

System development

Relationship management is usually supported by an IT process that incorporates a database, analysis of data (datamining) and a system to manage communications (CRM).

Database

A database is required to manage:

◆ Personal and profile data, including contact details

◆ Transaction data, including purchase quantities, channels, timing and locations

◆ Communications data, including response to campaigns.

There is a high initial investment in setting up databases, even when using in-house data, but maintaining data is also costly given that up to 20 per cent of the data will be out of date by the end of a year.

Datamining

Datamining is used to 'discover hidden facts contained in databases'. Identifying relationships between data contained in databases provides a basis for cost effectively targeting prospective customers, developing cooperative relationships with other companies and better understanding the patterns of customers' purchasing behaviour.

Customer relationship management

International consumer markets are characterized by their sheer size and the relative anonymity of their customers. Technology has been developed to try to integrate relationship marketing activity and manage the vast amounts of supporting information. CRM is an effective computer software coupled with defined management processes and procedures to enable staff throughout organizations to capture and use information about their customers to maintain and build relationships.

Question 9.5

Explain why relationship marketing is not appropriate for every marketing situation. Why has CRM sometimes failed to live up to expectations?

Challenges to relationship development

Relationship marketing requires a different philosophy in the firm and changes in the marketing and communications strategy objectives, budgets and performance measurements. Chaffey *et al.* (2003) explain that the key objectives are customer retention, customer extension (increasing the depth and range of customers) and customer selection (segmenting and targeting).

However, it is necessary to build relationships not only with the final customers but also with those other stakeholders who might influence the final purchase.

The problems arise when firms see CRM systems as a quick fix to try to manage vast amounts of data. They make broad generalizations about customer segments and are often too insensitive to different consumer cultures and concerns. Too often CRM is not adopted on an organization-wide basis and instead is adopted by individual departments for very specific reasons. It also gets modified because of the need to interface it with existing legacy systems and so becomes fragmented, and rather than reducing cost, actually increases it. The introduction of CRM leads to raised expectations of service levels, among customers and staff, and if this is not delivered then CRM can have a detrimental effect on the business.

Relationship marketing works if both customer and supplier gain from the relationship but they must also understand their duties. In B2C markets for FMCG it is questionable whether customers will derive much benefit from relationship marketing and whether the risks outweigh the benefits. Moreover, it is also difficult to measure the long-term benefits of relationship marketing in B2C markets when compared to traditional marketing.

In consumer markets, relationship marketing is becoming more relevant for organizations as one-to-one connections with customers through interactivity, and promoting and placing products and services in the appropriate media at just the right moment are likely to become more commonly used. Business relationship marketing is leading to ever-closer relationships and partnerships for essential supply-chain supplies, but at the same time, more transient purchasing relationships for commodity items.

Activity 9.4

Prepare a stakeholder map by listing the organization's stakeholders and their expectations. Evaluate the relationships that the organization has formed and is building with the stakeholders and decide whether the investment in relationship marketing is really adding value.

Privacy

It is important to recognize the problems with new communications technologies. There is a conflict between the interests of the firm and customer in developing databases. To offer more individually targeted, personalized and relevant communications the firm requires even more detailed and potentially sensitive information from the customer. However, customers are reluctant to give firms personal information that might be passed on deliberately or accidentally to other firms that will not be so scrupulous in its use. Customers are also concerned about Web security.

Unsolicited e-mail is becoming an increasing problem, not just because of the inconvenience, but also because a significant proportion is related to pornography, and children are routinely receiving inappropriate messages by e-mail and text.

Case study: Consumers redefining relationship marketing

The concept of relationship marketing was introduced as a strategy for achieving win–win between supplier and customer. In practice, relationship marketing has never really been about an 'equal' relationship at least not in the B2C market – the main aim has been for suppliers to find new, more subtle ways of promoting their products and services to consumers. By contrast consumers generally see little benefit from having a relationship with a 'major' organization The balance in the relationship however is changing. It was a lonely battle complaining individually but now consumers have technology which can help make their collective voice heard. 2007 has been hailed as 'the year of consumer power in the UK', as customers used the vast range of web-based information sources to fight back.

British Gas admitted losing 1.1 million customers in 12 months as price comparison websites made it easy to switch suppliers. Mars UK began using animal products in its confectionery products, Mars, Snickers, Maltesers and Galaxy in May 2007 but changed its mind after 60,000 protest calls and emails from vegetarians, who started an angry campaign. In August 6000 students used Facebook, the social networking site to protest about HSBC Bank's plans to scrap interest-free student overdrafts. In September, scared Northern Rock's customers flocked to withdraw their money from the crisis-hit bank. In response the UK government provided loans of more than £26 billion to keep the bank afloat. 1.8 million people signed a petition on the UK Prime Minister's website opposing a proposed national road pricing scheme, leading to it be shelved by the Department of Transport. After filming dolphins, albatrosses and turtles choking to death on plastic waste in the Pacific Ocean, a BBC camera woman started a successful campaign to ban plastic carrier bags in her home town, Modbury, pursuading 34 shopkeepers in the process. A futher 80 communities in Britain have followed the lead.

At little cost, customers can now campaign strongly enough to persuade large organizations to change their practices and this potential voice will become increasingly important as organizations plan their relationship and intergrated marketing communications strategies.

Adapted from: R Smithers, The year of consumer power, *Guardian Unlimited*, 2 January 2008

Question 9.6

Identify the challenges posed to organisations because of the increasing ease of complaining and campaigning.

Question 9.7

What are the critical success factors for an effective relationship marketing oriented communications strategy?

See CIM SMD Examination June 2006 Q.1

It is important to recognize at the outset that many of the concepts of Strategic Marketing Decisions apply as they are or in a modified form to case studies focusing on the not-for-profit sectors. It is important in the first question to provide evidence that you have a clear understanding of the objectives of the charity. Although question 1(a) focuses on money raising it is important to recognize that one of the success factors in this is that the charity must be seen by donors to be fulfilling their expectations of what the charity should achieve, effectively and efficiently. You therefore need to consider crisis and incremental interventions made by Oxfam.

The focus of 1(b) is integrated communications and to answer this question you need to explain the concept. It is not simply about trying to achieve greater co-ordination of messages and tools, and better management of crises, unintended messages and adverse communications. It is about putting each audience member at the centre of communications and working out what messages they are receiving and from where, and learning what are the best and most effective methods of communicating with them, recognising at all times that emphasis should be placed on the value that is created through the communications.

Summary

- Organizations must integrate their communications and ensure that, as far as possible, customers and other stakeholders receive consistent and coherent messages.

- Communications planning must focus on the target audiences and the use of appropriate tools to be most effective.

- Members of internal staff and those in the extended organization (distributors, supply chain and partners) must also be part of the communications plan, especially when staff are in remote locations.

- Winning new customers is extremely expensive and it is preferable, particularly in the B2B sector, to use communications to build long-term relationships with stakeholders.

- Relationship marketing involves integrating all aspects of marketing activity and using CRM to build mutually beneficial relationships between customers and suppliers.

Further study

Chaffey, D., Mayer, R., Johnston, K. and Ellis-Chadwick, F. (2003) *Internet Marketing: Strategy, Implementation and Practice*, FT Prentice Hall, provides more insights into electronic marketing communications

Doole, I. and Lowe, R. (2005) *Strategic Marketing Decisions in Global Markets*, Thomson Learning, Chapter 10

Fill, C. (1999) *Marketing Communications*, Prentice Hall

Shimp, T.A. (2003) *Advertising, Promotion and Supplemental Aspects of Integrated Marketing Communications*, Thomson South Western, provide additional reading on communications and relationship development

Hints and tips

It is useful to have a clear understanding of the advantages and disadvantages of the marketing communications tools, their availability and effectiveness. You could also build up some examples of international marketing communications failures.

Bibliography

Chaffey, D., Mayer, R., Johnston, K. and Ellis-Chadwick, F. (2003) *Internet Marketing: Strategy, Implementation and Practice*, FT Prentice Hall

Davidson, H. (2002) *Committed Enterprise: How to Make Values and Visions Work*, Oxford: Elsevier Butterworth-Heinemann

Doole, I. and Lowe, R. (2008) *International Marketing Strategy: Analysis, Development and Implementation*, Cengage Learning, 5th Edition, Chapters 2 and 3

Doole, I. and Lowe, R. (2008) *International Marketing Strategy*, Cengage Learning, 5th Edition

Doole, I. and Lowe, R. (2005) *Strategic Marketing Decisions in Global Markets*, Thomson Learning

Fill, C. (1999) *Marketing Communications*, Prentice Hall

Kotler, P. (2003) *Marketing Insights from A to Z*, Wiley

Shimp, T.A. (2003) *Advertising, Promotion and Supplemental Aspects of Integrated Marketing Communications*, Thomson South Western

Wilson, R. and Gilligan, C. (2004) *Strategic Marketing Management: Planning, Implementation and Control*, Oxford: Elsevier Butterworth-Heinemann, 3rd edition

Unit 10
Using the extended organization to add portfolio value

Learning objectives

The CIM syllabus for Strategic Marketing Decisions expects you to take a broad perspective that includes creative ways of adding value through the contributions of the extended organization and the way in which cost, often affected by outsourcing policies, and pricing can affect performance.

In studying this unit you will:

4.7 Examine the role of alliances and the creation of competitive advantage through supply-chain development and marketing partnerships.

4.8 Examine how pricing policies and strategies can be used to build competitive advantage.

4.9 Explain the strategic management of the global portfolio and the expanded marketing mix.

Having completed this unit you will be able to:

◆ Identify, compare and contrast strategic options and critically evaluate the implications of strategic marketing decisions in relation to the concept of 'shareholder value'.

◆ Evaluate the role of brands, innovation, integrated marketing communications, alliances, customer relationships and service in decisions for developing a differentiated positioning to create exceptional value for the customer.

◆ Demonstrate the ability to develop innovative and creative marketing solutions to enhance an organization's global competitive position in the context of changing product, market, and brand and customer life cycles.

◆ Demonstrate the ability to re-orientate the formulation and control of cost-effective competitive strategies, appropriate for the objectives and context of an organization operating in a dynamic global environment.

This unit relates to the statements of practice:

Fd.1 Promote the strategic and creative use of pricing.

Gd.1 Select and monitor channel criteria to meet the organization's needs in a changing environment.

Key definitions

The value chain – is the series of activities that create additional value for customers and comprises the use of materials, tangible and intangible assets.

A strategic alliance – is an informal arrangement between two or more organizations to pursue a common objective.

A joint venture – is a separate enterprise created using assets from two or more companies who share the equity and risk.

Study guide

This unit is concerned with the ways in which an organization builds value through the extended organization. Distribution channels should add value to the organization and its customers, but with the changes brought about by the Internet, increasing globalization and regionalization, market entry and distribution in international markets, strategies must be re-evaluated. Through the supply chain, strategic alliances and partnerships, the organization can further extend the portfolio and increase the impact and influence of the marketing mix and so increase the organization's presence and reach in the global market. We explore partnerships in both the supply and distribution chain.

The success of these partnerships in creating value will ultimately be determined by considerations of costing and pricing. In this unit the emphasis is placed on taking a strategic view when making pricing decisions.

The value chain and supply-chain management

The value chain concept

Porter (1985) introduced the concept of the value chain to identify the various strategically relevant activities that contribute to competitive advantage. The primary activity consists of:

◆ Inbound logistics

◆ Operations

◆ Outbound logistics

◆ Marketing and sales

◆ Service.

The support activity consists of:

◆ The firm's infrastructure

◆ Human resources management

◆ Technology development

◆ Procurement.

Marketing adds value in a number of areas of the value chain, and Doyle (2000) has explained the contributions.

The concept is intended to drive growth, through adding value and improving efficiency in the supply chain and distribution channel. It has helped firms to grow through:

◆ Reducing costs through eliminating duplication and unnecessary processes

◆ Benefiting from concentrating expertise and complementary activity

◆ Exploiting new market opportunities

◆ Reducing investment for organizations through outsourcing rather than manufacturing components

◆ Enabling small firms to have similar costs to large firms.

It is vital that each part of the value chain maximizes the added value contributions of each member by integrating the activities. A supply chain for a complex product might typically involve design, raw materials supply, manufacture of components, assembly, advertising, logistics and local servicing. The most efficient suppliers could be located in different points of the world.

E-business has provided the mechanism for integrating and further facilitating the contributions of supply-chain members. It has also led to e-procurement and virtual marketplace e-hubs, discussed in Unit 7, which substantially change the basis of competitive advantage particularly in the manufacture and supply of utilities, standard components and services.

The implications of using e-commerce for procurement is that partnerships can be set up and dissolved instantly. Suppliers are in completely open competition with other firms around the world. Of course, suppliers need to have huge flexibility and excellent systems to manage the rapid changes that are necessary to survive in this type of market.

Value chain integration decisions

The key question is how effectively can the individual supply-chain members around the world work in partnership to maximize the effectiveness of their contributions towards improving efficiency and adding value across the entire value chain, the so-called value chain integration. The value chain decisions are taken at two levels:

Operational – Assessing the individual contributions of members in the supply chain and making decisions about efficiency, transaction costs, just-in-time, quality management, information transfer and contributions to differentiating the products and services.

Strategic – Assessing the overall effectiveness of the value chain in adding customer value by making disintermediation and reintermediation decisions in the distribution channel and outsourcing decisions (make or buy) in the supply chain.

In other units of this coursebook we focus upon the organization's direct contribution to the value chain through its internal activities, and here we focus upon the contributions of the extended organization. First, we look at distribution channel management in terms of operational issues before considering the strategic issues. Second, we extend this further into a re-evaluation of routes to market and the use of strategic alliances, joint ventures and other mechanisms to 'extend' the organization. For a fuller discussion read Doole and Lowe (2005).

Activity 10.1

Using the value chain concept assess the contributions of your organization's value chain and identify three areas where there is scope for cost reduction or value enhancement.

Distribution channel management

Intermediaries often provide the only point of personal contact between the organization and the consumers, but they can also fulfil many other roles too. We therefore look at the traditional nature and role of intermediaries before considering the value of their contribution and considering the challenge of channel motivation and management.

The nature and role of intermediaries

The role of intermediaries is changing because of the high cost of physical intermediaries and the increasing acceptance and versatility of the Internet for doing business and carrying out many of these functions and roles more cost effectively.

Many organizations appear to be reviewing the nature of their partnerships with other members of the supply and distribution chain and either deciding to enhance the relationship through alliances and partnerships or making the relationships more at arm's length and transactional in nature.

There is also a less distinct demarcation between what might be considered to be market entry methods and distribution channels, not only for international markets but also for domestic markets, too.

The traditional roles of intermediaries expressed in terms of product distribution are included in Table 10.1.

Table 10.1 The traditional roles of intermediaries

- Be part of the organization's push strategy and make products available to customers when and where they want them
- Reduce the cost by efficiently performing distribution functions
- Manage discrepancies between the quantities manufacturers want to supply and the quantities customers want to buy (break bulk)
- Offer a greater range by using products from complementary suppliers
- Standardizing and managing smaller transactions
- Providing customer service and building relationships

A key consideration is to decide when the manufacturer and intermediary are best placed to supply the customer, and this comparison is made in Table 10.2.

Table 10.2: Who is best placed to supply the customer?	
Manufacturer best placed to supply	**Intermediaries best placed to supply**
Complex products with continuous development	Simple product with basic service levels
Made-to-order products	Standard stocked lines
Where a high level of service and support is required	
Where there is a small customer base	Large customer base
Where the transactions are of high volume or value	Smaller customers
Easy to cover locations	Geographically difficult to cover
Where shipments are large scale, planned and just-in-time	Small random deliveries from stock
High-level feedback is required	Low-level feedback

Value contributions of intermediaries

The intermediary role typically involves a number of responsibilities that add value:

◆ Collection of information

◆ Promotion of the products

◆ Financing of inventories

◆ Delivery and physical transfer

◆ Accepting a degree of risk sharing

◆ An ordering function.

Activity 10.2

List the key decision areas of channel management. Include the issues that relate to member recruitment, replacement, contributions, management and motivation. Assess the effectiveness of the channel management in your own organization and identify measurements that are made to monitor performance.

Channel motivation and management

A major problem for any organization is motivating and managing the intermediaries (Wilson and Gilligan, 2004) as it makes huge demands on management time. The organization must provide channel leadership to direct and influence the overall channel performance, build the channel as a competing system by encouraging cooperation between intermediaries that in other circumstances might be competing and manage channel conflicts by identifying and resolving the sources of conflict.

It is necessary to select channel members, evaluate them according to pre-set criteria, such as service levels, drop them if they underperform and replace them with others. Where appropriate, areas and product ranges must be allocated and the role of the intermediaries defined in terms of inventory, selling, marketing, invoicing, support services and so on.

Managing intermediaries in foreign markets is particularly problematic, given the differences in legal frameworks, culture, language, service expectations and communication distances that make motivation, management and development particularly problematic.

Insight: Inchcape

A few years ago, Inchcape was a poorly performing business, part of an earlier era, trading cars, business machines, medical products and bottles around the former colonies. Eight years ago, CEO Peter Johnson, put forward a strategy to exit from many of these disparate business areas and focus on car dealerships. Moreover, he decided to operate in six core countries, unlike other dealers that usually concentrate on just one country. The firm decided to concentrate on premium brands such as BMW and Lexus and aimed to build up a strong presence in an area. The firm would benefit from economies in delivering after-sales service.

The strategy delivered double-digit growth in profits and completed the turnaround, achieving a turnover of £4 billion in 2004. Johnson put the success down to sticking to what the firm was good at, and particularly, its strong partnerships with the key manufacturers. He cited his own 10-year relationships with manufacturers, such as Toyota, who supported Inchcape during its difficult turnaround period.

Other aspects of the strategy also worked well. The concentration on premium brands enabled the firm to avoid the worst price wars, and the presence of the company in more than one country helped to avoid the worst effects of a slowdown in the UK car business. Indeed two-thirds of Inchcapes's profits already come from overseas.

When Andre Lacroix took over from Johnson he continued the expansion, increasing from six to ten core markets, including the fast growing markets of Eastern Europe and China and, in August 2007, set up a Toyota dealership in Shaoxing. Inchcape's strategy focused on higher margin manufacturers and to fund the growth it was necessary to dispose of dealerships in the UK, including Land Rover, Volvo and Ferrari. The strategy was justified, however, because as Inchcape exceeded profit forecasts, their competitors in the UK market, Pendragon, announced profits warnings and Dixon Motors went into administration.

Adapted from: A. Davidson, Sales giant of the motor trade, *Sunday Times*, 16 January 2005 and M. Kleinman, Inchcape steers into China's fast lane, *Daily Telegraph*, 31 August 2007

Disintermediation and reintermediation

Increased competition is putting further pressure on prices, and this coupled with the burden of channel management, makes it obvious why organizations might be tempted to remove intermediaries, shorten the distribution channels and, using technology support, carry out the roles themselves. However, to maximize revenue from many products, organizations try to provide as many points as possible for customers to access products and services, and in some cases this is leading to reintermediation. It is the Internet that prompted a channel review for many organizations and an assessment of the potential benefits of new routes to market might prove to be more appealing to customers.

The Internet offers the possibility for an organization to efficiently handle many more transactions than was possible previously. An evaluation of the contribution of the channel has lead to a reassessment of the value of intermediaries and a decision to remove them. The benefits to the organization are the removal of channel infrastructure costs and intermediary margins and the opportunity to develop a direct relationship with the final customer. 'Cutting out the middleman' is described as 'disintermediation'. At the start of the e-business boom it was expected that there would be widespread disintermediation. In some sectors there has been, but in others the results have been disappointing with the organization incurring substantial additional IT, order management and logistics costs. Many organizations have failed to deliver the predicted savings or increase in sales.

'Reintermediation' is the creation of additional intermediaries in the distribution channel to provide the new Web-based points of access. While many consumer products, financial and travel services lend themselves to online selling, customers want to compare the many offerings from competing companies. The online intermediaries receive a click-through commission on sales or enquiries generated.

In many sectors there are now intermediary websites that enable potential customers to compare products for the home, holidays and travel. Of course this means that the Internet marketer must ensure that they are represented on key sites where there are high volumes of potential customers and ensure that they are offering competitive prices. This makes it difficult for firms to differentiate their offering and may not guarantee sales. Instead some organizations have set up their own intermediary to compete with the existing intermediaries, and this is referred to as 'countermediation'. A group of airlines set up www.Opodo.com as an alternative to www.expedia.com to offer airline tickets.

Question 10.1

Explain the terms disintermediation, reintermediation and countermediation and in what context they are used. Using examples, show their significance and value to customers and organizations.

Routes to market

So far we have discussed distribution channels, but, in practice, organizations have a much wider range of routes to global markets than simply relying on distributors and retailers. Figure 10.1 shows the main alternatives in terms of level of involvement, organizational perceived risk and marketing control. For a fuller discussion of international market entry read Doole and Lowe (2008), Chapter 7, to familiarize yourself with the advantages and disadvantages of each of the methods. E-commerce is not shown as an individual market entry method as it is used to support all of these market entry methods.

The key issue in thinking more broadly about routes to market is to achieve the optimum between the key criteria to best add value for the organization and the customer.

Level of market involvement – The level of market involvement is usually determined by the availability of financial resources for investment in operations and direct marketing activity. The greater the involvement, the more market knowledge and influence (as an insider) the company has.

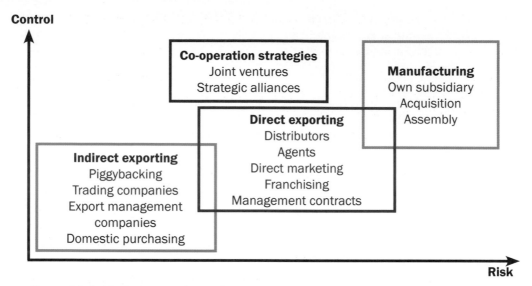

Figure 10.1 Market entry alternatives

Marketing control – The greater the level of direct involvement in a market the greater the degree of marketing control over how the company and its products are presented. Going through third parties dilutes the degree of control, and the customer can be left confused over mixed communication messages. In practice, however, even the most powerful global organizations, such as Coca-Cola and McDonald's, do not have the resources to do every-thing themselves and use franchising and joint ventures to pursue their objectives.

Perceived risk – The conventional view is that wholly-owned operations in foreign markets are the most risky as they involve the greatest financial exposure and in many cases do not benefit from committed local help and support. In practice, the routes to market with the lowest levels of involvement could present the highest risk, as the organization may not be aware of major market changes (and, because of self-interest, partners may not inform them). They may be unable to respond to these major changes quickly enough to save the business.

Firms entering markets and also new emerging markets based on technology change try to reduce their risk exposure, while maximizing their market involvement and control by building stronger partnerships with businesses that complement their competencies and assets. A number of traditional and more contemporary partnership mechanisms for achieving this are discussed in the next section.

Question 10.2

When seeking to build an international market, a small or medium sized firm must select its methods of market entry carefully. What methods could be used and, using these methods, what would the firm have to do to ensure that its international custom-ers receive a satisfactory product and service?

Extending the organization through alliances and network marketing

Following on from these considerations it becomes clear that closer collaborative working through a variety of arrangements can provide a solution to a number of problems that arise from the latest environmental trends:

◆ Greater unpredictability in the environment and the need for a faster and more effective specific market response.

◆ Increased global competition requiring a global response.

◆ Competition from new competitors attacking markets in new ways with new technology.

◆ The lack of resources of most organizations to cope with the increasing cost of R&D and marketing to develop distinctive positioning.

◆ Customer expectation of complete solutions, not simply individual products and services.

◆ Changes in supply-chain structures and power.

The main driver of collaboration is the inability of single organizations to be able to produce a complete response:

◆ Global marketing that is necessary but outside the individual resources of most companies.

◆ The need for composite solutions to meet the diverse nature of customer requirements and the increasing trend to global one-to-one marketing.

◆ The integration of technologies and convergence of industries with the consequence that market boundaries are becoming less defined.

On the one hand, organizations are forced to become more efficient, achieve higher returns from their assets and so focus on core competencies. However, at the same time they must offer an efficient consumer response on a global basis.

Hooley *et al.* (2004) explain the different types, nature and roles of network marketing and emphasize their role in different types of environment. They also discuss the closeness of the relationships and whether they are likely to be short or long lasting.

Outsourcing – tends to be seen as 'arm's length' purchasing, often long term, without any significant commitment or sharing of other than the essential information to complete each transaction. However, with greater interdependence between supplier and customer these arrangements may have to become closer. In times of crisis, for example, it is often recognized that the burden must be shared rather than being simply the responsibility of the other firm.

Partnerships or strategic alliances – involve close relationships but do not involve shared ownership, and examples of marketing alliances can be found in the B2B, B2C and institutional markets

Vertical and horizontal integration – There are a number of alliances formed to provide customers with better value offers or a package of complementary products or services.

167

This is achieved either through vertical integration of the supply chain or local operators that are carrying out similar tasks by sharing the development and delivery of mutually beneficial products and services. Sometimes this leads to a new jointly owned organization being set up.

Joint ventures – involve shared ownership of a project or operation by two or more organizations with a variety of objectives ranging from international market entry to technological collaboration.

Acquisition and reciprocal shareholdings – A number of partnerships and alliances lead to more formal arrangements, such as joint ventures and reciprocal shareholdings, but also in some cases they lead to full acquisition of a partner.

For a fuller discussion of collaborative arrangements read Doole and Lowe (2005), Chapter 11.

Effective collaborations can be a powerful market force, but there are a number of risks. Different studies have suggested that between 50 and 66 per cent of partners in strategic alliances are dissatisfied with their performance.

Case study: Renault's Russian partners

Many western businesses have used partnerships in some form to enter new markets. In December 2007 Renault announced that it had acquired a 25 per cent stake in Avtovaz, the producer of the Lada and Russia's largest car maker in a deal worth $1.25 billion. The move provided Renault with the opportunity to exploit the booming Russian market, which grew 20 per cent in 2007. CEO of Renault, Carlos Ghosn said that Avtovaz's main plant in Togliatti could expand output from 700,000 to 1.5 million cars, eventually producing Nissan and Renault cars. Avtovaz will have access to Renault technology and marketing expertise. Russian Technologies, owned by Rosoboronexport, the Russian State arms company will retain a 25 per cent stake to ensure continuous support from the Russian state. Russia could become Renault's main market, as it is expected to grow from 2.5 million units to 4 million in 2015. Avtovaz holds about 70 per cent of the market.

Renault surprisingly took a 40% stake in Nissan when it was on the edge of bankruptcy in the late 1990s. Ghosn, then an executive with Renault was credited with turning around Nissan by improving designs and marketing, before returning to boost performance in Renault by introducing quality and manufacturing improvements.

Adapted from: M Leroux, Renault breaks into market with stake in Avtovaz, *The Times*, 10 December 2007

Question 10.3

Major projects, which involve substantial investment, are often undertaken by two or more firms on a joint venture or strategic alliance basis. Explain why firms undertake partnership projects and outline the major advantages and disadvantages of the approach.

See CIM SMD Examination June 2006 Q.3

The starting point for this question is to explain what effect rapid change might have on organizations from a particular sector, for example, shorter product life cycles causing products and services to reach maturity quickly and technology to become obsolete more rapidly. New technological development is expensive and often cannot be funded by one organization alone. In a declining market firms might benefit from co-operation rather than competition. An explanation of the difference between alliances and joint ventures should be related to the context in which the co-operation is formed. Finally the advantages and disadvantages should be related to examples from the sector and should focus on such issues as resource, capability and intellectual property.

Cooperation and competition

One of the outcomes of developing partnerships is that for the very largest and most complex businesses this means that at an SBU level the organization may be cooperating and competing with another MNE. This poses challenges in deciding which firms to cooperate and compete with, in which markets and for what purpose.

One significant consequence of this is that firms must decide in these circumstances what information to share and what to keep secret. This is particularly problematic given the ease with which information is transferred and the lack of security of IT systems.

Pricing and costing

In this section we focus on reassessing pricing and costing strategies in the light of the changes in marketing strategy implementation discussed so far. In doing this we first review the nature and role of pricing and the relationship between pricing and costing, before going on to discuss strategic decisions to cut costs.

We finish the section by considering the factors that affect pricing before discussing the pricing strategies.

The nature and role of pricing

Many organizations believe that pricing is the most flexible, independent and controllable element of the marketing mix and that it plays the pivotal role in strategic marketing decisions. This view is largely based on the fact that pricing changes appear to prompt an immediate response in the market. For example, discounting a price might achieve an immediate attributable sale. However, despite the apparent simplicity of using pricing as a major marketing tool, many managers find pricing decisions difficult to make. This is in part due to the fact that while most firms recognize the importance of pricing at a tactical level in stimulating short-term demand, far fewer recognize the importance of the strategic role of pricing.

The nature of costing and its effect on pricing

In most organizations, costing is inextricably linked with pricing, but in practice the relationship between cost and price has changed considerably over the past few years. There are a number of new factors applying additional pressures on price, but there is also now considerably more scope for firms to change the cost base. Inevitably this changes the relationship between costing and pricing. Some of the most significant trends include:

Pricing transparency – Customers are able to compare prices with increasing ease, mainly due to the Internet, but also in Europe because of the introduction of the euro. Customers are much more knowledgeable and demanding and more willing to buy from more distant suppliers.

Supply chain cost considerations – Supply chains must now meet a target market price to compete with other suppliers rather than being able to simply add a margin on top of the total costs. Decisions need to be made about how the chain can optimize customer value while reducing costs.

Outsourcing and value chain decisions – Companies must reassess their value chain and decide whether to outsource components, manufacturing and services and evaluate the consequences this might have for customer value and company reputation.

The increase in R&D costs and overheads – The high R&D and marketing costs are unavoidable as firms seek to build competitive advantage, but this leads to very high initial investments that need to be recovered and very high fixed costs. This requires very high gross margins to be guaranteed. For example, software volume products can generate over 95 per cent gross margin but still fail to recover marketing and R&D investment.

See CIM SMD Examination December 2005 Q.4

When a question highlights a specific concept or technique – in this case absorption costing – it is essential to demonstrate an understanding of it by including an appropriate explanation and, where appropriate, applying it in the context described. In part (a) of this question it is possible then to explain how it impacts on the pricing strategy and how it works in conjunction with non-price factors to create competitive advantage. By combining price and non-price factors, a number of options can be highlighted in part (b) but the key here is to ensure that the options are linked to developing longer-term competitive advantage, particularly by using examples to illustrate the points made.

Actions to reduce costs

A feature of most management is cost reduction and the need to:

◆ Have a real understanding of what exactly are variable and fixed costs in the organization.

◆ Appreciate the step change nature of fixed costs and the impact on performance.

◆ The opportunity cost of no-hopers and the drain on resources.

◆ The sensitivity of the allocation of overhead and fixed costs across products and product categories.

◆ The precise nature of cost-savings that are claimed through bundling, deals and so on.

Managers need to be clear about the action that they can take to improve profitability by cost reductions, obtaining benefits from the economies of scale and the experience curve effect.

Activity 10.3

Undertake an audit of one product and service category in your own organization with the aim of making a substantial cost saving – 10 per cent not 1 per cent.

Yield management

The challenge for firms delivering services is to try to balance supply and demand order to obtain the maximum output for their expensive assets. It is well known that there is not a constant demand from customers for services, and so there needs to be some management of demand, wherever possible. One approach is to obtain the best yield for each service delivery occurrence by maximizing the revenue generated. This has been the basis of the business model of low-cost airlines, which offer low prices to early bookers and high prices for the 'late comers'. This is the reverse of the traditional airlines, which maintain high published prices but attempt to offload spare tickets close to the time of departure.

Pricing decisions

Reassessment of the pricing strategy within the organization

To make good pricing strategy decisions it is necessary to have a clear understanding of both the uncontrollable factors in the market environment, such as customer expectations and competitor pressures, and the factors that the organization can control, such as the other marketing mix factors.

Price making and price taking

In developing pricing strategies, organizations tend to be either price takers or price makers. Price takers have only limited ability or willingness to control prices and so follow the market leader's pricing strategy and respond reactively to changes in price. Because of their power, size, market leadership or competitive advantage, price makers are able to set prices. For example, powerful organizations are able to temporarily set prices so low that they are able to force a competitor out of business. Over the years, too, there have been many examples of oligopolies illegally running a cartel to fix prices artificially high to maximize their profits.

Price makers can add value and, within reason, recover the costs through higher prices. By contrast a price taker tends to think of making a product that will undercut the market's price by an amount that is attractive to potential purchasers. To make the required profit there will be a limit on the costs allowed in the supply chain.

Pricing objectives

Because of their different current market positions and future business development aspirations, organizations must adopt pricing objectives that will drive their strategic marketing decisions. These alternative pricing objectives are detailed in Table 10.3.

Question 10.4

The Internet is increasing price transparency across international markets. Fully evaluate the problems and opportunities this brings to a company trying to build a global competitive advantage.

Portfolio integration decisions

In Units 8 and 9 and in this unit we have discussed a number of decision areas relating to the marketing mix. We have emphasized throughout the need to add customer value with the intention of increasing prices and revenue and making cost reductions to increase profitability. In practice these activities should not be undertaken in isolation and need to be integrated. Table 10.4 provides the starting point.

Table 10.4: Portfolio integration

	Providing opportunity to increase prices (or revenue)	Making cost reductions to increase revenue or profitability
Product portfolio		Better sourcing
		Better plant utilization
		Better use of raw materials and labour
		Design or specification changes
Service enhancement		Better use of labour and processes
		Better use of assets (yield management)
Promotion		Better choice of communication methods from mix elements
		More targeted, less mass communications
Channel		More value from channel
	Reintermediation	Disintermediation
Relationship		Cost effective one-to-one marketing
	Value chain contribution	Supply-chain efficiency

Activity 10.4

What factors affect your organization's pricing strategy? What scope is there for the organization to adopt a more offensive approach to pricing?

Summary

◆ Analysis of the value contributions of the supply chain should lead to development work to increase customer value and reduce unnecessary costs.

◆ Evaluation of channel effectiveness and new channel opportunities leads to disintermediation and reintermediation decisions.

◆ The choice of route to market in international markets will be determined by the organization's desire for market involvement and control, set against the perceived risk.

◆ Organizations can extend their reach and influence in markets by developing closer partnerships.

◆ Costing and pricing decisions are often made with short-term objectives in mind, but the consequences can be long term.

◆ It is essential to fully integrate the marketing mix decisions with the costing and pricing strategy.

Case study: New pricing models in the music industry

For years consumers have complained about the high price of music CDs and when an alternative technology, music downloading, became available it was inevitable that it would become popular. However, in 2007, Radiohead came up with a further new pricing model. When they released their new album 'In Rainbows' to download online they asked customers to pay what they thought it was worth. There was some logic behind this experiment. Clearly sales increase if the price is low – 10 people might pay $10 a copy, 100 will pay $2 and 1000 would pay zero. But here customers were asked to pay their own valuation and so, in theory at least, the maximum revenue is obtained. Moreover, there was considerable publicity generated for the group too.

It was estimated that 62 per cent of customers downloading the album paid zero and the remaining 38 per cent paid an average price of $6, totalling overall an average price of $2.28 (£1.29 in the UK). The interesting comparison is with the costing of CDs marketed by record companies which, of course, Radiohead avoided. An estimate by William Fisher of Stanford University, a short time ago, showed retailers took 38 per cent, the distributors 8 per cent and marketing 8 per cent, whilst the artist got 12 per cent and the music pubisher 4 per cent. For a conventionally marketed CD priced at £8 in the UK the artist would therefore get £1.28 – the same as the estimate of Radiohead's average price!

Other pricing models have been tried too. Despite a contract with Sony BMG, Prince decide to give away his 'Planet Earth' album for free with the *Mail on Sunday* newspaper. This shrewd move gave him money up front and helped him sell out 21 nights for his concert at the O_2 arena at Greenwich.

Sir Cliff Richard, celebrating 50 years after his first rock and roll hit, 'Move it', came up with another model. A website collected download pre-orders for his 78th new album, the compilation 'Love, the Album'. For every person who ordered a download album the price dropped by a penny. The maximum price was set at £7.99 and the minimum £3.99. The advantage of this approach was that it allowed the selling price to be reduced without harming the perceived value of the music. It also encouraged his older fan base to try downloading the music.

Adapted from: J. Naughton, Radiohead find their gold at the end of the Rainbows, *The Observer*, 18 November 2007 and O. Gibson, Cliff Richard pulls a Radiohead, *Guardian Unlimited*, 30 October 2007

Question 10.5

What do you consider to be the main factors and the key strategic marketing decisions that will determine success or failure in pricing downloaded music?

Question 10.6

Who are likely to be the winners in this market and why?

Further study

Doole, I. and Lowe, R. (2008) *International Marketing Strategy*, Cengage Learning, 5th edition, Chapters 7, 10, 11 and 12 for the international dimension to market entry, channels, pricing and value chain

Doole, I. and Lowe, R. (2005) *Strategic Marketing Decisions in Global Markets*, Thomson Learning, Chapters 9 and 11

Wilson, R.M.S. and Gilligan, C. (2004) *Strategic Marketing Management*, Oxford: Elsevier Butterworth-Heinemann for further discussion on pricing, value chain and distribution strategies

Bibliography

Doole, I. and Lowe, R. (2008) *International Marketing Strategy*, Cengage Learning, 5th edition

Doole, I. and Lowe, R. (2005) *Strategic Marketing Decisions in Global Markets*, Thomson learning

Doyle, P. (2000) *Value-Based Marketing*, Wiley

Hooley, G., Saunders, J. and Piercy, N. (2004) *Marketing Strategy and Competitive Positioning*, FT Prentice Hall

Porter, M.E. (1985) *Competitive Advantage: Creating and Sustaining Superior Performance*, Free Press

Wilson, R.M.S. and Gilligan, C. (2004) *Strategic Marketing Management, planning, implementation and control*, Oxford: Elsevier Butterworth-Heinemann

Unit 11
Financial appraisal for strategic marketing decisions

Learning objectives

The CIM Postgraduate Diploma in Marketing requires candidates to show they have the financial skills to demonstrate the contribution marketing strategies make to the business, to financially justify the budgets needed in their strategic marketing decisions and to financially evaluate potential investment decisions so they are able to focus on those marketing activities that offer the best returns.

In this unit you will:

5.1 Examine the implications of strategic marketing decisions for implementation and control.

5.3 Apply investment appraisal techniques to marketing investment decisions.

5.4 Examine alternative approaches to modelling potential investment decisions in the deployment of marketing resources.

5.6 Define budgetary and planning control techniques for use in the control of marketing plans and explain the pitfalls of control systems and how they may be overcome.

Having completed this unit you will be able to:

◆ Identify, compare and contrast strategic options and critically evaluate the implications of strategic marketing decisions in relation to the concept of 'shareholder value'.

◆ Define and contribute to investment decisions concerning the marketing assets of an organization.

◆ Demonstrate the ability to reorientate the formulation and control of cost-effective competitive strategies, appropriate for the objectives and context of an organization operating in a dynamic global environment.

This unit relates to the statements of practice:

Bd.1 Promote a strong market orientation and influence/contribute to strategy formulation and investment decisions

Fd.1 Promote the strategic and creative use of pricing.

Key definitions

Return on capital employed – is a measure commonly used by companies to assess the added value to shareholders resulting from the capital invested.

Payback – measures the number of years it will take to recover the original investment from the net cash flows resulting from a project. The method is based on being able to estimate a future flow of funds.

Cost/Volume/Profit (CVP) analysis – is used to help a company understand the relationship between volume, costs and profits and used to budget and forecast the break-even point.

A ratio – takes two variables (e.g. profit/sales) and compares them with other measures of the same variable in another time period or in another company to assess the performance of the company and the efficiency of its operations.

Study guide

Examination candidates of Strategic Marketing Decisions will be expected to demonstrate an understanding of the financial implications of the decisions they make. Finance is the common language of business enabling the costs and benefits of the different strategic options you may be considering to be quantified, evaluated and compared. Thus in studying this unit you need to develop the skills to understand the impact of the decisions you make on the financial health of the company and be able to use financial techniques to assess the decisions you make.

Assessing owner/shareholder value

The main objective of a business is to maximize the shareholders'/owners' wealth. Much has been said in previous units about the importance of value-based marketing and the need for marketing managers to be able to quantify the economic benefits to the company of the strategic marketing decisions taken and contribute to shareholder/owners' added value. However, the question we need to ask in this unit is how added value to the company is measured. The share price as an indicator of improvements in shareholder value has major shortcomings in that it is essentially a *second-hand market* trading in stocks and shares, the market certainly determines a price for a company's shares, but it is questionable whether this is a true assessment of the value. Doyle (2000) suggests two approaches to assess shareholder value: the cash flow valuation method and the calculation of economic profit or what Stern, Stewart & Co. branded 'economic value added' (EVA). In this section we also include return on capital employed (ROCE) as a method for calculating added value.

Economic value added

Economic value added is used to assess ongoing performance and help managers to determine whether the current policies are creating value. It is used in the development of a position appraisal by the company – in other words assessing what the position is now in terms of the creation of value by the past and current marketing strategies being employed. Basically if a company achieves a positive EVA then the investment will have generated a surplus greater than the firm's weighted average cost of capital and therefore created value for the owners/shareholders. The calculation of EVA is:

EVA = adjusted profits after tax − (adjusted invested capital × weighted average cost of capital)

Cash flow valuation

The cash flow valuation approach is useful in assessing how investment decisions contribute to the building of shareholder value and so is useful in the financial evaluation of strategic options. Essentially the principle of this method is that a strategy creates value when it produces returns that exceed the cost of capital and therefore generates a positive net present value (NPV). However, in using cash flow valuation for shareholder added value, measuring the long-term value may be difficult as the investment input may be creating long-term value but in any one year shows a negative or declining cash flow. Thus the measure used in assessing the cash flow is the continuing value of cash flow.

Doyle (2000) splits the calculation of the continuing value of cash flow into two parts: the value created in the initial forecast period and the present value created after the explicit forecast period:

Continuing value = present value of cash flow during the forecast period + present value of cash flow after the forecast period.

Return on capital employed

This is a measure commonly used by companies to assess the added value to them resulting from the capital invested. It is criticized as a technique for measuring shareholder value by Doyle (2000) as it is difficult to take into account the fact that returns today may be the results of a gradual investment built over many years and not just a result of the most recent injection of capital. ROCE is used to evaluate the efficient use of capital. A company may make a profit of $100,000, however, that is only meaningful if we know how much capital was invested to achieve that profit.

ROCE is the amount of profit expressed as a percentage of the capital employed. It is calculated as follows:

ROCE = estimated profit before interest/capital employed

Activity 11.1

For a company known to you calculate the ROCE and the profit margin.

Question 11.1

A company operates in three distinct market segments. For each segment calculate the percentage profit on sales turnover.

	Sales ($k)	Profit ($k)
Segment A	600	36
Segment B	1000	200
Segment C	3000	450

Financial analysis for long-term decision-making

Insight: The challenge of the digital cost model

In fast-changing digital markets the business model and the costs associated with products can change significantly and very rapidly too. These are major concerns for organizations that are planning their future strategy and taking marketing decisions that are concerned with implementing that strategy. The games market has changed substantially over the last few years. In 1982, the Japanese company Namco produced one of the first successful games, Pacman, for $100,000. Comparing that game with cutting-edge games that are shown off to their best effect by the latest games consoles, such as Sony Playstation 3 and Microsoft Xbox 360 illustrates the astonishing progress that has been made. The cost of the average Playstation 3 title is now estimated to be $15 million and Halo 3, produced by Microsoft, is estimated to have cost $30 million. Of course the rewards can be equally astonishing. Halo 3 brought in $170 million on its first day of sales, setting the record for the most money earned in a day by an entertainment product. It far exceeded the first day income for Spiderman 3, the biggest grossing Hollywood film.

The costs to produce the games are rocketing because of the increased size of the games-writing teams, the cost of new tools and of the graphics needed to cope with the challenges of high definition video. Consequently margins decrease. For smaller firms the problems are compounded by the fact that a quarter of games in the UK and Europe are sold at Christmas. Most digital products incur huge up-front costs in research and development, but once developed, cost almost nothing to reproduce it in billions. Big companies, such as Sony and Microsoft are at a great advantage over smaller companies because they can afford these huge upfront costs and can accept the risk of some games failing if the successes sell in the millions of copies.

Adapted from: Y. Takatsuki, Cost headache for game developers, *BBC News Online*, 27 December 2007

Activity 11.2

For a company of your choice investigate the criteria used in financially evaluating the feasibility of a new product being developed.

There are many financial approaches to investment appraisal in the context of this course-book, we will consider two – *payback* and *discounted cash flow*.

Question 11.2

What options are there for the smaller players with less flexible supply chains? How would you construct a business case for investing in a more globally flexible supply chain to sustain a competitive advantage in the longer term?

Payback

Payback simply measures the number of years it will take to recover the original invest-ment from the net cash flows resulting from a project. The method is based on being able to estimate a future flow of funds. Thus a marketing manager evaluating two strategic op-tions both requiring $100k investment would estimate net cash in-flows for each project and for the life of the projects. If payback was the sole evaluation criterion the company would choose the option which resulted in the shortest payback period. The advantage of using payback is that the calculations are simple, and it focuses on the company's liquidity position and minimizing cash flow risk. However, the overall profitability is not considered and no account is taken of the long-term value of the strategic options being evaluated.

Question 11.3

The following information relates to an enterprise producing and selling one product:

Selling price per unit   £60

Variable costs per unit   £42

Total fixed expenses   £900

Find:

a   Contribution per unit

b   Break-even sales (in units)

c   Sales (in units) which will produce a net profit of £360

d   Sales (in units) which will produce a net profit margin of 20 per cent of sales

e   Net profit if 80 units are sold

f   The break-even sales (in units) if variable expenses are increased by £4 per unit and if fixed expenses are reduced by £340

g   If the company requires a net profit of £700 on a sales volume of 200 units, what must the selling price per unit be, assuming no changes in the variable expenses of £42 per unit or in the fixed expenses of £900?

Net present value and discounted cash flow

Discounted cash flow (DCF) is based on the principle that money received today is worth more than money received next year because of the opportunity to invest and consequently earn a return. Thus DCF concentrates on cash flows rather than profits.

An investment appraisal using DCF would involve the following steps:

1   identifying the cash flows that would result from the investment in the project

2   identifying when the cash flows will take place

3   applying the appropriate discount factor to the cash flows

4   calculating NPV by aggregating the DCFs

5   comparing the NPV of one project with another.

In calculating NPV there are three possible outcomes to the analysis:

1.	NPV = 0	In which case you would be indifferent to the investment
2.	NPV = negative	In this case the project would fail to generate sufficient funds to cover the cost of capital. Thus it would destroy shareholder value
3.	NPV = positive	In this case the project would most likely generate a return greater than the cost of capital and so would be considered. Only if there is a positive NPV is there any possibility of increasing shareholder value

The following illustration is given in Chapter 4 of Doole and Lowe (2005) where a more detailed treatment of the concepts introduced in this unit can be found.

A company has a choice of two projects A or B, the firm's cost of capital is 10 per cent. Both projects involve an investment of £800 and have the following profits and cash flows.

Projects	Year	A (£)	B (£)
Initial sum invested	0	800	800
Cash flow generated by the project	1	100	900
	2	900	100

Discounted cash flows – using a 10 per cent discount rate

	A			B		
	CF (£)	DR	DCF (£)	CF (£)	DR	DCF (£)
Year 1	100 ×	0.909 =	90	900 ×	0.909 =	818
Year 2	900 ×	0.826 =	743	100 ×	0.826 =	83
			834			901
Initial investment		(800)			(800)	
Net present value		34			101	

Using the NPV of the cash flows the enterprise would select project B. For project B, NPV is greater because the bulk of the cash flow from the project occurs in year 1.

See CIM SMD Examination June 2006 Q.5

This question requires the candidate to have an understanding of the analysis of cost, volume and profit and to be confident in handling the information supplied in the questions. The questions involve relatively straightforward calculations and credit is given for a logical approach as well as demonstrating numeracy and accuracy in the calculation. However, a higher proportion of the marks were allocated to the non-numerical questions, where an understanding of hard-edged marketing should be demonstrated, particularly focusing on the pros and cons of a particular approach and the risks associated with it.

Financial analysis for short-term decision-making

Activity 11.3

Consider a decision to change the price of a product/service in your company. What financial analysis did the company undertake in making the appropriate decision?

Insight

Sales and marketing managers who are busy making sales often assume that they are also making a profit. Yet this is not always the case, particularly in smaller businesses whose owners are technically competent but who are not familiar with the basic accounting methods used to determine whether a profit is being generated by the organization. If a company's cost structure is too high, the organization will be unlikely to generate a profit because any increase in volume also generates a high increase in costs. Understanding the relationship among costs, volume and profit is critical if a company is going to be able to make strategic marketing decisions to develop strategies which will promote long-term growth.

Cost/Volume/Profit analysis

Cost/Volume/Profit analysis provides a company with a decision support system allowing management to test out the implications of their plans without committing the company to expensive experiments. CVP analysis incorporates break-even analysis; the reason for this is that one of the main functions of the CVP analysis is to predict the volume of sales that must be achieved for the company to make neither a profit nor a loss (i.e. break-even). Understanding the relationship between volume, costs and profits is essential for any marketing manager. In high fixed costs businesses, volume is the key to success! CVP analysis evaluates:

◆　　The impact of volume on costs and profits

◆　　The volume of sales required to achieve a target profit

◆　　The required break-even volume for the range of products being assessed.

CVP analysis is based on the assumption that costs can be accurately divided into their fixed and variable elements. A fixed cost does not change with the volume of production, whereas a variable cost will change directly with the volume of production. The profits are calculated on a variable cost basis, this means they will reflect the firm's cash flow.

Thus the contribution is sales revenue, less variable costs.

The break-even point will occur where the contribution exceeds fixed costs.

CVP analysis enables the manager to calculate the break-even level of activity for the company using the following formula:

$$\text{Break-even volume} \quad = \quad \frac{\text{total fixed costs}}{\text{contribution per unit}}$$

Thus if fixed costs are £10,000 and the contribution is £20, the company would need to sell 500 units to break even.

If the company wished to make a profit of £5000 then the volume required can be calculated by treating the target profit as an additional fixed cost.

$$\text{Required sales units to be sold} = \frac{\text{total fixed costs}}{\text{contribution per unit}}$$

$$= \frac{£10,000 + £5000}{20}$$

$$= \text{750 units}$$

A break-even chart for the above example would look as in Figure 11.1.

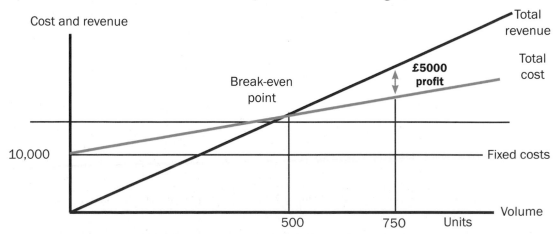

Figure 11.1: Break-even analysis

There are several assumptions applied in CVP analysis:

◆ the sales price is constant over the relevant range of products

◆ production outputs and sales outputs are the same

◆ variable costs do not change in the short run

◆ fixed costs are constant.

Cost/Volume/Profit ratios

Cost/Volume/Profit analysis also provides a number of ratios for the analysis of the performance of a product.

◆ The margin of safety ratio (MOS) indicates by how much sales may fall before a company will suffer a loss.

$$\text{Percentage margin of safety} = \frac{(\text{expected sales} - \text{break-even sales}) \times 100}{\text{expected sales}}$$

◆ The margin of safety is an indicator of the risk profile of a product, the smaller the margin of safety the greater is the risk that the enterprise's level of activity may fall below the break-even point.

$$\text{Contribution sales ratio (CSR)} = \frac{\text{selling price} - \text{total variable cost}}{\text{selling price}}$$

$$\text{Profit volume ratio (PVR)} = \frac{\text{sales revenue} - \text{total variable cost}}{\text{sales revenue}}$$

CSR and PVR are simply different ways of calculating the same ratio. The ratio tells us what percentage from an additional £1 of sale will go towards covering the fixed costs and providing profit.

The CSR/PVR ratio can be used to calculate the break-even level of sales revenue for an enterprise.

$$\text{Break-even sales revenue} = \frac{\text{fixed costs}}{\text{CSR}}$$

Question 11.4

Last year, the trading company Nig Yabmob achieved sales of £100,000 and a profit of £6000 on a capital employed of £18,000. The company wishes to increase their profit margin to 10 per cent and believes if they raise prices and inject £50,000 extra capital they could increase sales turnover to $150,000.

Evaluate the decision in terms of profit margin and ROCE.

Case study: Control in a low-cost airline

Ryanair claims to have more cash and lower costs than its competitors.

In the 6 months to Nov 2007 passenger numbers rose 20 per cent to 26.6 million and interim profits rose 23 per cent, despite a 5 per cent rise in unit costs caused by higher fuel and airport landing costs. Part of the profit increase is attributed to 'ancillary services' such as car hire, hotel bookings and insurance products.

Ryanair announced in December 2007 a further 50 new routes bringing the total routes to 600. However, during the period Ryanair's load factor – a measure of seats sold as a proportion of seats available on each flight – reduced slightly leading some analysts to suggest that the company might be expanding too quickly. Analysts suggested that maybe there was some redistribution here. Given the increased choice customers were simply choosing other routes – rather than many more customers being attracted to the airline.

The industry body IATA has given a pessimistic view of future profitability in the industry due to weaker sales growth, higher fuel costs and a surge in capacity – driven by significant aircraft orders and this will reduce global profit. Moreover, they expressed concern that such an indebted industry, under pressure on profits is poorly placed to cope with any downturns in business. Flying in the face of this Ryanair, one of the more profitable companies, remains optimistic and expects by 2012 to have doubled its fleet to 260 planes.

Adapted from: D Milmo, Ryanair to add 50 new routes despite industry gloom, *Guardian Unlimited*, 18 December 2007

Question 11.5

What performance ratios could Ryanair use to enable it to take further control of its performance?

Adapted from: K. Done, *Financial Times*, 4 November 2003

See CIM SMD Examination December 2004 Q.5

It is interesting to observe that frequently the last question on the SMD paper is a financially based question. Financial appraisal techniques are central to the SMD syllabus and so questions such as this one are important to practise. You need to ensure you understand the differences between short-term and long-term decision-making and that in each area you understand which financial appraisal techniques are most relevant.

Financial techniques for evaluating performance

Activity 11.4

For a company of your choice find out what financial ratios are calculated in assessing performance. Which ratios are viewed as the most critical by the company as indicators of performance?

All of the techniques explored in the previous sections, while discussed in the context of making strategic marketing decisions, can also be used for assessing performance. In addition to the techniques identified in previous sections the use of ratios is the common financial technique for evaluating performance. Ratios measure the various interrelationships in a company and are used to assess corporate performance and the effectiveness of marketing programmes as well as other operational activities. The calculation of certain ratios enables the performance of an activity to be compared year on year so that trends or potential problems can be identified. It also allows the comparison of actual performance against the budgeted/forecasted performance, as well as enabling businesses to compare their performance with others in their industry. Any variance from the expected norm can then be investigated and decisions on the relevant corrective action taken. A fuller discussion of control and evaluation techniques is given in Unit 12. In this section we will focus on identifying some of the main ratios used by companies to assess and evaluate marketing performance.

Ratios fall into three main groups: profit, sales and operational ratios.

Profit ratios

The main profit ratio is the profit margin: the ratio of profit before interest + tax (PBIT) over sales turnover.

Other profit ratios include profit/net assets, gross profit/sales and net profit/sales.

Related to profit expectations is the share price/earnings (P/E) ratio which reflects the investors' view of the future prosperity of the company.

Sales ratios

The main sales ratio is asset turnover = sales/net assets; other sales ratios used by firms involve sales turnover being calculated as a ratio of fixed assets, working capital, selling costs or perhaps such things as admin costs, overheads, and so on. All these ratios either tracked over time or compared against competitors or the standards set can give a company a measure of the efficiency of their performance in these areas.

Operational ratios

Operational ratios help a company assess its ability to generate cash on which to run the business. Without cash, a company cannot operate its business, therefore the liquidity of the company and its amount of working capital will be regularly monitored. In these ratios the turnover periods in which cash will be generated are calculated, usually expressed in terms of days of how many times the business is exchanging cash. The main liquidity ratios are:

◆   Debt collection period   level of debt/sales turnover

◆   Stock turnover period – average stock level/total cost of goods sold

◆   Creditors turnover period – average trade credit/cost of sales

◆   Current ratio – current assets/current liabilities.

Any increase in any of these ratios will warn the company that cash is being tied up in funding the work in progress. As stated previously any of these ratios alone is not terribly meaningful, it is by tracking these measures over time and with other metrics that trends and changes can be identified.

See CIM SMD Examination June 2005 Q.5

This non-numerical finance question allows you test your knowledge of the financial criteria used to assess strategic options. Invariably in all SMD examinations these will some type of question testing your skills to assess there financial viability of marketing plans. The more you can practise these questions, the better prepared you will be.

Question 11.6

Fully explain how variance analysis can be used in the assessment of marketing performance.

See CIM SMD Examination December 2005 Q.1

This case study emphasizes that strategic marketing decisions must often take into account financial considerations as well as qualitative assessments of the market, competition, and customer requirements and expectations. Question 1(a) should consider these elements but also reflect on how these influence the competencies, assets and ambitions of the company. To fully evaluate the situation it is necessary to explain the business model for the development of games which involves very high up-front development costs and the implications for a smaller company's strategy.

In Question 1(b.i) it is particularly important not only to carry out the calculations correctly, but also to explain and justify the formulae that are being used for the calculations. This helps to provide evidence that you fully appreciate the decision-making process. It is then necessary to provide additional information and highlight other factors that the company would consider in reaching its decision. Again it is necessary to consider environment, market and company factors. In doing this it important to demonstrate that you understand the limitations but also the advantages that Wizzgames has, as a smaller company with limited resources.

In Question 1 (b.ii) you should provide evidence of your ability to critically evaluate the analytical tools that are available for decision-making. Conceptual tools are valuable but must be used with caution!

Summary

◆ Three approaches assess shareholder value: the cash flow valuation method, the calculation of EVA and ROCE.

◆ The two financial approaches to investment appraisal considered in this unit were payback and DCF.

◆ Discounted cash flow is based on the principle that money received today is worth more than money received next year because of the opportunity to invest and earn a return. Thus DCF concentrates on cash flows rather than profits.

◆ Understanding the relationship between volume, costs and profits is essential for any marketing manager and is used in evaluating the options available particularly in short-term decision-making.

◆ Ratios measure the interrelationships of various input and output factors in a company and are used to assess corporate performance and the effectiveness of marketing programmes as well as other operational activities.

Further study

Doole, I. and Lowe, R. (2005) *Strategic Marketing Decisions in Global Markets*, Thomson Learning

Doyle, P. (2000) *Value-Based Marketing: Marketing Strategies for Corporate Growth and Shareholder Value*, Wiley, Chapter 2

Hints and tips

In preparing for the Postgraduate CIM Diploma it is important you learn how the concepts examined in this unit would be used in the strategic marketing decision process. The three major areas are the appraisal of investment decisions, short-term decision dilemmas and dilemmas in assessing and tracking the performance of the programmes resulting from those decisions. In the Strategic Marketing Decisions examination it is unlikely you will be expected to make any complex calculations. What is important is that you can show the examiner that you have the knowledge and understanding to apply the relevant approaches to the specific situation you may be given. However, you will certainly be expected to use and apply, in appropriate manner, a number of the approaches identified in this unit in strategic marketing in practice. Thus it is important you practise using these techniques and develop the ability to use them in the analysis of the case study on which the examination for strategic marketing in practice is based.

Bibliography

Doole, I. and Lowe, R. (2005) *Strategic Marketing Decisions in Global Markets*, Thomson Learning

Doyle, P. (2000) *Value-Based Marketing: Marketing Strategies for Corporate Growth and Shareholder Value*, Wiley

Unit 12 Achieving a sustainable competitive advantage

Learning objectives

In this unit we examine the decisions a company has to make in its approaches to its evaluation of marketing performance. We also explore the wider dimensions of strategic marketing decision-making and discuss the goals and expectations of its stakeholders and the impact they have on strategic marketing decisions and the achievement of a sustainable competitive advantage.

In this unit you will:

4.10 Assess the issues of corporate and social responsibility (CSR), sustainability and ethics in achieving competitive advantage, enhancing corporate reputation and creating stakeholder value.

5.2 Explain the concept of, and evaluate methods such as Balanced Scorecard for, stakeholder value measurement.

5.5 Define performance measurement systems for the deployment of marketing assets and the implementation of marketing plans.

5.6 Define budgetary and planning control techniques for use in the control of marketing plans and explain the pitfalls of control systems and how they may be overcome.

Having completed this unit you will be able to:

◆ Identify, compare and contrast strategic options and critically evaluate the implications of strategic marketing decisions in relation to the concept of 'shareholder value'.

◆ Demonstrate the ability to reorientate the formulation and control of cost-effective competitive strategies, appropriate for the objectives and context of an organization operating in a dynamic global environment.

This unit relates to the statement of practice:

Bd.1 Promote a strong market orientation and influence/contribute to strategy formulation and investment decisions.

Key definitions

Evaluation and control mechanisms – set standards to which marketing strategies should aspire, measure performance and take corrective action when the measurement varies from the level of performance required.

The balanced scorecard – is a management system to measure current performance and to set priorities for future performance. It incorporates four perspectives: financial perspective, the customer perspective, the internal business perspective and the innovation and learning perspective.

Corporate social responsibility – is the term used to describe the level of awareness shown by companies of their social responsibility and the values exhibited with regard to the societal impact of strategic marketing decisions.

Study guide

In this final unit we examine the issues in establishing evaluation and control mechanisms in strategic marketing decision-making and discuss the wider implications of assessing added value for all stakeholders in the company. Increasingly the CIM examinations are expecting candidates to show they have an appreciation of the wider dimensions of a company's efforts to achieve a sustainable competitive advantage over the longer term. In studying this unit, therefore, you need to consider how issues discussed would impact on the evaluation of strategic options and the marketing decisions you make as a marketing manager. A fundamental value underpinning all the subjects at the Postgraduate CIM Diploma is the belief that to drive business success, the marketing decision process has to be a disciplined process which achieves demonstrable added value for all stakeholders and is supported in its application by robust marketing metrics. In studying this unit you need to consider how you can therefore incorporate such values into your own strategic marketing decisions.

Approaches to measuring performance

Companies are continually striving to find relevant and appropriate measures by which to measure and control the complexity of marketing programmes and show how they contribute to the economic value of a company and in turn to shareholder/owner added value. If marketing managers are to take a more strategic role in marketing at board level they need to talk the language of the CEO. This means there has to be a demonstrable link between marketing expenditure and its contribution to the profitability of the company. In the past, marketing has been accused of regarding marketing activities as beyond measurement. Examiners of the CIM Diploma are constantly bemoaning the fact that examination candidates recommend marketing strategies without taking any regard of the resource implications or how their proposals will be controlled and evaluated. It is therefore important that you ensure you have an understanding of the implications of the strategic marketing decisions you take in examinations and how the resultant programmes will be controlled and evaluated.

Control systems have four primary objectives:

◆ To set standards to which marketing strategies should aspire

◆ To measure performance in a meaningful way

◆ To assess areas of strengths and weaknesses in marketing programmes

◆ To establish mechanisms for taking corrective action when required.

If standards are to be set, it presupposes that there is a marketing plan which has targeted budgeted outcomes. The standards set are essentially the guidelines towards which all the personnel involved in the implementation of the marketing programme are aiming. Performance against those standards will then be measured by comparing actual performance against the predetermined standards. Variance from the standards set will be analysed to identify the reasons for the shortfall and to identify the strengths and weaknesses in the programme. Therefore a feedback mechanism is an essential component if the control system is to be effective. The results need to be fed back to management, to enable decisions to be taken as to what corrective action is needed to control the planned outputs of the marketing programme. The results also need to be fed back to the strategic marketing decision-makers as the variance identified could well have implications for the marketing strategy itself. If the variance is due to a change in environmental factors then to maintain a competitive advantage, decisions as to what strategic changes are necessary need to be made. For a much fuller treatment of this subject the reader is directed to Chapter 12 of the accompanying textbook, Doole and Lowe (2005).

Activity 12.1

Identify six critical success factors which you consider drive the marketing performance of your company.

Performance metrics

In establishing a performance evaluation process there are some basic but fundamental questions which managers need to ask.

◆ What are they going to measure?

◆ What are the organizational mechanisms for the measuring activities?

◆ How to ensure performance is measured against a balanced range of goals and objectives?

What are we going to measure?

In choosing the metrics to apply, the CIM (2003) suggests, metrics need to be robust and reliable and have the following characteristics:

◆ Be clearly linked to business objectives of economic added value.

◆ Be focused on measuring the key indicators in a clear way so they are easily understood.

◆ Encompass broad and balanced factors and incorporate a range of marketing measures.

◆ Be able to track performance reliably over time and so visibly signal changes in performance.

◆   Be cost-effective in that the financial and staff time resources required to collect and analyse the data should not outweigh the benefits.

The type of metrics that can be used in performance measurement can be either non-financial or financial. Table 12.1 gives an indication of some of the more common metrics used by companies.

Table 12.1: Financial and non-financial metrics

Financial	Non-financial
Shareholder added value	External rankings
Economic added value	Market share
Return on capital employed	Sales volume/growth
Return on investment	Unfulfilled orders
Return on net assets	Meeting delivery schedules
Cost/revenue/profit ratios	Market penetration levels
Profits and profitability	Customer commitment/loyalty
Cash flow/liquidity	Number of customer complaints
Return on sales	Market image and awareness levels
Production costs	Employee motivation
Unit costs of marketing activities	Employee turnover

In deciding the particular metrics to measure, companies need to consider what they view as the critical success factors that drive performance in their market/industry. The metrics chosen need to assess performance in these areas. Thus if a critical success factor is superior customer value, then level of customer satisfaction and level of customer loyalty may be key measures. If the source of competitive advantage is of lower relative costs to a competitor, then production capacity utilization, quality standards and CVP ratios will be key measures.

What are the organizational mechanisms for the measuring activities?

Benchmarking

Benchmarks can be set against key competitors or in a large multinational against performance in other subsidiaries. If, however, competitor benchmarks are to be the main organizational mechanism for measuring performance then marketing research and competitor intelligence would be needed. There are two main types of competitor benchmarking processes:

Industry-based benchmarking – In this case the company is comparing their performance against the average known performance in the industry. In industry-based benchmarking data is exchanged between companies, usually by an independent industry or trade association so that companies can benchmark their activities while maintaining confidentiality of information.

Competitor benchmarking – In this case the company is identifying key competitors and acquiring information on their performance on specific measures. Targets are then set of either matching or perhaps outperforming them in particular measures.

The annual budgeting procedures

In the implementation programmes of marketing strategies, the goals and objectives set will be translated into annual budgeted targets for the operational performance of the marketing programme. These will usually comprise targets for the achievement of the overall financial objective for each of the planning periods, as well as budgeted financial targets for marketing activities. These budgets will then be broken down to specific activities within the marketing programme (sales budget, advertising budget, etc.). Budgeted performance targets will also be set for product/brand strategies as well as performance targets for each element of the marketing mix. Performance will then be evaluated and the marketing programme controlled by measuring actual results against the target for each period. The advantage of using the annual budgeting procedures to control marketing strategies is that it facilitates the co-ordination of a different range of activities by setting either financial or numerical targets which have a common language across functional activities. Furthermore if managers are involved in the budget-setting process then it can act also as a key motivational device. Most budgets are prepared over a one-year period, which enables managers to plan and control activities in line with the process of preparing the annual accounts of the company.

The major problem with using the budgeting process, however, is that the very first task of the budgeting process is the sales forecast on which all subsidiary budgets and targets will be based. The accuracy in forecasting future sales therefore is critical to the meaningfulness of any budgets set to control activities. If this forecast is wrong, for whatever reason, using the budgeting process can become a dispiriting exercise for marketing managers.

Auditing as a control mechanism

As we have said in previous units, strategic marketing decision-making is an iterative and continuous process. Marketing auditing is also a continuous process and an integral part of evaluating the current position as well as controlling the activities of the company. The auditing process is intertwined with the decision-making process, which itself is intertwined with the control and evaluation process. Thus the auditing processes established by a company are important for signalling likely changes and problems in the marketplace in the strategy development process and ensuring performance standards are met. Auditing processes need to be established to monitor the marketing environment, the marketing strategy, the organization and systems set up to deliver the strategy as well as the functions and profitability of different aspects of the marketing programme. In setting up control and evaluation procedures, all the above areas will be regularly monitored and performance assessed against the objectives and standards articulated in the marketing strategy.

Question 12.1

Identify the barriers to measuring and evaluating performance that marketing managers may encounter. Suggest how these barriers might be reduced.

How to ensure performance is measured against a balanced range of stakeholder goals and objectives?

Kaplan and Norton (2006) suggested the use of the Balanced Scorecard (Figure 12.1) to ensure a balanced range of metrics to measure the added value of a company to all stakeholders. The Balanced Scorecard is essentially a management system to measure current performance and to set priorities for future performance. It takes companies beyond the conventional metrics of sales, profit and cash flow and incorporates the many vital goals and measures against which a company can evaluate their performance rather than simply relying on one measure alone. It addresses four elements:

1   The financial perspective – what is our added value to shareholders/owners?

2   The customer perspective – what is our added value to customers?

3   The internal business perspective – what must we excel at to create value?

4   The innovation and learning perspective – how can we create and improve added value?

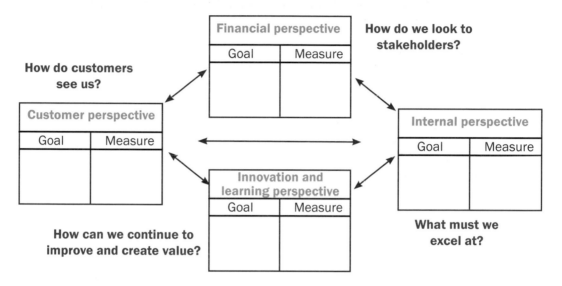

Figure 12.1: The Balanced Scorecard

Source: CIM Professional Postgraduate Diploma in Marketing Tutor pack: Adapted from Kaplan and Norton (1992)

The Balanced Scorecard can be used by companies to measure stakeholder value and so assess company performance against their goals and expectations. If used in the manner suggested in Figure 12.2, for each component, standards will be set, then measures established by which the company can evaluate the performance in each area against the goals.

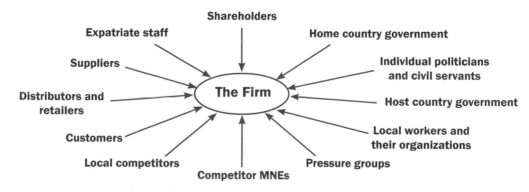

Figure 12.2: Typical stakeholders of a company

Does the Royal Mail have a healthy Balanced Scorecard?

The Royal Mail made a profit of £220 million in 2004 compared to a loss of £200 million in 2003. The turnaround reflects tough cost-cutting measures, including large-scale job losses and a programme of post office closures.

But the financial recovery was marred by the fact that it missed all 15 delivery targets as late deliveries increased. Royal Mail aims to deliver 92.5 per cent of first class letters on the day after they were posted but has undershot the target. As a result Royal Mail is now due to make compensation payments of about £80 million.

Such a lacklustre performance on non-financial targets poses a huge competitive threat to Royal Mail. Overseas competitors, who will soon enter the market, will have much more cash to plough into their operations. The company is still only making returns of 2 per cent while the Dutch and Germans who are intending to move into the UK market are making 20 per cent plus. Chief executive Adam Crozier warns that they still need to radically change the company if they are to deliver the necessary profits over the longer term and fight off overseas competition.

Adapted from: Newing, R. (2007) Role of managers, www.ft.com, accessed 2 May 2008

Question 12.2

What performance measures would you recommend the Royal Mail should use to develop a Balanced Scorecard that would allow the company to more effectively assess its competitive performance?

Activity 12.2

How does your company ensure a balanced and integrated approach to its system of performance measurement?

Question 12.3

For a company of your choice develop a Balanced Scorecard that would allow the company to effectively and efficiently manage the marketing process. Justify the performance measures you have selected.

Managing stakeholder expectations

A stakeholder is anyone who has an interest in, or an impact on, the organization. In making marketing decisions managers need to appreciate that different stakeholders have different perceptions of the value they expect to receive from the strategic marketing decisions made. Shareholders/owners will perceive value in terms of the financial benefit they hope to receive, while customers will perceive value in terms of the benefits consumption of the product or service will give them. Employees' perception of value, on the other hand, will be couched in terms of the rewards they receive due to their efforts.

Activity 12.3

Using Figure 12.2, the stakeholder framework, draw up a diagram of the stakeholders of an organization known to you.

Stakeholders

According to Doyle (2000) stakeholders fall into a number of major groups:

◆ **Shareholders/owners** – From the perspective of shareholder/owner value, the first priority of any strategic marketing decision is that they result in activities which create economic benefits which in turn translate into economic value.

◆ **Employees** – The knowledge and skills that employees have are the intangible assets of an organization that can help a company create and deliver superior value to the customer.

◆ **Managers** – Managers may well have priorities relating to how they are paid, promotion prospects as well as their political motivations for status and power within an organization which may sometimes conflict with the interests of other stakeholders.

◆ **Customers** – The sustainable competitive advantage that will deliver economic value added has to be achieved by maximizing customer value at a cost that generates cash for the company. Customers are interested in obtaining value. If the company fails to meet their value expectations then they will switch suppliers.

◆ **Suppliers** – A totally integrated marketing effort requires the cooperation and commitment of all the partners involved in the route to market of the products and services being offered by the company.

◆ **Community and society** – Companies today are seen to have a social responsibility to ensure that their actions are in line with the expectations of the society and in keeping with the public interest and the regulations set down by governments.

The typical stakeholders of a company were depicted in Figure 12.2.

In making strategic marketing decisions a company has to assess the varying interests of their stakeholders and evaluate the risks that the different strategic options they are considering in terms of the potential reaction of the different stakeholder groups. The risk that a stakeholder group may react in an adverse way may make the proposed marketing decisions less attractive. Thus to ensure the effective implementation of marketing programmes, managers have to manage their relationships with their stakeholders and ensure they meet their expectations. If a company has a high retention rate among employees it is much more likely to be able to retain customers and deliver superior value. If it has a continuous and stable relationship with its suppliers, the government and the wider community it will be more able to develop appropriate responses to challenges in the marketplace.

Question 12.4

Show how a multinational enterprise can incorporate a consideration of its stakeholders into its strategic marketing decision-making process.

Issues of corporate social responsibility

Activity 12.4

Discuss with a senior manager within your organization how corporate social responsibility is managed within your organization and how it influences the marketing decision-making process.

If a company is to manage the varying demands of its stakeholders then it has to be seen as a company that exhibits a strong sense of corporate social responsibility. Fundamental to achieving this are the shared values between the company and its stakeholders. This is the heart of the societal marketing concept which proposes that in determining the needs and wants of target markets, the strategic marketing decisions made must enhance the well-being of the society as well as that of the consumer. Thus to sustain a long-term competitive advantage the decisions made must take into account the social impact of these decisions on the well-being of the society.

Insight: Is CSR really at the top of the agenda

The challenge of global poverty is now on the agenda of the world's top companies. Whereas the Indian Ocean tsunami focused recent attention on philanthropy, there has been a quieter change of tide in the opinion of key marketing strategists who now see poorer regions of the world as potential markets to be developed while at the same time helping the local populations combat poverty. Many companies have seized opportunities by designing products and services that can be consumed by the world's poor.

However, how far is this evidence of CSR or, is it just another form of relationship marketing? There are some suggestions that much of the profitable business with lower income markets involves products such as mobile phones, not the provision of basic nutrition, sanitation, education and shelter, so the current expansion of profitable business in the global South does not necessarily imply poverty reduction. The type of 'development' that is promoted by marketing consumer products to the poor is also questioned. The environmental impacts of changing consumption patterns need to be looked at, as well as the potential displacement of local companies and increasing resource drain from local economies, as larger foreign corporations become more active.

Society increasingly expects companies to show an ethical responsibility in the decisions they take and share their social responsibility with their stakeholders. Thus it is becoming increasingly apparent that to sustain a long-term competitive advantage companies need to show at a corporate level they have a strong awareness of their social responsibility and that it is a key component of the values on which they build their marketing strategies and an integral consideration in the decisions they make. This means that companies have to consciously engender a culture of shared responsibility among all their stakeholders: shareholders, employees, customers, suppliers as well as the wider community. This involves developing in the strategic marketing decision process an ethic of collective good which is marked by a voluntarily accepted solidarity among stakeholders that the company, with them, holds a common interest in achieving a sustainable future.

Question 12.5

To what extent should marketing managers recognize the social responsibility of their marketing decisions beyond the boundaries of their organization?

See CIM SMD Examination December 2005 Q.5

Corporate social responsibility (CSR) is a well publicised current issue and familiar now to most people. Whilst it is important to explain the concept and explain the potential conflict between shareholder and other stakeholder value, the answer to the question requires more depth particularly in critically evaluating the arguments for investing in a sustainable and ethical strategy rather than being solely focused on profitable operations. Some discussion is required of the opposing views of CSR as an investment to achieve strategic competitive sustainability with significant potential benefits for all stakeholders compared to CSR being seen as a marketing cost, typically involving public relations and sponsorship activity that demonstrates an ethical or philanthropic approach to operations.

Ethical implications of decision-making

Activity 12.5

Draw up an ethical code of conduct with the aim of instilling ethical values for your company sales personnel.

The ethical dimensions of strategic marketing decision-making have become more visibly important due to the increased sense of corporate social responsibility. In response to this companies have introduced codes of ethical conduct to guide decision-making and also invite independent auditors to review their ethical performance, which is increasingly used to help companies differentiate themselves from competitors. The prevalence of consumer watchdogs, industry ombudsmen and consumer television programmes have all encouraged companies to take a positive stance on these issues so they can defend themselves publicly on such issues if a controversy does arise.

Insight: The dilemma of the long supply chain

Whitline sells a range of premium kitchen accessories. Their principal international markets are the USA, Australia and Northern Europe. They have become aware that a number of their competitors, particularly in the USA have become enthusiastic members of the ethical trading initiative (ETI). Whitline's own company research has shown indications that a growing number of consumers across their priority international markets are concerned about the ethical origins of the goods they purchase. However, to become a member of the ETI would require a comprehensive and costly series of verification visits to suppliers with repeated visits at regular intervals. Over 60 per cent of the products sold by Whitline are sourced in China and East Asia. Often their products are bought through intermediaries and so they have little contact with the original manufacturers. The process then of verifying the ethical practices of the original supplier could involve the company in considerable cost and effort.

The question to be considered are how such ethical issues impact on a company when trying to build a global brand image and should Whitline make the necessary investment.

Adapted from: Doole and Lowe (2008)

In today's markets a number of the ethical dimensions of marketing decisions are backed by law, both domestic and international. However, ultimately ethics really comes down to the moral behaviour of managers within a company and the importance they place on acting and behaving in an ethical manner. Managers need to form a view as to what constitutes ethical decision-making within an organization. In taking such a view mangers need to reflect on how their views on what constitutes ethical behaviour reflects changing societal views of acceptable behaviour, how decisions will be viewed by stakeholders and the perceived and real impact upon the organization of making those decisions. Central to their concerns is the importance the company places on the need for an ethically responsible approach to their operations on the global markets. However, interwoven within this are the commercial concerns of the business and how they meet the expectations of their stakeholders with regard to their ethical behaviour while delivering added value to their shareholders/owners and their customers.

Question 12.6

A large household furniture retailer recently received criticism for its policy of sourcing its rugs and carpets from unregulated sources of supply in India. Suggestions have been made that the rug manufacturers pay very low wages and are guilty of exploitative employment practices. The furniture retailer defended their ethical integrity.

How should the company deal with such criticism?

Case study: Aveda conserving the nuts

For Peru, Brazil nut processing is an important economic activity reliant on the demand from major international companies that effectively carry out domestic purchasing from local people. In the past many community enterprises of this type have been exploited by unscrupulous buyers.

Aveda, the personal-care product company, has formed a partnership with Conservation International (CI) to add sustainability to the activity by taking a nut by-product and using it in a hair-care product. Aveda's interest is to source plant-based ingredients for its developing product range. The unique ingredient for Aveda is the protein Morikue. CI's objective is to help local communities create sustainable, environmentally-friendly businesses and avoid damaging the natural resources upon which they depend. Activities of this type add value to the nut-processing operation.

The enterprise is based in the Tambopata-Candamo reserve zone, an area rich in bio-diversity and claiming the highest single-site species diversity records for woody plants, birds, butterflies, mammals and dragonflies. The nut collection and processing activities directly affect conservation and natural resource management, and so Aveda supports training activities for Brazil nut collectors and has run enterprise development workshops to show how sourcing guidelines can be used to establish reliable supply chains and improve product quality necessary for enterprises aiming to develop new markets.

Aveda has also helped to fund Profores, a business founded in 2000, to produce and market sustainable forest products, such as fruit nectars. The funding has been used to improve the quality of manufacturing and establish the systems necessary for quality recognition that will enable the company to develop new markets.

Adapted from: Corporate partnerships, Conservation International, www.conservation.org, accessed 1 Feb 2007.

Question 12.7

What benefits do partnerships of this type offer to CI?

Question 12.8

Evaluate the marketing benefits of this example of CSR at Aveda and the impact on its marketing activity.

Summary

◆ Managers have to ensure a demonstrable link between marketing expenditure and its contribution to the profitability of the company.

◆ In establishing a control and evaluation process managers need to decide what they are going to measure and how they are going to measure activities and ensure performance against a balanced range of goals and objectives.

◆ In making marketing decisions managers need to appreciate that different stakeholders have different perceptions of the value they expect to receive from the strategic marketing decisions made, and these varying expectations have to be managed.

◆ If a company is to manage the varying demands of its stakeholders then it has to be seen as a company that exhibits a strong sense of corporate social responsibility.

◆ Managers' views on what constitutes ethical behaviour need to reflect the changing societal views of what is acceptable ethical behaviour.

Further study

Doole, I. and Lowe, R. (2005) *Strategic Marketing Decisions in Global Markets*, Thomson Learning, Chapter 12

Doole, P. (2000) *Value-Based Marketing: Marketing Strategies for Corporate Growth and Shareholder Value*, Wiley, Chapter 2

Wilson, R.M.S. and Gilligan, C.T. (2004) *Strategic Marketing Management: Planning Implementation and Control*, Elsevier Butterworth-Heinemann, 3rd edition, Chapter 19

Hints and tips

Any marketing decisions you are asked to make in the examination are incomplete without consideration of how those decisions can be evaluated. In the Strategic Marketing Decision examination it is the process and the approaches that you would recommend that are important. In the examination it is unlikely there will be a detailed financial question on the setting up and implementation of a control system. Such questions are more likely in Managing Marketing Performance and the Marketing in Practice paper. However, you will be expected to consider the implications of your strategic marketing decisions for control and evaluation. In the evaluation of those decisions it is also important for the wider perspective and to consider how you would measure the added value to stakeholders as well as shareholders/owners.

Bibliography

CIM (2003) *Shape the Agenda: Hard Edged Marketing*, Chartered Institute of Marketing, September

Doole, I. and Lowe, R. (2008) *International Marketing Strategy*, Cengage Learning, 5th edition

Doole, I. and Lowe, R. (2005) *Strategic Marketing Decisions in Global Markets*, Thomson Learning

Doyle, P. (2000) *Value-Based Marketing: Marketing Strategies for Corporate Growth and Shareholder Value*, Wiley

Kaplan, R.S. and Norton, D.P. (2006) *Alignment: How to Apply the Balanced Scorecard to Corporate Strategy*, Harvard University Business Press

Appendix Feedback and answers

Unit 1

Question 1.1

This is meant as an introductory general question to help you think about some of the issues you will be studying in this module. Use your learning from Professional Diploma in Marketing of the CIM syllabus and your learning in the previous modules that you have studied at Professional Postgraduate Diploma in Marketing to consider some of the capabilities you consider important if a company is to make effective strategic decisions. You may want to reflect on the stages of the strategy development process and consider the capabilities in the companies you have studied in case studies. Some of the capabilities you may consider are such things as:

♦   Knowledge management capabilities
♦   Innovative and open culture in an organization
♦   Appropriate performance metrics
♦   The flexibility to be responsive to environmental changes.

Question 1.2

This is an open question to allow you to think further about the context in which strategic marketing decisions are made and the changing dimensions in the environment that are influencing the way in which companies build a competitive advantage. You need to consider such factors as increasing customer sophistication, increasing turbulence in global markets, the fast pace of change in some markets and the increasing interdependency of economies across the globe. You could also discuss the impact of shrinking communications and the impact of the Internet on the way a company's competitive advantage is achieved in the market place.

Activity 1.1

Consider the basis of your company's competitive advantage and ask yourself whether it is based on the actual transaction, whether it has been built by achieving brand leadership or whether it has been built through the relationships the company has formed with its customers or members of the supply chain. The concept of value-based marketing is discussed in Unit 2, but at this stage perhaps you might want to consider how successful your company is in offering superior value to its customers and does it differentiate itself from its competitors through the integration of its total marketing effort or one aspect, perhaps either the product or the service attributes it offers.

Question 1.3

Innovative and creative thinking requires managers to develop the mindset where they can reflect on the information presented, reorientate their thinking in the light of the analysis and then use their learning of the new situation to reinvent the basis on which they develop their competitive advantage. Such thinking therefore means managers have to step outside the formal strictures of the traditional rational linear planning models and approach their strategic marketing decisions from an entirely new angle. In view of the changing dimensions of competitive advantage discussed previously it is becoming ever harder to achieve a sustainable competitive advantage. There are some schools of thought that propose the only sustainable basis for competitive advantage is innovative leadership in the market, be this through the product or services offered, the route to market or in the way a company builds and uses its relationships with customers to offer superior value.

Activity 1.2

In completing this activity you need to first consider what the important elements of hard-edged strategic marketing decisions are. In considering how hard-edged your company is perhaps you may want to think about:

♦ The process in which marketing decisions are made

♦ The different management functions that are involved in making those decisions

♦ Whether marketing decisions are made at board level

♦ Whether creative and innovative thinking are encouraged in the organization

♦ How far do the marketing decisions create superior value for customers

♦ Whether marketing decisions are financially appraised prior to the decision being taken

♦ Whether marketing metrics are used to assess the performance of decisions.

Activity 1.3

The shape of the life cycle will vary enormously depending on the industry or market chosen. If this activity is carried out in a classroom situation, it would be interesting to note the varying shapes of the life cycles identified and reflect on the similarities and differences between the industries where the differences in shape are most pronounced. Likewise in some industries it will be possible to discern quite clear stages that have existed for considerable time periods, whereas in perhaps high-tech markets, stages of the life cycle are more difficult to discern and the time periods at each stage more difficult to isolate. In carrying out this activity perhaps the easiest way is to consider the competitive activity at each stage and the way the market structure has developed in the period of time being observed.

Question 1.4

In answering this question you need to consider the changing competitive landscape of mail-related business services. Royal Mail have lost market share as competitors enter the market but customer needs and expectations have also changed and this must be reflected in the portfolio offer (products and services). You should consider what the future focus should be for the organization, recognizing its existing assets and capabilities, decide what in the portfolio needs to be retained, reduced and enhanced and what implications this has for marketing strategies and decisions.

Question 1.5

The life cycle concept, for many scholars, is useful in explaining the past structure of the market/product/demand life cycle. However, given all that has been said with regard to the changing dimensions of competitive advantage it may well be that just because a certain cycle has been followed in the past there is no guarantee that it will follow the same pattern in the future. Managers making decisions for future time horizons need to do more than simply extrapolate what has happened in the past. A large number of companies operate in global markets and so there is not necessarily one life cycle but a multitude of cycles to understand. It is thought therefore that the life cycle concept is a two-dimensional one that has little value in explaining a market structure that is multidimensional and complex. In managing life cycles in global markets, managers need to recognize that life cycles do not always follow such a set pattern. Competition today in many markets is global rather than domestic for many products and services. Consequently, there is a reduced time lag between product research, development and production, leading to the simultaneous appearance of a standardized product in major world markets. Nor does the model go very far in explaining the rapid development of transnational companies networking production and marketing facilities across many countries and targeting transnational consumer segments. Such developments impact on the shape and characteristics of all life cycles, be they market/competitive/demand or product life cycles.

Activity 1.4

This may be quite a difficult activity to complete if you do not have access to the required information. In that case try to talk to a manager of another company who operates in global markets and discuss the life cycle concept with them. See if you can identify the different stages each of the various countries is at and justify why you think you would plot them in that particular position. In other words consider the characteristics you are identifying as being relevant to the particular stages of the global product life cycle.

Question 1.6

Operational excellence – This is about efficiency not necessarily about effectiveness and so can only be a basis of obtaining customer preference if it is geared to a strategy that delivers superior value to the customer. Operational excellence is usually a major strategic thrust in markets where it is difficult to differentiate on product benefits and so competitive advantage has to be built on being cheaper, faster and more efficient. The problem is how to sustain such an advantage over time.

Customer intimacy – Can be extremely effective not only in the service sector but in industries that have the capability to build detailed individual profiles on customers through da-tamining. This allows for a mass-customization strategy that if effective can almost deliver a one-to-one targeted personalized strategy. Supermarket retailers and online retailers such as Amazon are examples of companies that have such a capability.

Brand leadership – Companies basing their strategic positioning on brand leadership need to work actively to deliver an extra value proposition that is valued by the customer to sustain brand leadership over a period of time. Price transparency, the growth of Internet marketing and the growth of grey marketing have led in some markets to the deteriorating perception of the value of some designer brands.

Question 1.7

The high-tech market is a fast moving and changing market where the cost of R&D is constantly spiralling and technical progress is at such a pace that it is difficult for companies in such markets to resource and build the capability to develop a sufficiently robust R&D programme on their own in all the speciality technology areas. In answering this question you need to consider the synergies that partners can bring to the relationship and how these can be exploited in the market. However, it would also be good to consider the potential difficulties in forming such a joint venture across two disparate company cultures and consider some of the strategies and techniques the JV company could exercise to minimize such difficulties.

Activity 1.5

Consider the relationships, if any, your company has with companies that it may be in direct or indirect competition with. If your company does not have any relationships, see if you can ascertain why and what the senior management view is of such relationships. If you work for a large company, it could well be that you have a complex web of such relationships. If this is the case, it would be interesting to categorize the relationships and examine the purpose and objectives of them, the time span of the relationship and whether it is a simple bilateral or a complex multilateral relationship.

Unit 2

Activity 2.1

The reader should consider changes in competitor activity that have rendered a firm's strategy obsolete or perhaps changes in the market that have impacted on the competitive landscape. This activity builds upon Question 1.2 in Unit 1, but here the emphasis is on drivers that you anticipate are affecting the company in its future direction and should be specific to the market or industry you have specified.

Question 2.1

The drivers include the cyclical nature of defence spending, the political stance of governments, the degree of turbulence in the world – including political instability and perceptions of the prospect of conflict. Clearly revenue in military markets comes from innovation and it is necessary for BAe to remain a leading edge technology player in order to benefit from future spending. Competitors will seek to defend their markets against competitors that might come and go, according to the defence demands. BAe must maintain flexibility in order to maintain its performance against a background of fluctuating demand.

Question 2.2

For many companies the Internet has broken down barriers of access to markets and enabled them to redefine the geographical boundaries of their market. It is now considerably easier for companies to access disparate and fragmented markets across the world through the Internet. It has meant that they are able to build knowledge on individual customers that has given them the ability to develop mass customization strategies, changing the way many companies approach their marketing strategy. However, it has become much harder for companies to identify and track competitors, as in the virtual competitive landscape of e-marketing it is much more difficult to identify and locate competitors and keep track of their movements. Thus the way in which a differentiated position is built and maintained has required considerable rethinking for many companies operating Web-based marketing strategies.

Question 2.3

Companies in their offline marketing activities have had to consider the changes in consumer behaviour that the impact of the Internet has brought. However, marketing, whether it be online or offline, is about how a company achieves the competitive advantage and sustains that advantage over time. Thus the principles of marketing remain the same, in that it is about anticipating and satisfying customer needs and building an added value proposition in the market. However, in many markets the Internet has changed the expectations of consumers and changed the way they seek information and the way they evaluate the options available. Such changes have in some markets, therefore, led to companies reconsidering their offline marketing strategies.

Activity 2.2

The breakpoints themselves may be easy to identify and for any company you may in fact be able to identify several. However, what may be more difficult to ascertain are the decisions and actions the company took to overcome the breakpoints. It may be that the company did nothing. If this is the case, then consider what the consequence of their inaction was? Did the company survive or was it ultimately forced to realign its strategic thinking? You may also want to consider the strategic marketing decision process in the company and whether this facilitated or inhibited the company's ability to react to the breakpoint.

Question 2.4

A totally integrated marketing effort reflects the ability to take a long-term perspective to its strategic marketing decisions and ensure that the customer proposition in the marketplace is clear, that it has an explicit positioning strategy and a high level of resource coordination in the delivery of that strategy to the market. To achieve this, there needs to be a good understanding within the organization of the needs, wants and behaviour patterns of the customers. There also needs to be a clear direction from senior management that is understood by all the employees of the company. In this way all the company will understand what is required of the marketing effort and they will be able to work to the same goal. Of course to achieve this, the company has to be effectively organized and have a good knowledge management system and strong marketing orientation.

Question 2.5

The shareholder value principle asserts that marketing strategies should be judged by the economic returns they generate for shareholders and company owners. It is important for marketing managers in their drive to gain more representation at board level of companies. There is a strong view that marketing is not adequately represented at senior management level as what the value-added marketing brings to an organization has been difficult to quantify in financial terms. Value-based marketing offers a way for managers to show how marketing strategies increase the value of the firm as well as providing a framework and language for integrating marketing more effectively with other functions of the business.

Question 2.6

In high-tech markets, the pricing dilemma faced by companies is how to maximize revenues when they have gone through a highly expensive R&D programme and the cost of producing one product is incredibly high, but the marginal cost of producing large numbers is incrementally very low, hence the pressure to reduce process quickly. The reader needs to consider in such a market how the company can best employ strategies that will maintain long-term shareholder value while maintaining competitiveness in the market.

Activity 2.3

Obstacles in applying the economic value-added principle are:

♦	Absence of clear objectives from senior management

♦	No clear lines of responsibility for the accountability of marketing decisions taken

♦	Lack of integration between departments

♦	No effective knowledge management system

♦	The lack of performance metrics within the organization.

The implications for strategic marketing decisions are that the principle implies a clearer decision making process by providing a more evaluative approach to choosing options. However there can be tensions created, for example between decisions that focus on short and long term strategies

Question 2.7

The main components of value-based marketing are:

♦	A deep understanding of customer needs, operating procedures and decision-making processes

♦	Value propositions that meet the needs of customers and create a differential advantage

♦	Long-term relationships with customers so a level of loyalty and trust is built based on satisfaction and confidence in the supplier

♦ The delivery of superior value to customers requires superior knowledge, skills, systems and marketing assets.

Activity 2.4

Some companies clearly articulate their value disciplines and ensure they are known and understood by all employees. If this is the case, then it gives clear criteria against which strategic options can be evaluated when companies are making strategic decisions and helps them to clarify which decision is in line with their values. However, a company where such values are not evident does not have the same strategic steer. This means in making strategic decisions in difficult and complex circumstances it is much harder to clarify a clear path forward and so harder to judge the appropriateness of decisions.

Question 2.8

Both the approaches outlined have validity, and the approach taken may well be determined by the core ideology expressed by the senior management of the company as well as the competitive and market situation. However, all approaches have to have inbuilt flexibility to respond to challenges in the marketing environment. Thus in the view of Mintzberg, strategy development processes need to be an iterative process allowing a company to reflect and respond to challenges so the company has to be proactive in seeking knowledge to anticipate future developments but also have the ability to react and change the strategic basis should the market demand it.

Activity 2.5

In many SMEs the managing director may have sole responsibility for all marketing decisions. One of the problems they have in making decisions is that unlike in a large firm they do not have the capacity to generate ideas, assess options and clarify the best route forward by bringing together teams of experts and professionals within the organizations. Thus the responsibility of making strategic decisions can be a lonely and onerous one. This is why SMEs build an almost virtual organization through a network of relationships with external partners who play a huge part not only in advising on any decision to be made but also in the provision of information on which to base decisions and helping to validate any decisions that are made as appropriate to the market conditions.

Unit 3

Activity 3.1

To complete this activity, draw a grid with the names of the five companies along the top and then down the side the components of a customer value-based philosophy, that is marketing orientation, continuous learning and a commitment to innovation. For each of these components assess what evidence there is that the company gives priority to these components. In what way do you see these three activities being implemented by each of the companies identified?

Question 3.1

To create a learning environment a company needs to:

♦ Remove the barriers to learning that may exist between departments

♦ Have a top-management commitment to the process of learning

♦ Define widely the scope of their learning activities

♦ Develop mechanisms for leveraging the learning by the company to gain competitive advantage

♦ Be flexible and be prepared to respond to the learning gained.

Activity 3.2

The key indicators identified will vary depending on the characteristics of the market and the type of product/service being offered in that market. They will also vary depending on whether the company is operating in the business to business (B2B) market or the business to consumer (B2C) market and the route to market used by the company.

Generally speaking, however, the indicators may include such factors as:Macro environmental changes

♦ Changes in legislation

♦ Changes in industry/competitive structures

♦ Changing consumer demographics

♦ Market segment changes

♦ Level of customer satisfaction

♦ Operational efficiency measures

♦ Level of repeat purchase.

Question 3.2

3R learning is an important component of strategic marketing decision-making in that it helps companies to develop the capability to:

♦ Develop advance knowledge of key events in markets

♦ Build the flexibility to quickly reconfigure operations and reallocate resources

♦ Focus on an emergent opportunity

♦ Identify threats in the environment

♦ Achieve a rapid response to competitive challenges.

However, in evaluating the role of 3R learning you need to consider the time, resources and expertise required to carry out the role and the possible cost/benefits to an organization. It may be that in a firm with limited financial resources, the role of 3R learning in strategic decision-making takes on a very different character to a much larger organization.

Question 3.3

The starting point in answering this question is to reflect on the nature of political decision-making and the possibility that some decisions (often short term) and backed up by substantial publicity are taken for political reasons to give the appearance of doing something to respond to concerns of the public. An approach based on reactive initiatives accompanied by publicity can give the appearance of dynamism. This should be set against a more considered approach that would take into account the various factors affecting the decision. Both signal and 3R learning should be used.

It is essential that the cost of a new initiative is set against its potential stakeholder benefits and value. An assessment needs to be made of the value of promoting and carrying through initiatives, including both the short-term and the long-term benefits and their impact on different stakeholders. Then it becomes the role of marketing communicators to ensure that the stakeholders really understand the message.

Question 3.4

You should begin by explaining why an understanding of customers and competitors is so important. You should distinguish between, direct, indirect and potential competitors, and for each of the different types of competitors consider the factors that need to be analysed. However, in carrying out such an analysis, the following are important:

♦ Identification of competitors is closely related to the definition of market boundaries.

♦ In a global market it is difficult to ascertain who competitors are and where the future competitive threat is coming from.

♦ Collecting reliable information on competitor activity is notoriously difficult.

♦ It is the direction of future competitive activity that it is important to try and anticipate, not past behaviour.

Question 3.5

What is happening in the mobile phone industry is not dissimilar to what happened previously in the car industry. To gain cost efficiencies companies outsourced a number of operations that brought them huge benefits in terms of their access to markets and the speed of bringing new innovations to market. However, the barriers to entry to the mobile phone market are somewhat less than in the car industry. As a fashion market, the mobile phone market moves very quickly and it has become increasingly fragmented. Thus the emerging specialists that have grown up as a result of the outsourcing policies are now looking for ways to grow by themselves and are able to cherry-pick segments in which to compete. Motorola, who outsource 35 per cent of their production, is particularly vulnerable. Equally it provides the opportunity, as in the car industry, for 'leading edge' component makers such as software suppliers to become global niche players, capable of supplying many of the major industry players.

Activity 3.3

To start this activity you may want to draw up a grid detailing:

♦ Your organization's products and services

♦   The principal competitors for each of them

♦   Your own organization's position

♦   The intensity and the basis of the competitor activity

♦   The likely new entrants

♦   The level of similarity between competitors.

Then draw the matrix as illustrated in Figure 3.2 and plot the competitors as to the degree of their resource similarity and market commonality to assess whether they are direct, indirect or potential competitors.

Activity 3.4

In completing this activity it may be better if you choose a purchase that involved you in making a number of decisions and where you had a choice of alternatives. Consider when it was that you recognized you had a buying need or a problem that required a solution. Ask yourself how you searched for the relevant information, where you searched for it and what media did you use. Did you search the Internet? Once you had the information, what specific criteria did you use to help you decide among the alternatives on offer? Did you rank the alternatives and arrive at a final shortlist? Did you seek advice from other people? If so what sort of people did you consult? How did you reduce the risk of making a wrong decision? Did you seek reassurance after the purchase that the decision made was the correct one?

Question 3.6

The major barriers to the integration of knowledge management and learning activities are:

♦   Lack of involvement of marketing decision-makers in the development of a knowledge management system

♦   The inability to access relevant information required for decision-making

♦   Lack of cooperation between departments as to the inputting of relevant information

♦   Lack of commitment from top management to the integration of knowledge management into decision-making

♦   The time and resources required to allow integration of the two activities to develop

♦   Inadequate expertise within the company.

In considering how these may be overcome you may want to refer to the obstacles you have identified and consider possible solutions for each of them.

Activity 3.5

For some companies the growth of Internet-based strategies has played a significant role in the way they compete on the marketplace and has impacted on all aspects of the marketing process and the way decisions are made. Other companies simply view the Internet as a medium for them to advertise their products and services. Consider which category your company falls into and think about how this has, or has not, changed their approach to marketing decision-making. You could also consider how the Internet has added value to the various stages of the marketing process and what changes this has brought in the company. You could also consider how the use of the Internet has impacted on the way your customers behave and whether it has meant new and changing demands have been made on the company.

Question 3.7

Disintermediation is one of the latest buzzwords. It describes the process by which middlemen in the supply chain are progressively being cut out as companies more and more deal directly with their customers. This is not a trend necessarily started by the Internet, but it is a process that has been further stimulated by its growth. By giving companies the capacity to deal direct with customers across geographical boundaries the need for agents and distributors with local market knowledge has for some industries become much less important. Thus for intermediaries in the supply chain the Internet has been a breakpoint that has meant the traditional basis on which they compete has been made obsolete. Many of these companies, therefore, to survive, have had to reinvent their competitive strategies. In this question you need to discuss the new services being offered by intermediaries and explore the way they have tried to reposition themselves in the market so they can still offer value-added services to traditional customers.

Question 3.8

Here is a good example of a global company choosing one business model over others that it has in its portfolio to enter a new market. It has been able to escape the limitations of its core supermarket model and adapt its smaller store format for this market. It has recognized that a new set of rules for the game are emerging (Hamel and Prahalad – see Unit 3). Tesco is demonstrating the 3R learning approach, rather than signal learning, and it has been used in this situation to identify the new set of rules. The new game rules are needed in response to the drivers from the macro and micro environment and particularly the change in expectations of what gives customer value.

Question 3.9

The key to answering this question is to identify the indicators that will show whether the chosen business model is working with customers and how competitors are responding. Because Tesco is still small in the USA it could still be vulnerable to competition and it is essential that continual changes are made to keep the format fresh. You should explain what signal learning can contribute to monitoring progress and development and how 3R learning should be used to identify potentially significant changes that may lead to further reinvention of the model.

Unit 4

Question 4.1

The starting point is to define technological discontinuities and industry breakpoints and explain the effect they have on the competitive offerings within a market. You should explain the nature of incremental change in technology and markets and then discuss the nature and effect of visionary leaps forward. There are a number of reasons for the break-points and you should explain how they occur. You should emphasize that many of the reasons for the change in the sector originate from the external environment. Even the breakpoints that are driven by individual companies may be initiated by environmental change as discussed above.

The marketing strategy of firms in any market should include environmental scanning, and customer and competitive analysis that will anticipate breakpoints and either take advantage of them or prepare a response when competitive products enter the market. The challenge for the firms is to develop the characteristics of a market pioneer or concentrate on being rapidly responsive to benefit from opportunities that breakpoints generate.

Activity 4.1

You should assess the dimensions of innovation capability including:

♦ How generally proactive the firm is in innovation.

♦ Whether the firm tends to introduce more, or less, innovations than its competitors.

♦ An approximate ratio of innovations that succeed compared with those that fail.

♦ The nature of innovation and whether it tends to create breakthroughs or is continuous incremental change.

♦ How long it takes to get innovations to market and whether the firm is typically first to the market with new ideas.

♦ How successfully the organization is able to anticipate customer needs, and launch and market the innovation.

You should also make some assessment of where the capability (or lack of) resides: whether it is technologically or marketing based.

Activity 4.2

If you are unable to think of an organization or market sector, you may wish to use the case study on page 58.

You should begin by listing the various techniques for opportunity identification and identify some of the sources of innovation that have been discussed. Then go on to assess their advantages and disadvantages in the market and company that you are studying. It is important to distinguish between the types of opportunity because the way that each might be identified and exploited will require a different technique.

Most managers have tried brainstorming, researching customer needs and evaluating complaints, so it might be useful to try the exercise in generating a 'quantum leap in customer benefits'. At first, most managers find this difficult, as the whole basis of the technique is overcoming the industry assumptions and challenging preconceived ideas that familiarity with the industry brings. For this reason you might start by carrying out the technique on a quite different organization first.

Activity 4.3

The starting point is to list the stages in the innovation process discussed earlier and then objectively assess the effectiveness of the organization at each stage, for example:

♦ Are sufficient ideas encouraged and generated?

♦ Is there an effective process for acknowledging ideas and reporting progress back to the initiator?

♦ Is there an objective process for assessing ideas?

♦ Does the business case contain a realistic assessment of the potential market or is it based purely on (largely hypothetical) financial calculations?

You should then consider whether the whole process is overly bureaucratic and time consuming and whether this is simply a reflection of the culture of the organization. Once you have been through the process, it should then be possible to identify areas where the process could be better managed.

Question 4.3

Clearly, the critical factor is achieving fast diffusion of the product or service into the market. But this starts with knowing who the innovators of the diffusion curve in the market are and what will make them adopt the product right at the start of the innovation process. The same questions can then be applied to the other groups of the diffusion curve. Answers are needed to the following questions:

♦ Who are the customers?

♦ How many of them can you switch?

♦ How quickly?

♦ Who needs to be influenced (the customers or the distribution channel)?

♦ What are the best routes to market?

♦ What are the barriers to introduction that must be overcome?

♦ How will competitors react? Will you be a threat?

Activity 4.4

Your organization might fall into this category in which case the evidence of a poor record is probably easily obtained, but the solutions are more difficult. In other, more innovative companies you might think about the steps the organization takes to avoid becoming bureaucratic. The actions that you would propose taking should include:

♦ The nature and effectiveness of the process

♦ The innovation culture within the organization and the absence of a 'blame' culture

♦ Developing the firm's capability, for example, in marketing research, technical expertise (where appropriate), project management and marketing promotion.

Question 4.4

The diffusion curve provides the basic concept of spreading new products into the market through persuading successive segments of the market that a product and service solves a problem and fulfils a need. It would seem to be quite clear that third-generation telephones were a technology looking for an application that would appeal and be useful to customers. It has taken some time and substantial discounting for the mass of the market to be prepared to purchase the product. There was a lack of services that were needed to provide the customer solutions, and this should be explained.

In the case of the Internet consumer purchasing, the marketers appear not to have fully educated customers about the benefits and reassured them about the risks of buying in this way. There is considerable interest among the computer-literate consumers, and this has led to the success of companies such as eBay.

Question 4.5

The marketing aims reflect the vision of the Eden project and particularly the personal vision of Tim Smit. This requires some discussion before the objectives can then be articulated in terms of meeting a number of different criteria, including financial requirements, value for visitors, organization sustainability, continued employment and business for local suppliers as well as the environmental sustainability and education issues.

Question 4.6

At Eden there are some conflicting stakeholder expectations and these can be spelled out by evaluating each stakeholder in turn. It is necessary to explain how, in these circumstances, decisions might be taken but, more importantly, implemented with some sensitivity to individual stakeholders so as to manage rather than alienate them. The criteria for decision-making needs to be explained in such a way that the stakeholders who are adversely affected might at least understand the reasoning behind the decisions.

Question 4.7

Some creativity is needed to suggest ways in which the lessons and good practice might be exploited. In part 1 of the answer (within Cornwall) some explanation of the benefit of network marketing, the use of 'exemplar projects' and 'spin off' benefits to the wider community might be discussed. In part 2 some discussion of exploiting the capability, expertise and knowledge being built could provide some structure to the answer. Refer to the resource-based view of marketing.

Unit 5

Question 5.1

You should decide whether the management claims that the reasons were unexpected and outside their control were correct or whether the reasons given are a change in customer demand or the emergence of new competition. If this is the case, then you should decide if the management should have foreseen the changes and reacted to them.

Use the factors discussed above as a checklist in making your judgement. What should the management have done to protect themselves? For example, was the cause ultimately a weakness in their marketing information system and poor environmental scanning?

Activity 5.1

The factors that are discussed at the start of this unit provide a checklist for carrying out the evaluation. You should then prioritize the factors in terms of the level of probability and the likely effect they would have on the firm's performance. You should think about the external factors, such as the potential changes to the market sector, and decide whether the organization is capable of responding to changes and managing the new situation.

In assessing risk, again, there are external factors, such as customers moving elsewhere, competitors becoming much more powerful or the structure of the market changing to exclude the business, and these will have an effect on every aspect of the marketing strategy, but there are also internal management issues, such as the inability of the organization to respond to external factors as fast as competitors.

Question 5.2

For IBM a main benefit is releasing financial and management resources from an under-performing area of business so that they can be focused on the new direction and opportunities. The challenge is to demonstrate the wisdom of this move by showing improvements in profitability and Return of Capital Employed (ROCE) and so on. Normally there would be a number of threats including narrowing the customer base from the consumer into the business market, reducing the portfolio and the loss of synergy between the PC division and the remainder of the business, but the focus on outsourced IT services means there is a large replacement market available.

For Lenovo this is an opportunity to establish a strong global presence and improve its financial and marketing performance. The threats include the market not proving to be as buoyant as it has been, competition forcing prices down further or new innovations changing the balance between suppliers. A specific challenge for Levono is to effectively integrate the two parts of the business and benefit from the potential synergies.

Activity 5.2

The strategy definitions and criteria for success provide a checklist for answering this question. However, it is important to try to take an objective view of the situation to focus future actions more effectively and so consider the checklist in the light of the competitive market situation. In thinking what action can be taken to achieve future success, you need to consider the strategy itself but also the implications for communication of the strategy internally as well as externally, and you might obtain some additional ideas from Unit 9.

Activity 5.3

It is easy to simply jump to conclusions about whether the strategy is a cost, focus or differentiation strategy, but you need to decide first what the intended generic strategy is and then how well it is being implemented. You should list the criteria that characterize the generic strategies and then look for evidence from the organization's actions as to which is being followed. Today most firms will claim to be following a cost containment strategy, in addition to clear focus or differentiation. You should use the evidence to decide what is correct.

Question 5.3

The introduction should start by explaining that segmentation is a concept that underpins the marketing strategy and that to be effective it requires a deep understanding of customers. Using the appropriate bases of segmentation it is possible to develop a targeting and positioning strategy that enables the marketing mix to be developed, which is distinctive from competitor offerings. By developing a hierarchy of segmentation, an international marketing strategy can be developed that achieves economies of scale and experience. You might contrast a transnational segmentation approach with the deficiencies of a country-by-country approach.

Question 5.4

The introduction should begin with an explanation of the traditional approaches to segmentation in the B2B markets and an explanation of the typical bases used. Strategies are changing in the B2B market and you should take into account the factors that are affecting them to explain more innovative ways of market segmentation before explaining the implications for targeting and positioning. In the case of B2B markets, which are driven by Internet developments, the segmentation might also drive the business model used, or the business model might self-select the target segments.

Question 5.5

You should explain the characteristics of the different marketing approaches, expanding upon the material detailed above and provide examples from different sectors, including not-for-profit and international marketing examples. It is necessary to provide some insights into the types of organizations that adopt these approaches and the examples should help in the identification of competitive advantage. It is important to provide a clear explanation of the resource-based view of firms, focusing on assets and competencies.

Question 5.6

These developments might be seen as incremental changes intended to maintain revenue growth for Apple between the industry breakpoints (such as after the introduction of iPod and iTunes, the music download service) and before the iPhone. More importantly, however, Apple targeted another segment of customers that want Apple products but are unwilling or unable to pay the price of the existing products.

Clearly, there were dangers of cannibalization, brand and price erosion of the Apple products, but the potential benefit of widening the number of Apple users outweighed this. The key to success was continuing to build the 'added value' product range and ensuring that the firm was seen to be introducing products at the leading edge of technology rather than simply 'dumbing down' a successful product. Enhancing this is the powerful Apple brand identity.

Activity 5.4

Using the additional reading you should assess the organization in terms of one of these categories. In practice you might find that different strategic business units are in different positions in the market. You should decide whether the organization is proactive and has made a conscious decision to adopt a particular stance (even to be a follower), in which case you will see plenty of evidence of one of the categories. You may find that the picture is confusing with evidence of inconsistencies in the company's stance. You should then try to work out which competitive marketing strategy (attacking and defensive) it is pursuing and again you might find inconsistencies in the strategy, in which case you might decide whether this is an intended or an emergent strategy.

Question 5.7

In a fast-changing market it is essential that eBay monitors the changes in the environment. However, simply observing trends is not enough. The company will have to continue to make strategic marketing decisions about which direction to go in. There are disadvantages in taking bold steps, as is shown in the case of the purchase of Skype, when perhaps it was not really clear how the cost of purchase would be recouped. However simply doing nothing and relying on the growth in retail spending is also highly risky. Furthermore it is necessary to consider the competitive position and consider whether new competitors or new, alternatives business models might be launched that customers would find attractive.

Question 5.8

To answer this question, it is necessary to separate clearly between two elements. There is a need to create and maintain a fresh up-to-date vision that will attract customers and retain their interest through the development and delivery of value. In this market, customers are also continually looking for something new. eBay must have the competencies and assets that will enable them to provide interesting, innovative and relevant services.

The second element is that of being a learning organis=zation. It can be argued that whether or not eBay have paid too much for Skype, the most important outcome is what they have learned from the whole episode. If it has led to more innovations, if staff have learned good (or even bad) practice in purchasing and integrating a company into eBay and if, as a result, their future identification and delivery of competitive advantage and strategic marketing decision-making has been improved then it will have been worthwhile.

Unit 6

Activity 6.1

You should decide to what degree the organization is already exploiting the opportunities that globalization offers and protecting itself from the threats. Is the organization robust against global competitors and what might it do to better exploit the opportunities and deal with the threats?

Question 6.1

This requires a presentation of the arguments for standardization, including:

♦ Economies of scale

♦ The experience curve effect

♦ The increase in customer value of a consistent image and brand

♦ The advantages of a simpler planning process

♦ and then an explanation of the reasons why products are adapted to local needs, including

♦ Legislation, such as health and safety and promotion

♦ Cultural and usage factors

♦ The lack of 'buy in' to the standard product by local managers.

Question 6.2

Start off by listing the methods and outline the characteristics then explain how the following criteria will affect the choice at each stage:

♦ Existing company operations and resources

♦ Existing foreign market involvement

♦ Management expertise and attitudes to internationalization

♦ Nature and size of competition

♦ Legal, tariff and non-tariff

♦ The nature of the market and the products and services.

You should also give some thought to any scope for more innovative (e.g. e-commerce approaches) and explain the reasons for including them.

Activity 6.2

There will be fairly obvious reasons why the majority of the elements are adapted, but you should pick two or three examples where you think that the arguments for adaptation are less clear and try to determine whether the justification was really market-based or whether it was a fairly arbitrary management decision. In the areas of standardization check whether there is market 'logic' for it or whether it is a head office dictating!

Question 6.3

Markets are changing ever faster because of:

♦ Rapid changes in fashion and consumer attitudes

♦ Changes in the environment: technology, the economic situation and legislation

♦ Shorter product life cycles and faster copying by competitors

♦ More rapid innovations and new product introductions.

The implications are that the traditional systems are:

♦ Too slow, as the environment has changed by the time the plan is ready for implementation

♦ Too many activities and people are involved in the process

♦ Unresponsive as too much information is collected

♦ General and unresponsive to specific situations

♦ Ineffective in their feedback and control mechanisms.

Improve the process by better use of:

♦ Marketing information systems

♦ Environmental scanning and expert knowledge

♦ Benchmarking and best practice

♦ Emergent strategies facilitated by a 'top down' strategy and 'bottom up' local action.

Question 6.4

It is important to explain the various global strategy options: multi-domestic, regional and global, and then how these strategies can be used in a complementary way in a trans-national firm. You should focus on the segmentation approaches, and differentiate between them. You should then go on to explain the competencies in terms of global efficiency and competitiveness, local sensitivity and global learning.

Question 6.5

At the moment many universities and colleges are operating a simplistic product-push strategy (see Unit 5). Others are more service oriented and are attempting to move on from that into a more customer-led marketing strategy. However, both these strategies are short term and fail to address the changing nature of the environment, competition and customer expectation in the market.

A more fundamental review is required to decide a long-term sustainable international marketing strategy. For different institutions in various different situations resource-based, entrepreneurial and network marketing approaches may offer more substantial benefits, particularly in terms of identifying the most appropriate market entry strategies and marketing mix offer to potential students. You should reflect on where students are expecting to gain value from the experience, including living in a new location, gaining exposure to a new culture, mixing with others from different nationalities, the quality of the learning experience, the course content, the possibility and experience of working in the host country and overall value for money from the expenditure incurred.

Activity 6.3

You should regard the model as a continuum between exporting and niche international marketing and assess the overall pattern that emerges as this is a reflection of the company's attitude to international marketing as well as strategy.

It is likely that some functions or business units within the organization will operate rather differently from others. Probably what would be more revealing is assessing the organization on a periodic basis to see how it is progressing.

Activity 6.4

What is important to remember is that informal learning through reflection on practice, good or bad, and using informal information networks can be extremely powerful for more entrepreneurial firms. They are quite willing to experiment on the basis of new information and adapt if things do not go exactly right.

Equally important if the firm is at an early stage of internationalization is whether the firm is progressing quickly to the next level of internationalization and becoming more proactive.

Unit 7

Activity 7.1

You should base your assessment on evidence rather than an instinctive feel. You should see what pattern emerges from the evidence as it may show that your organization and its competitors behave differently in different market sectors (or they may behave exactly the same). You might find that your organisation and certain competitors are becoming more proactive. The evidence that you identify may well provide a strong indication of the competitors' future priorities, intentions and even what future strategies they are likely to pursue. You might also consider whether the proactive competitors show the characteristics of fast growth, discussed next, and whether they will be able to sustain any potential lead they might gain over your own company.

Activity 7.2

Remember that the organization should be seeking to deliver a memorable customer experience that will ensure that it is the first choice for future purchases. You should begin by drawing a flow chart of the various interactions between customers and the organization throughout the purchasing and consumption process. At each interaction you should examine the criteria that will determine whether the customer is disappointed or entirely satisfied. You should think about what pattern emerges from this and decide what should be the focus for improvements. You could make a start by thinking about the three service Ps, any gaps between the customer expectations set and the quality of delivery through staff–customer interactions and the process that customers are taken through.

You should then decide whether the organization has a customer service strategy. To check whether a strategy is being enthusiastically implemented use an assessment based on Table 7.1.

Question 7.1

A number of characteristics of fast growth are included in this unit, and it is useful to group them under a number of headings such as:

◆ Market awareness

♦ Speed and focus in new opportunity identification and exploitation

♦ Recognition of the nature and source of competitive advantage and a recognition of the importance of marketing innovation

♦ A focus on creating customer value

♦ The attitude and ambition of the organization.

Using some examples from fast-growth organizations will help to identify the key factors.

You should then consider each of the factors and explain the difficulty each presents for larger, more administratively (rather than entrepreneurially) managed organizations.

Question 7.2

You should begin by explaining the nature of fast growth and draw a distinction between early stage development and then maintaining growth as the organization matures. Figures 7.4 and 7.5 provide the basis for a discussion of the early stages of fast-growth development. You should then go on to explain how organizations can generate fast growth in sectors that have reached the mature phase of the life cycle. Clearly, there may or may not be the opportunity for a breakthrough, discussed in Unit 4. If there is no possibility of visionary leaps forward, then the approaches discussed earlier in this unit and, particularly, improving the customer management process to provide exceptional customer value can be the competitive advantage driver and lead to fast growth. Again you should think of organizations in a mature market that have increased market share at the expense of the competition.

Question 7.3

Clearly, the timing of Sony's entry, covered in the early part of the case study, was right, but the main success factor was achieving a breakpoint in the industry by adopting a strategy that makes the product desirable for a new customer segment and then building further incremental growth through providing for these new segments new innovative designs for games. Whilst Sony created and benefited from one breakpoint, Wii focused on a different area of innovation to build competitive advantage that enabled them to create a new industry breakpoint.

With quite different demands emerging from different customer segments the market could now fragment with different suppliers adopting niche strategies by targeting different segment needs.

Activity 7.3

You should avoid undertaking this activity in a relatively superficial way unless the organization has already reflected on its position and already carried out a full re-evaluation of its products and services and defined its future source of competitive advantage. If this has not been done, then you should think about the way you have classified the products and services. You should take a market perspective (customer and competitive viewpoints) and not fall into the trap of focusing on products and services alone (and especially products that are easy to make). You should focus on what customers will want in the future – solutions that they value, not simply products and services. You can then identify the types of knowledge, competencies and assets that will be needed to exploit future opportunities, without defining them precisely in terms of specific products.

For example, your markets may become more volatile, in which case the ability to respond to new opportunities and withdraw from yesterday's successes may be critical. In this case the organization must become more flexible, adaptable and responsive.

Question 7.4

A number of the previous activities provide the background to answering this question and you should list the good practice lessons that you have already identified from companies that have succeeded in the past and are succeeding now, and you should add some examples. You should then think about the sources of competitive advantage that have been highlighted before deciding which of these will be important in the future. You should then use the list of possible areas of knowledge for competitive advantage discussed above to identify what will be important in the industry that you have selected.

Activity 7.4

It is essential to critically analyse the reasons for visiting the sites, think about exactly what the customer is looking for and whether this can be better obtained from other websites or alternative information sources. It is useful to assess other sites before concentrating on your organization's site. The use of the customer management process characteristics provides a checklist to assess satisfaction. In thinking about innovation you should decide whether the improvements are really innovative, the application of existing good practice or applying technology for no real customer or company benefit.

Question 7.5

This is a straightforward question that requires the advantages and disadvantages to be listed from different viewpoints, including the buyer, seller and supply-chain leader. You should comment on the different situations, such as using hubs for core and peripheral components and services, simple and complex purchasing situations and the consequences of successful suppliers putting out of business less-successful companies.

In explaining the characteristics of the companies that are likely to be successful you should both focus on the 'hard' issues, such as systems, organizations and operational efficiency, and then discuss the importance of 'soft' issues, such as organizational skills, knowledge and capability, management style and the overall culture, given the need to be quicker to respond to new opportunities and challenges.

Question 7.6

Companies that operate within one or more key technologies can dominate and dictate to their market. Whilst stakeholders, particularly customers, obtain products and services that they perceive to be valuable, the situation is stable. However, when the stakeholders believe the dominant player is abusing their position they will feel resentful and take action where possible. If an alternative technology comes along then the dominant player's position can be considerably weakened.

It is important to recognize that a co-operation strategy should not replace building competitive advantage, as a company should not adopt a co-operative strategy from a weak position. This issue should be considered when identifying advantages and disadvantages. Within a co-operation strategy it is important to define and agree the specific contributions made (and added value created) by partners at the outset, so that the contributions are distinctive. Competitive advantage can be built by the participating companies by increasing value added by their offer.

Unit 8

Question 8.1

The answer requires an explanation of the role that branding plays in the purchasing decision for customers and the value proposition made to customers by organizations. It is important to discuss the nature of intangible benefit and the contribution of attribute branding to this, especially in areas where customers are unable to assess the quality and specification of products and services themselves and have to rely on the brand to provide the assurance. Aspirational and experience branding also deliver benefits in other customer situations, and these should be explained. Examples should be provided to reinforce the points made.

It might be useful to refer to research (de Chernatony, 2001) among consultants that highlighted different interpretations of 'brand':

♦   The input perspectives: logo, legal instrument, company, shorthand, risk reducer, positioning, personality, cluster of values, vision, adding value and identity.

♦   The output perspectives: image and relationship.

♦   The time perspective: the evolving identity.

Activity 8.1

Question 8.1 provides the starting point for this activity, but you should then move on to the list above entitled 'specific benefits to the organization' and use these criteria to assess the brands. From the research quoted, the atomic model of the brand is proposed by de Chernatony (2001) as a planning approach to branding. In that he suggests that the brand essence consists of a distinctive name, sign of ownership, functional capabilities, service component, risk reducer, legal protection, shorthand notation and symbolic feature, and these might be used for evaluating the organization's brands.

Activity 8.2

You should start by contrasting the customer's view of the brand with the organization's view (by asking them) and decide whether or not the organization is 'milking' the brand and stretching it inappropriately over too many dissimilar products or investing and building the brand through effective portfolio and communications management.

Question 8.2

In addressing the purpose of rationalization it is important to explain the need to use scarce resources effectively and provide the contrasting arguments that might be offered for and against rationalization. It is necessary to use the portfolio analysis tools referred to earlier to make the case for retaining or rationalizing products, but you should also refer to other parts of the marketing mix and portfolio dependencies. For example, we have listed some reasons why loss-making products might be retained, and these include the potential damage to communications, more effective use of distribution channels and recovery of overheads.

Activity 8.3

Use your answers to Activity 8.2 and Question 8.2 as a basis for evaluation based on value addition.

Question 8.3

The introduction to the answer should include an explanation of the management of the service elements in the banking situation and how services differ in different markets. Against the background of the difficulties of managing services and the need to provide tangible evidence it is necessary to explain the standardization and adaptation issues.

◆ Physical evidence such as corporate identity, branches and Internet capability

◆ People such as staff, advisers and so on and different response to and expectations of service

◆ Processes such as how customers are managed, their experience in dealing with the bank and the supporting 'back office' processes

You should also refer to any relevant 4P issues such as advertising and promotion campaigns and the range of products.

You should then go on to explain how competitive advantage can be built through an understanding of the various markets and routes to market, the different products and processes that are needed, interest rates and the knowledge and capabilities of the staff.

Question 8.4

In answering this question you should return to some of the concepts discussed earlier and consider, for example, the diffusion curve. It is necessary to be quite objective about the assessment of the willingness and ability of customers to buy even an apparently 'too good to miss offer'. Where political decisions are required anticipating outcomes is even more difficult. The G1G1, for example, has a number of potential benefits but you should decide again quite objectively what the customer segments are, what the criteria for choosing the product might be (and alternatives) and where competition might come from in the future.

Activity 8.4

You should start by taking a period, say the previous two years, and list the projects that have been started, been launched and achieved commercial success. You should think about not just the major products but also the line extensions and product upgrades. If you are able to do it, it would be useful to compare at least the number of successes of your competitors too.

You should think about what pattern emerges from this, particularly in the light of the investment that is made, and think about what aspect of the process is being done well and what not so well. For example, you may wish to think about the effectiveness of outsourced services as well as in-house activity.

Question 8.5

You should use the section headings in this unit to provide a checklist for your work on the portfolio, but you should supplement this with additional areas outside this unit including, for example customer requirements, branding, communications, supply chain and distribution.

Question 8.6

The introduction might start by explaining the concepts behind Unilever's strategy and comparing it with other strategies in the industry, for example that of Nestlé and Heinz, who have taken a less centralized approach.

One way to answer this question is to carry out a brief situation analysis, including environmental analysis (PEST), changes in customer purchasing and usage behaviour and fashions, competition and the market structure – particularly the shift in power in the distribution channels to the retailers. This might include the globalization drivers and focus on converging and diverging customer needs. You should then consider the internal management issues and particularly the opportunity cost of management of local brands and local innovation against global brand dvelopment.

Question 8.7

Strategies do not last for ever in the marketing world and Unilever has constantly changed its strategy in line with changes in the environment and market. Clearly the current strategy seems to be working, but what you should consider is what criteria you should use to decide if it is appropriate, and other options that will meet the criteria. You might consider how to deliver the best shareholder value, for example further acquisitions and further rationalization of underperforming products. You might consider whether the emphasis should be on other product and brand developments.

Unit 9

Activity 9.1

You should take the viewpoint of the customer and list all the messages received, including the direct and indirect communications, then again compare what you think the customer might be expecting and what they receive. Where appropriate you might undertake a survey to find out exactly what their impressions are. You should particularly take notice to see whether the communications are integrated or sent out separately.

Activity 9.2

In carrying out this activity consider the intended and unintended messages, the formal and informal communications, process, people and content problems, the controllable and uncontrollable elements. Think particularly about the physical aspects, appearances and locations that made an impression on you (good or bad).

Think about how many of the negative communications would benefit from better discipline and management, better training or more substantial changes that require significant investment.

Question 9.1

The introduction should start with a definition of integrated marketing communications that emphasizes the need to put the customer at the heart of the communications and to assess the communications from the customer perspective.

The communications come from all parts of the marketing mix and include every intended and unintended interaction. Using examples, the communication problems and failures can then be explained. Methods to improve the integration can be discussed, including customer relationship management (CRM).

Question 9.2

The important thing to note here is that a plan is not needed, but a planning framework would be useful as this would highlight the areas where decisions would be required. While decisions would be needed for each section of the plan you may decide that certain factors will be critical in the decision, such as the available budget, location and competition. It would also be important to know which customer segment should be targeted and by which media.

Question 9.3

Clearly a key part of Google's competitive advantage to date has been to provide a valuable free service to customers and enhance it with additional service offerings. By providing a connection to potentially lucrative customers, Google had a very attractive offering for advertisers who provided the revenue to support the free services.

However, the key for advertisers is not simply to be where potential customers are but to find cost-effective ways of persuading them to make purchases. Within the value chain Google has to ensure that it continues to be an essential part of the integrated marketing communications process, which itself will be subject to change as consumer fashions change and competition increases.

Question 9.4

The important thing with this question is to explain the importance of setting clear objectives for the use of each communications tool and how they might be used within an integrated communications strategy. Explain the advantages and disadvantages and where the use of each tool might be appropriate or inappropriate. Finally identify the generic criteria for communications evaluation and explain how the tools deliver against these criteria.

Activity 9.3

The following checklist might start your evaluation:

♦ Communication objectives delivered

♦ Contribution to marketing strategy (integration)

♦ Efficiency and value for money

♦ Message effectiveness

♦ Success with the target audience

♦ Impact on other audiences

♦ Communication tool/media effectiveness

♦ Was success quantified?

♦ Was process effective and efficient?

♦ Could it have been done in a different/better way?

Then you should decide what was learned from the campaign. Finally you should think about what would have been lost if the communication had not been used and whether this could be justified as an investment rather than an expenditure.

Question 9.5

The concept of relationship marketing is based on the idea that both sides, customer and supplier, benefit from the relationship, but it is often the supplier that pushes the 'relationship'. You should explain when relationship marketing works well (e.g. B2B and certain types of retailing) and when it works less well (e.g. FMCG). The critical success factors can then be listed and an explanation given of how CRM might deliver these. There are a number of reasons why CRM has not always worked. Often CRM installations are technology-led rather than customer-led, and because relationship marketing demands a different philosophy, organizations have not developed and implemented suitable strategies to make it work.

Activity 9.4

It is important to assess the level of resource put into each relationship and decide whether it is appropriate to the value the relationship is expected to deliver. Very often organizations put considerable effort into developing close relationships with stakeholders that are not influential or have little power but fail to invest in more important relationships. Because it is difficult, they fail to develop the most important relationships. Moreover, you might question whether some of your relationships are one-sided and therefore are not relationships according to the definition.

Question 9.6

In identifying the challenges, you should use some concepts of relationship marketing and integrated communications to structure and focus your answer. For example, it is worthwhile considering the balance between the power, influence and degree of control of organizations and their stakeholders. The challenge to organisations is whether they can really place the receiver at the centre of all messages and media. In this way the organisation should understand the what communications their audiences are receiving and should therefore be able to influence them.

Question 9.7

A key success factor is to adopt a consistent approach to communications and relationship building. This means that the organization needs to consider all aspect of the communications strategy: internal, external and interactive marketing. It needs to develop a deep understanding of customer needs and expectations. Most particularly, however, the organization needs to consider the nature of its decision making and the consequences of it, with the examples of British Gas and Mars in the case study being particularly relevant.

Unit 10

Activity 10.1

First list in detail the value chain contributions and the role of your own organization within it. Define the activities or interfaces carefully as they are now and specify exactly what value is obtained and at what relative cost. Think carefully about whether this offers value for money and consider whether the contributions are both appropriate now and relevant in the future market. Think particularly of issues such as response time, constraints, duplication, flexibility, complaints and feedback of information.

Activity 10.2

The key decision areas in setting up or reassessing the channel include the (re)formulation of the channel strategy, designing the channel structure after considering the options, selecting channel members, motivating and managing the channel members, co-ordinating the channel strategy with the marketing mix and evaluating channel member performance. Measurement should include comparative costs and sales of different channels, qualitative and quantitative assessment of channel members and customer satisfaction.

Question 10.1

The answer should build on the explanation earlier in the text and list the key drivers of the three approaches as well as the advantages and disadvantages. By using examples it is possible to provide detailed explanation of the different strategies and challenges posed in each sector. Consider B2B, B2C and different market sectors. To do this you should refer to other units and the additional reading.

Question 10.2

The answer should start with an explanation of the limitations of SMEs in international markets and the problems of entering markets, including their lack of resources, market knowledge and expertise. It is then necessary to outline the concepts of the market entry alternatives in relation to SMEs and the criteria that might be used to choose between the options.

The alternatives are direct-entry methods, including e-commerce, or indirect including the use of intermediaries (agents and distributors), the use of partnerships or licensing. The specific advantages and disadvantages for SMEs should be explained.

In ensuring that customers receive a satisfactory offer, firms should recognize the importance of adapting to local needs, cultural sensitivity if using these methods, in adapting the product/service mix.

Question 10.3

The introduction should include a definition of different forms of partnership and their use in the global market. Typically for a major project, no single partner has the necessary technology, marketing and financial capability. Moreover, the risk of failure is often too great for a single organization.

Advantages include:

♦ Reduction through sharing of market/product risk

♦ Synergy of combined skills and capabilities

♦ Delivery of complex project with different requirements

♦ Complementary marketing, technological and financial assets and competencies

♦ Filling resource and skills gaps.

Disadvantages include:

♦ The decline of interest by one partner

♦ A conflict of interests between the activities included in the collaboration and in the separate corporate activities

♦ Cultural differences between the two organisations' managements

♦ Lack of clear decision making, where ownership is shared

♦ Changes in the individual strategic requirements of the partners

♦ The difficulties of managing a collaborative venture that might be viewed critically by the 'parents'

♦ Giving away intellectual property, commercial secrets and competitive advantage

Activity 10.3

This level of cost reduction requires the elimination of some activities, possibly by outsourcing, and benefiting from economies of scale and the experience effect. It might be possible to take an entirely radical approach, such as yield management:

♦ Greater labour efficiency

♦ Work specialization and methods of improvement

♦ New production processes

♦ Better performance from existing equipment

♦ Changes to resource mix

♦ Greater product standardization

♦ Faster product redesigns

♦ Process standardization.

Question 10.4

The problems include:

♦ Difficulties in keeping international markets separate

♦ Grey marketing/parallel importing

♦ Commoditization of brands

♦ Sustaining a competitive advantage

♦ Low-entry barriers

♦ Monitoring fragmented competition.

The opportunities include:

♦ Huge cost savings through removing intermediaries

♦ The ease of response to random requests

♦ The ease of processing orders

♦ JIT and reduced stockholding.

Global competitive advantages are achieved through:

♦ Transnational segments

♦ Low-cost market entry opportunities

♦ Closer and cost-effective global communications through supply chain

♦ Intranets for tendering and global sourcing

♦ Development of integrated supply chain

♦ Competing the supply chain

♦ Creating worldwide call centres

♦ Impact on the time element in logistics.

Activity 10.4

The organization might adopt a very simple cost-plus or competitor matching approach, so ignoring most of the factors, or the approach is more considered.

The more offensive approach can be considered in two stages, first, the market considerations of customer and competitor factors. You should then consider the portfolio integration issues (Table 10.4) as potential sources of additional customer value and the possibility to increase prices.

Question 10.5

The starting point is to consider the market (consumer, competition and market structure) and technology factors that will affect the business. Then it is necessary to work out the nature of the different possible business models and decide how value is created. You should therefore consider the package of benefits for the consumer and what they are prepared to pay. You should consider the value for the artist and the adding value roles of other members of the supply chain. Once this has been completed then the extended organization should be considered and, particularly, the value (if any) that could be created in the supply chain (both tangible, such as combining hardware and software, and intangible, such as brand associations) through the co-operation of one or more partners.

Question 10.6

You should be prepared for questions that require some speculation or innovation on your part, albeit still underpinned by appropriate concepts. You need to consider what success and value looks like both in financial and non-financial terms. It is also important to consider the short and long term. A 'loss leader' might be useful in the short term to raise awareness but there is a need for reliable income streams too within the portfolio of products and services. Is it live performances, music downloads or something else that should be the cash generators. Is there a role for music producers, distributors and retailers?

Unit 11

Activity 11.1

To start this activity you will need to find out the operating profit, the total capital employed and the sales turnover.

Then:

profit margin = profit/sales

ROCE = Estimated profit before interest and tax/capital employed.

Question 11.1

You need to calculate profit/sales turnover as a percentage:

A 6 per cent

B 20 per cent

C 25 per cent

Activity 11.2

The company could perhaps use a range of techniques: break-even analysis, discounted cash flow (DCF) projections and the calculation of the projected ROCE.

Before an investment project in marketing is undertaken the company must attempt to establish the financial viability of the project. This means estimating the probable return from the investment, the potential increase in profits or for that matter the potential reduction in costs. Any investment must create value: the purpose of investment appraisal is to assess the likely value by:

♦ Forecasting the results of potential projects.

♦ Financially evaluating potential projects.

♦ Financially controlling the development of the project.

♦ Carrying out a post-decision audit to assess performance against the estimates made.

Question 11.2

Smaller players need to consider how they are going to compete in what is forecast to be a deflationary pricing cycle. They perhaps need to consider developing a more flexible supply chain sourcing on a more global scale. In building a business case you need to consider the tools and techniques you would use to evaluate the options you identify. In this you will also need to consider the pricing architecture the company has and how they can use their pricing strategy to deliver economic added value.

Question 11.3

a) Contribution per unit = Selling price – Variable cost

$$= £60 - £42$$

$$= £18$$

(b) Break-even in units $= \dfrac{\text{Fixed costs}}{\text{Contribution}}$

$$= \dfrac{£900}{£18} = 50 \text{ units}$$

(c) Break-even + profit $= \dfrac{£900 + £360}{£18} = 50 \text{ units}$

(d) Volume of sales to give a net profit of 20 per cent

£60 Selling price × .20 = £12 per unit profit

Contribution per unit to fixed o/hds = Contribution - profit margin

$$= £18 - £12$$

$$= £6$$

Break-even + profit $= \dfrac{£900 + £360}{£18} = 50 \text{ units}$

(e) Net profit if 80 units sold = (Expected sales - Break-even volume) × Contribution

$$= (80 - 15 \text{ units}) × £18$$

$$= £540 \text{ profit}$$

(f)   Increase in variable costs = £42 + £4 = £46

Reduction in fixed costs £900 – £340 $= \dfrac{£560}{£46}$

Break-even   = 40 units

(g)   Selling price per unit for sales of 200 units to give a £700 profit

Variable cost   =   £900 ÷ 200 units   =   42.00

Fixed costs   =   £900 ÷ 200 units   =   £4.50

Profit   =   £700 ÷ 200 units   =   £3.50

                                          Selling price   =   £50.00

Activity 11.3

You need to ask what cash flow forecasting took place. Did the company use break-even analysis? What financial ratios were calculated? You also could investigate the ways they evaluated the impact of the change. What method of costing was used, marginal or absorption?

Question 11.4

The current situation is that the company has a profit margin of 6 per cent and the capital employed is £18k. This means their current ROCE is $6/18 \times 100 = 33$ per cent.

In making the changes the profit would be 10 per cent $\times £150k = £15k$. The increased capital figure is now $18k + 50k$, therefore the ROCE is $15/68 \times 100 = 22$ per cent.

Question 11.5

A range of ratios could be used by Ryanair. Consider the ratios outlined in this unit for evaluating profit, sales and operations. Which of these can be applied to the airline industry? You should also be able to think of other ratios that have particular relevance to the airline industry. Further detailed information on performance ratios can be found in Chapter 4, Doole and Lowe, *Strategic Marketing Decisions for Global Markets*, Thomson Learning.

Activity 11.4

A ratio takes two variables (e.g. profit/sales) and compares them with other measures for the same variable. In assessing marketing performance a variety of financial ratios may be used, such as profitability, ROCE, revenue/sales personnel, revenue/advertising budget, contribution per sales call, average mileage per sales and contribution by customer/market segment. Essentially the ratios used will vary from firm to firm depending on the critical success factors identified, and the key operational performance measures the company wishes to assess.

Question 11.6

Variance analysis is a control device used to assess performance against budgets and standards set. For instance, if the forecasted sales budget is $500k but the actual sales turnover achieved is $460k, the sales variance is $40k. On its own, this gives little information and so the actual price achieved, and the volume achieved will also be examined. The variance to the budgeted forecasts will help to identify the reasons for the sales variance.

Unit 12

Activity 12.1

The critical success factors identified may well be financial as well as non-financial measures and capable of giving the company key insights to the important measures indicating their level of performance in key areas. Identifying such factors will enable the company to develop an efficient and effective methodology to control and evaluate marketing programmes.

Question 12.1

There are many barriers a company may face in measuring and evaluating performance. The most significant are:

♦ The environment in which the company operated is too complex to monitor efficiently.

♦ The set-up costs, in terms of finance and time, are difficult resources to obtain.

♦ Internal departmental resistance.

♦ Lack of appropriate information system to facilitate the monitoring and evaluation.

You need then to suggest ways in which companies can overcome such barriers. These should include such factors as, commitment from the top, wide participative discussions with departments, identification of critical success factors, relating the mechanism for measuring performance to the reward system in the company and so on.

Question 12.2

You need to start by considering the specific measures you see as appropriate for a service company such as the Royal Mail. As you can see from the text, a Balanced Scorecard incorporates four perspectives. Construct a scorecard which will give the company a balanced view of the four perspectives. You need to consider how far this will allow the company to evaluate the factors that will be important in beating overseas competition.

Activity 12.2

Does your company use a Balanced Scorecard approach? You could look at what measures they use in each of the categories and where they place highest priority. Is it in the financial or non-financial measures? Perhaps you could make a judgement as to whether you think the system used by your company enables it to obtain a balanced view of the organization or are there particular problems they face in the collection of the data for the analysis?

Question 12.3

You would need to start the answer to such a question by introducing the specific company on which you are going to base the Balanced Scorecard to enable the examiner to understand the context of your answer. The Balanced Scorecard consists of four parts: the financial perspective, the customer perspective, the internal business perspective and the learning perspective. However, within each of those parts the specific measures you choose to use are up to you. They must, however, be relevant to the context and you must show the examiner why you think they are appropriate to the company you have specified. Thus the application of the techniques in this question is critical.

Activity 12.3

Think widely when considering the stakeholders, and if the organization operates internationally it is important you consider the stakeholders from a global perspective.

Question 12.4

The problem for a global MNE is that across the varying cultures within which it operates there will also be highly different views as to what business practices constitute ethical behaviour, what the priorities are in terms of corporate social responsibility, as well as a huge number of different political priorities. How to incorporate these into decision-making on a global basis is indeed a challenge. To a certain extent it will depend on whether the company follows a decentralized approach to marketing decision-making or a centralized approach. In a centralized approach the company may well have an ethnocentric view of the world and work to instil the values and priorities of the stakeholders in the country of the HQ on the rest of its subsidiaries. A more decentralized company will have a much more polycentric view and be more concerned with achieving a harmony of values than dictating a global corporate policy.

Activity 12.4

In tackling this activity consider the expectations different managers have within the organization and their relationship to the marketing decision-making process. You may in your interview ask how the company manages the expectations of different stakeholders and whether or not such consideration is formally integrated into the marketing decision-making process. There are also issues of how the policy of corporate social responsibility is managed, resources allocated and decisions made as to where the priorities lie. It may also be interesting to assess how the policy contributes to the long-term reputation and image of the company.

Question 12.5

Strategic marketing decisions impact on a whole range of parties who may not be constituent parts of the organization but have an interest in the outcome of the strategic decisions made. Such bodies constitute the stakeholders of a company. Internally they comprise employees and managers and externally, customers, shareholders, suppliers as well as the local community, government and wider members of society, all of whom have an interest in the organization. To sustain a competitive advantage over time, the company may well have to consider how its policy of corporate social responsibility is aligned to the goals and aspirations of its stakeholders. A good answer will recognize the varying demands of the different stakeholders and the conflict their varying aspirations of corporate social responsibility may cause the company in its decision-making.

Activity 12.5

In completing this activity you need to consider the feasibility of implementing your proposed code of conduct and the market situation your sales staff have to compete in. You would also need to ensure the code does not demotivate sales staff and act as a barrier to them achieving company objectives. You would also need to consider how you would introduce such a code and what changes it would require to the ways in which sales personnel were controlled and evaluated.

Question 12.6

There is never a simple approach to the handling of ethical issues of this nature. If the company has a code of ethical conduct and is clear that it is in full compliance with this then a proactive and positive policy to handling the publicity surrounding such criticism is vital. The inclusion of the senior management and a constructive attitude to the dissemination of information would also be important. Often, however, such issues are not as clear-cut as they may appear and the retailer may feel they have been judged unfairly and harshly. Such a situation can be difficult for companies. Defending their position may appear callous and show they lack an acceptance of their responsibilities. Even if the criticism is unfounded the company needs to protect its long-term reputation and image and so be proactive in dealing with such issues.

Question 12.7

The starting point should be to reflect on the aims and objectives of CI and then systematically identify their stakeholders and their expectations. It is then necessary to consider the different roles and influences that the stakeholders can bring to implementing the CI strategy. For example, CI is unlikely to have sufficient finances to both carry out its intervention work in individual projects as well as gaining the wider publicity for its work that could lead to further companies and individuals becoming involved. Partners of this kind also provide complementary skills, knowledge and resources, for example maintaining the commercial focus necessary to maximize the revenue from projects, which in turn helps CI to achieve the greatest impact locally.

Question 12.8

The starting point here is to address the issue of how Aveda can add stakeholder value and set it against the incurred costs. A substantial and growing customer segment is more aware of sustainability issues and will seek to buy products that are produced by companies with an ethical stance. A far larger segment is emerging that regards sustainability as a 'hygiene factor' in that these customers do not preferentially select products that are produced using environmentally sound process but will expect all producers to produce products using ethical processes. Organizations will need to invest in developing the appropriate processes in the supply chain as they target new customer segments, develop and promote new and existing products and services and communicate with their stakeholders.

A further consideration is internal marketing. It is necessary to explain the aims and objectives to internal stakeholders, but this can also be a benefit. For example, demonstrating an ethical approach can be important in recruitment as well as motivating existing staff.

Index